D0420708

About CROP

CROP, the Comparative Research Programme on Poverty, is a response from the academic community to the problems of poverty. The programme was initiated in 1992, and the CROP Secretariat was officially opened in June 1993 by the Director General of UNESCO, Dr Frederico Mayor.

In recent years, poverty alleviation, poverty reduction and the eradication of poverty have moved up on the international agenda, with poverty eradication now defined as the greatest global challenge facing the world today. In co-operation with its sponsors, the International Social Science Council (ISSC) and the University of Bergen (UiB), CROP works in collaboration with knowledge networks, institutions and scholars to establish independent, alternative and critical poverty research in order to help shape policies for long-term poverty prevention and eradication.

The CROP network comprises scholars engaged in poverty-related research across a variety of academic disciplines. Researchers from more than a hundred different countries are represented in the network, which is coordinated by the CROP Secretariat at the University of Bergen, Norway.

The CROP series on International Studies in Poverty Research presents expert research and essential analyses of different aspects of poverty worldwide. By promoting a fuller understanding of the nature, extent, depth, distribution, trends, causes and effects of poverty, this series will contribute to knowledge concerning the reduction and eradication of poverty at global, regional, national and local levels.

For more information contact:

CROP Secretariat
PO Box 7800, 5020 Bergen, NORWAY
Phone: +47 55 58 97 44
Email: crop@uib.no
Visiting address: Jekteviksbakken 31
www.crop.org

Series editors

Juliana Martínez Franzoni, associate professor of political science, University of Costa Rica

Thomas Pogge, Leitner professor of philosophy and international affairs, Yale University

WATER AND DEVELOPMENT

GOOD GOVERNANCE AFTER NEOLIBERALISM

edited by Ronaldo Munck, Narathius Asingwire,
Honor Fagan and Consolata Kabonesa

Zed Books
LONDON

Water and Development: Good governance after neoliberalism was first published in 2015 by Zed Books Ltd, Unit 2.8, The Foundry, 17 Oval Way, London, SE11 5RR, UK

www.zedbooks.co.uk

Editorial copyright © CROP 2015

Set in Monotype Plantin and FFKievit by Ewan Smith, London NW5
Index: ed.emery@thefreeuniversity.net
Cover designed by www.kikamiller.com

A catalogue record for this book is available from the British Library

ISBN 978-1-78360-493-7 hb
ISBN 978-1-78360-492-0 pb
ISBN 978-1-78360-494-4 pdf
ISBN 978-1-78360-495-1 epub
ISBN 978-1-78360-496-8 mobi

Printed and bound by CPI Group (UK) Ltd, Croydon, CR0 4YY

MIX
Paper from
responsible sources
FSC
www.fsc.org   FSC® C013604

CONTENTS

FIGURES AND TABLES

Figures

Tables

ACKNOWLEDGEMENTS

The editors would like to thank Irish Aid and the Higher Education Authority of Ireland for their funding of the research which underpins Chapters 5 through to 10. Water Is Life: *Amazzi Bulamu* was an inter-institutional action research project completed in 2014. The project was funded through the Irish Aid Programme of Strategic Co-operation, which was launched in 2006 to support Irish Aid's mission to develop the capacity of the higher education sector in the global South.

Thanks to John Wiley and Sons for permission to republish Chapter 2, 'Liquid dynamics: challenges for sustainability in the water domain', which was originally published in *Wiley Interdisciplinary Reviews: Water*, 1(4), 2014.

We would also like to thank Mary Hyland, who went beyond the normal copy-editing role to really get the best out of the work submitted for this volume.

ABBREVIATIONS AND ACRONYMS

AREX	Department of Agriculture and Rural Extension, Zimbabwe
CBMS	community-based management system
CMA	catchment management agency
DfID	Department for International Development, UK
DWAF	Department of Water Affairs and Forestry, South Africa
EU	European Union
FAO	Food and Agriculture Organization of the United Nations
FGD	focus group discussion
GGWG	Good Governance Working Group
GIS	Geographical Information Systems
GIZ	German Federal Enterprise for International Cooperation
GoU	Government of Uganda
GPS	global positioning system
HPM	hand pump mechanics
IDWSSD	International Drinking Water Supply and Sanitation Decade
INGO	international non-governmental organization
IPCC	Intergovernmental Panel on Climate Change
IWRM	Integrated Water Resource Management
JMP	Joint Monitoring Programme
LG	local government
MDG	Millennium Development Goal
MWE	Ministry of Water and the Environment, Uganda
NGO	non-governmental organization
O&M	operation and maintenance
OMVS	Senegal River Basin Development Authority
PMA	Programme for the Modernization of Agriculture
SADC	Southern African Development Community
SPSS	Statistical Package for the Social Sciences
TPC	Technical Planning Committee
TSU	Technical Support Units
UGX	Ugandan shillings
UN	United Nations

UNDP	United Nations Development Programme
UNESCO	United Nations Educational, Scientific and Cultural Organization
UNFOMRWS	Uganda National Framework for Operation and Maintenance of Rural Water Supplies
UNICEF	United Nations Children's Fund
USAID	United States Agency for International Development
VLOM	village-led operation and maintenance
WCD	World Commission on Dams

PART ONE
CONTEXT

INTRODUCTION

Water is an indispensable element for life and social development. It is also an underpinning enabler for many of the Millennium Development Goals. Sustainable development, without free access to potable water, is quite simply inconceivable. From these imperatives the Integrated Water Resource Management (IWRM) paradigm has emerged in recent years as part of the drive for 'good governance'. This book will critically examine this paradigm as part of the wider debates around water and development from an African perspective. It is in sub-Saharan Africa that many of the water and development debates have played out most dramatically, so it is appropriate that this region is our focus. A particular feature of this book is the cluster of Uganda-based PhD research projects run as part of the Irish inter-university research programme Water Is Life, funded by Irish Aid and the Higher Education Authority under the Programme for Strategic Co-operation. Other contributors also came at our topic from a wider African perspective, which helps us provide a grounded focus on water and development in the global South.

The various chapters of this book deal with a wide range of issues – from gender to water pumps, from governance to climate adaptation – and deploy a wide range of research methods – from participant observation to SPSS and GIS data analysis. But throughout there is a unifying thread, aimed at developing a participatory and sustainable approach to water, which recognizes that it is an invaluable public good. Taken as a whole, the chapters seek to provide a locally grounded picture but one set in terms of much wider theoretical and political reference points. There can be little doubt about the importance of our shared topic – water and development in an African context. Whether it is in relation to agriculture, industry, power generating or poverty alleviation, water remains a critical challenge to water managers and the diverse, and often competing, communities of water users alike. While the focus is on sub-Saharan Africa we are seeking solutions to a shared problem across the developing world. We do not believe we have all the answers but we hope we are asking the right questions to create an effective, equitable and sustainable water management system.

Chapter 1, by Ronaldo Munck, sets the context through a wide-ranginf analysis of water development and governance in the era of neoliberalism and beyond. Water has always been a crucial catalyst for human development given its diverse, but always interlinked, functions in sustaining human life. Inequitable access to water – which can be traced back to the colonial era when it acted as a key divide – is always a serious impediment to sustainable development. This chapter opens with the developmentalist era of the Water Decade (1980–90), which did achieve an overall increase in average rural water access from 30 to 50 per cent. However, this era was followed by the market-driven era of the 1990s, especially following the 1992 Dublin Principles declaration, which established water as an economic commodity and not a social right. While the lucrative water market promised by the proponents of commodification never materialized, the debate shifted irreversibly (see Barlow 2001). Thus the current debates around the Integrated Water Management paradigm develop a more participatory, woman friendly and appropriate technology based approach while accepting the overarching role of the market in reforming existing water provision architecture.

In Chapter 2, Lyla Mehta and Synne Movik examine the challenges to sustainability and sanitation from a 'liquid dynamics' perspective. This approach refers to the patterns of complexity and interaction between the social, the chemical and the ecological/hydrological aspects of water and sanitation in rapidly changing situations. It is argued that current debates around access to water pay insufficient attention to the elements of uncertainty and dynamics, missing out on the long-term sustainability issues. Thus the dominant discourse seems quite disconnected from the lived realities of poor and marginalized people. Furthermore, it tends to downplay the complex interconnections between the social and technical dimensions across different scales of human activity. An underlying problem in the discourse is the neglect of the issue of agency and formalized notions of community. A conclusion that can usefully frame the analysis in subsequent chapters is that contested knowledge, equity and power are at the heart of water futures and that this needs to be our inescapable starting point.

Larry A. Swatuk in Chapter 3 continues the task of critical

deconstruction of accepted truths in the water and development domain. We are often told that there is not a 'water crisis' but, rather, a 'crisis of water management'. This is the logic informing the dominant IWRM paradigm. It appears to be all things to all people. For the state it justifies sometimes dubious mega-projects; for the private sector it encourages profit-driven water delivery systems; and for the civic society, or NGO, sector, it validates their 'bottom-up' activities. Yet it is all at an extremely high level of generality. This chapter sets the rhetoric against the reality of development and underdevelopment in sub-Saharan Africa from the colonial era to the present. Its conclusion is that we cannot float IWRM on a sea of underdevelopment. It goes farther, though, and uses the IWRM stated goals of social equity, economic efficiency and environmental sustainability to critically situate current water resources access, use and management in both rural and urban contexts.

Chapter 4 by Sobona Mtisi and Alan Nicol further concretizes this analysis with a focused overview of water politics in eastern and southern Africa. It shows how the IWRM perspective brought about a radical transformation in the governance and development of water resources in the region. It notes in particular how water development, allocation, use and management are deeply embedded in the historical and social processes of the region. Water is clearly not separate from the wider politics of land use, political enfranchisement and national development in their fully formed and informal complexities. The authors find that IWRM is all but oblivious to the multidimensional nature of politics in the region. They analyse how the new water governance mechanisms put in place were contested in both the formal and informal political domains. Far from being a solution to the widely recognized water crisis of the region, many of these reforms have created new and powerful economic interests within a context of increasing poverty and water insecurity.

Following the wide-ranging perspectives opened up in Part One, there is a narrowing of focus in Part Two, which is dedicated to 'close-up' studies of a community in Uganda that was the focus of an Irish project called 'Water Is Life' (www.waterislife.org). This project, funded by Irish Aid, Ireland's national development agency, worked with local community organizations to develop an integrated research-action programme for better and more sustainable access to potable water. This work is reflected in the chapters that follow on governance, gender, climate change and appropriate technology issues. Water Is Life was informed by a community participation approach and a foregrounding of agency. It could be characterized as a critical grounded perspective based very much on the realities of a relatively circumscribed geographical area but from the standpoint of the 'big issues' and a critical position which seeks to uncover what lies behind the progressive-sounding rhetoric of national governments and international agencies.

In Chapter 5, Gloria Macri, Firmnus Mugumya and Áine Rickard set the scene for the detailed 'on the ground' accounts of water and development in one Ugandan community which follow. Uganda represents a good example of countries in sub-Saharan Africa that have undertaken reforms and devoted resources to their water supply sectors with the aim of scaling up efficiency and effectiveness in the delivery of services. However, despite a recovery from very poor service delivery in the 1980s and 1990s, Uganda's rural safe access water figures show there is still a challenge to be met. The second half of this chapter focuses on the specific region where the Water Is Life project was based, where access to safe water stood at around 65 per cent, close to the national average. The authors provide a detailed overview of the profile of the households of the study area, a rural parish in the province of Lwengo. This statistical and GIS mapping exercise provides a rich account of the various sources of water used by households and the major problems encountered in collecting and transporting water from the main water sources. The politics of water usage, and in particular its gender dimension, is introduced here, to be taken up in more detail in subsequent chapters.

Chapter 6 by Firminus Mugumya and Narathius Asingwire tackles the vital question of governance, both in theory and in practice, in relation to water in Uganda. The main focus is on the currently dominant community-based management system (CBMS) model of water supply and services. The CBMS model is situated in terms of the neoliberal turns towards reduction of the role of the state and the promotion of a decentralized or multi-stakeholder approach to water. While the CBMS model is deemed to have achieved a degree of sustainability for rural water delivery in Uganda, the government has not been successful in bringing together the resources to create greater equity. The authors argue for the need for public authorities to pay closer attention to context-specific circumstances and conditions that might disable good policy and programme proposals. They call for a more effective central and local government engagement with water issues that would genuinely fulfil the role conceived for it under the community-based management model, and so become an enabler of good, rather than a passive player ceding control to the market.

In Chapter 7, Richard Bagonza Asaba and G. Honor Fagan provide a detailed account of water and gender from a sociological perspective. They examine the dynamics at play in the operation of the proposed equal participation of women in community water management as their role is expanded from that of domestic water-keeper to community water-keeper. The gender dynamics of the management process and access to water provide a profound insight into the uneven power dynamics involved in the politics of water. Gender is an essential element in the social relations governing all aspects of water collection, distribution and use. There is a multifaceted sociocultural, environmental and health-related set of conditions which pattern the male and female roles in the complex relations between water and development. This chapter, based on a series of interviews, observations and surveys conducted in the study area, provides insights into the broader issues surrounding women and development. It concludes that, despite legislative provision, women's participation in management of water resources remains peripheral and is deeply marked by patriarchal domestic structures.

Chapter 8 by Joyce Mpalanyi Magala, Consolata Kabonesa and Anthony Staines takes a more anthropological approach to gender and development and is focused on women as gatekeepers. The day-to-day role of women in water management, at both household and community level, is examined through ethnographic data and observations. A picture is built up of the daily experiences of women with regard to water and how this impacts on their lives and perceptions of themselves. The gendered perspective on power and masculinity is developed as a theoretical frame to understand water management and also women's health. Women are presented as gatekeepers to water access, at both community and household levels, but always within an overarching patriarchal social and value system. The responsibility women have with regard to water is a major determinant, impacting on the realization of a woman's full potential and self-actualization. This chapter argues that development workers need to go beyond the biomedical model of health and engage with the more complex sociocultural processes that impact on women's role with regard to water and development.

In Chapter 9, Mavuto D. Tembo focuses on the adaptive capacity of agro-pastoralists to climate change in the rural study area. It takes a close look at the realities facing agro-pastoralists on the ground, in order to establish how adaptive capacity emerges. Using a wide range of research methods, this study gets close to a social group which tends to be excluded from mainstream social and political life in the villages. Though small in number, the agro-pastoralists play a role in shaping the adaptive capacity of villagers to cope with seasonal water variation. Living as they do in the wetland valleys between villages, they display great context-framed adaptive ability based on how to apply local knowledge when deciding where to dig a well. Their role in exchanging milk-based products for cash or other products leads them to travel across the area, thus picking up much local intelligence. Overall, the chapter argues that adaptive capacity to climate change occurs through a complex web of relationships. However, the capacity of agro-pastoralists to respond is being increasingly constrained by enclosures and by the micro-scale practices to which they lead.

Chapter 10, by Michael Lubwama, Brian Corcoran and Kimmitt Sayers, tackles the role of appropriate technology and sustainable development through a case study of hand pumps in a rural Ugandan setting. Appropriate technology is often articulated, in development research and practice, as a means to foster social and environmental sustainability. It also tends to stress the importance of a people-centred technology. Its aim is to promote small-scale, decentralized, energy-efficient and locally controlled initiatives. This chapter provides a concrete example of these debates through a detailed examination of sustainable water pump technology at community level. The problems associated with on-the-ground maintenance of hand pumps are examined in terms of policy and financial issues, as well as the social and community aspects. The technology transfer of modernized hand pumps from an Indian to an African context is critically examined. The chapter is a contribution to sustainable development from an engineering perspective, in that it presents a novel, holistic and workable approach to maintenance and repair of non-functioning hand pumps *in situ*.

This set of case study chapters, based around a specific experience in rural Uganda, represents a change of register compared to the opening section, which is worth reflecting on. What is clear is that water and development as a problematic covers a very wide range of issues, going from the management and politics of great river systems to the use of water in a domestic setting. Of course, water is used also for agriculture, something referenced only in one of these case studies, that in relation to the irrigation problems faced by agro-pastoralists. These chapters have focused mainly on domestic water use in a 'traditional' rural setting, given that it is where the majority of the population in sub-Saharan Africa still live and from where they face the challenges of creating a livelihood and combating extreme poverty. They deal with only a subset of the broader water and development debates outlined in Part One of the book. Another apparent disconnect is between the focus on the international paradigms of integrated water management and the MDGs in Part One and the much more grounded focus on local government issues and local actors in the case studies. This is, to some extent, due to the politics of scale, insofar as the 'high-level' problematics might seem remote from a local parish setting. But it may also signal a certain disconnect between the global policy level (e.g. MDGs) and the reality on the ground. Indeed, this can be seen to be in keeping with critical development theory, which posits just such a disconnect between the managers of globalization and those impacted by their policies and practices. In Part Three we move towards bridging that gap, returning to the broader issues discussed in Part One, but now enriched by the local-level case studies of Part Two.

It is there, in Chapter 11, that David Hemson rounds off the collection in a wide-ranging 'balance sheet' chapter. He calls for a more holistic approach to the development of sustainable water systems. We need to pay greater attention to the water resource itself, which is being depleted steadily through more intensive use of the land and deforestation. The focus needs to shift from the local to the regional level to improve access to water and to build better support structures for rural communities and for the development of new techniques for the recharging of ground water. The post-MDG policy prescriptions need to acknowledge the relevance of climate change and its impact on water supply and prioritize the development of renewable energy technologies for pumping water. Above all, water must be seen as part of the broader issue of rural development. Consistent with some of the chapters that have gone before, this final afterword argues that we must move beyond technicist quick fixes with regard to water. It points to the need to focus more on how effective and empowering social mobilization can be in promoting the provision of potable water for all in the developing world.

This book is appearing as the post-2015 MDG scenario becomes clearer. Whatever its precise outcome, it is obvious that water will be a central element in the new global development strategy. Securing sustainable water for all will be a key objective, and this will need to be supported by a coherent and mutually reinforcing set of targets. Improved water governance, supported by a comprehensive package of legislative and policy reforms, is essential to any such strategy. As we see in this volume – taking the chapters as a whole – water is a crucial element for development across the board, in terms of food production, energy, education and health, to name but a few sectors. Any post-2015 aspirations for poverty reduction and the achievement of gender equity, also critically depend on sustainable water for all. We hope that this volume will contribute to the ongoing debate through theoretical innovation, grounded empirical observation and keen awareness that research needs to feed into development policy and practice.

Reference

Barlow, M. (2001) *Blue Gold: The Global Water Crisis and the Commodification of the World's Water Supply*, San Francisco, CA: Committee on the Globalization of Water, International Forum on Globalization.

1 | WATER, DEVELOPMENT AND GOOD GOVERNANCE

Ronaldo Munck

Water has always been a crucial catalyst for human development given its diverse but crucial functions. Inequitable access to water – which can be traced back to the colonial period – is a serious challenge to sustainable development (Petrella 2001; Kansiime 2002; Conway and Waage 2010; Showers 2002). Today the dominant discourse on water and development stresses the need for its good governance (Bakker et al. 2008). This chapter sets current debates around water, development and governance in context.

Following a brief introduction of the issues, it examines the phase of developmentalism which sets the water debates of the 1980s in the context of the Brandt Report and the emphasis on Southern development to allay Northern security concerns and to open up markets to its goods. In particular, it examines the promises and the achievements of the Water Decade (1980–90). While overall the Decade achieved an increase in rural water coverage from 30 to 50 per cent, its premises were challenged by the new emerging market-driven neoliberal model (Hemson et al. 2008; Dagdeviren 2008).

The second section, 'Market miracles', deals with the privatization drive of the 1990s following the Dublin Principles declaration of 1992, making water an economic good. While the lucrative water market promised by commodification never really materialized, this period did leave a legacy in terms of a stated commitment to good governance and community involvement as priorities (Nicol et al. 2012; Finger and Allouche 2002). This approach is still very much an influence on current water and development paradigms.

The third section deals with the emerging post-neoliberal Soft Solutions, as advocated most notably by the integrated water management systems paradigm (Allan 2003; Biswas 2004). This represents a move away from traditional large-scale and capital-intensive solutions towards a more sustainable, low-tech approach which also emphasizes the gender dimension (Wade 2012; Swatuk 2008; Conca 2006). To what extent it will, in practice, alter the earlier reliance on market mechanisms remains to be seen.

Throughout, a critical deconstruction approach is followed, stressing the political context of water and development. A final section then outlines some of the ways forward, assessing the prospects of a pragmatic 'go with what works' approach while also positing an analytical distinction between 'practical' and 'strategic' water needs. The chapters in this book add much-needed empirical detail and analytical richness to this debate.

Introduction

The provision of fresh potable water to the global majorities is widely regarded as a major development challenge and, for many, one of the most visible failures of the development project. As Conway and Waage (2010: 258) note, 'Despite its critical importance to international development, and its scarcity in many poor countries, there is no headline MDG [Millennium Development Goal] for water.' Clearly, however, MDG1 (halving the number of the world's poor by 2015) depends on water insofar as it is essential for food security. Water is, of course, also vital to the health MDGs, and access to safe drinking water is referred to under MDG7 on ensuring environmental sustainability. Overall, however, I would agree with Gourisankar Ghosh (2012: 12), for whom 'the emphasis in the MDGs on focusing on the indicators rather than the process and direction of development has led to hasty, often top-down approaches that ultimately fail because they do not take people's actual needs into consideration'. That is a general lesson we need to bear in mind when examining the whole water, development and good governance problematic.

This chapter does not deal with water as a technical issue – the hydraulic paradigm, we might call it – but, rather, as a social and political issue, ultimately determined by unequal power and wealth relations. Even a cursory look at the issues would show that access to safe water is quite clearly governed by overarching social, gender and ethnic power differentials. All of the wider water and development paradigms – including the most recent Integrated Water Resource Management perspective – are determined by national and international political processes and have clear political effects on the ground. In my view, too often the water efficiency arguments mask water equity issues in a discursive sleight of hand that is not always noticed. A techno-centric approach to water and development almost inevitably, given its focus on the technical dimension, evades the question of social and political power. The scarcity of water and its uneven accessibility are inseparable from the history of colonialism, the development of autocratic and often predatory post-colonial regimes and the ever-present class and gender differentials. In brief, water is a political issue and thus needs to be set in that context.

Developmentalism

The development project has always envisaged a one-way path towards modernity that all countries must follow. The diffusion of capital and modern values into what were deemed backward or traditional areas was seen as the key to development. The path to modernity was guided by the compass of science and enlightenment values. As a recent influential text on *Science and Innovation for Development* puts it, the sequence is quite clear: 'The goal of international development is to reduce poverty and to help poor people build a better life for themselves ... Science can make a valuable contribution to this goal, scientific knowledge and technology can be applied to specific technical challenges, like achieving the Millennium Development Goals (MDGs)' (Conway and Waage 2010: 7). Except, of course, the challenge is not just 'technical' but goes to the heart of the uneven development of capitalism and a globalization that created great wealth only by generating great inequality between and within countries (see Arrighi et al. 2003).

The dominant focus in regard to both water and Africa is deeply imbued with this myopic vision of a Western science which would banish both underdevelopment and thirst. In relation to Africa, the colonialist imagination still rides high: 'joining the world economy' will lead to development and well-meaning Western NGOs will explain the importance of clean water. Of course, as James Ferguson (2006: 14) and others have shown, Africa's 'highly selective and spatially encapsulated forms of global connection [are] combined with widespread disconnection and exclusion'. In relation to water, the quite recent colonial heritage of water distribution and control is ignored and replaced by a simple gap in knowledge and understanding to be filled by Northern science, the World Bank and the international NGOs.

Water was often a key component in the development mission. In the 1950s Karl Wittfogel (1957) developed a model of 'hydraulic despotism' (or Water Monopoly Empire) for societies and political systems where power was based on elite control of access to water. The scale is always huge and we need only think of the huge remit of the apex river basin management systems such as the six major systems in Africa. The pressing problem of food security places a greater emphasis on the need to increase irrigation efficiency, and we should always bear in mind that agriculture accounts for 85 per cent of water use in Africa. Thus, not surprisingly, the 2005 Commission for Africa placed all its emphasis on the need to increase spending on physical irrigation infrastructure to meet its target of doubling the areas under irrigation. The social and institutional aspects of water management – in short, the governance problematic – were essentially pushed to one side, thus storing up problems in terms of legitimacy and 'buy-in'.

In regard to water, the developmentalist paradigm follows a long tradition of modernist thinking which sees nature – including water resources – as something to be tamed and harvested for the good of development. The Promethean myth runs deep across Western science and philosophy, not least in the missionary zeal of developmentalism. After all, industrial modernity, through a revolution in science and industry, had harnessed the resources of labour, capital and the environment. In terms of development discourse – the twentieth-century global counterpart – there could be a similar virtuous synergy between health, income, education and housing, leading to a satisfactory outcome. This was, of course, before the environmental turn of the 1970s which brought the hubris to an end, but developmentalism lingers on, not least with regard to water, where a techno-centric lens prevails over an ecocentric one, not least in Africa.

For Tony Allan (2003: 10), the modern-era 'hydraulic mission' regarding water runs from the late nineteenth century to at least 1980. This model portrays water as a purely technical issue beyond politics and thus subsequent ecocentric and market-centric paradigms are but recent arrivals by comparison. Across the water sector there is an abiding belief in science, technology and engineering as drivers of progress. One need only add the right mix of private and state investment and generate the right attitude among the population for success to be achieved. In a context of underdevelopment – whether that is caused by internal failings or neocolonial structures – it is not surprising that the hydraulic mission still holds sway and marginalizes the 'anti-dam' community or discourse. Water use commodification – as we shall see in the next sections – could easily be accommodated within this perspective, not least in Africa, where the 'water challenge' is at its most severe and growing.

The rise and fall (and rise again) of the dam as a major water management instrument symbolizes all the contradictions of developmentalism. The Report of the World Commission on Dams in 2000 sought to demystify previous uncritical reliance on large dam technology. Kader Asmal, as former minister for water in post-apartheid South Africa, was well placed to lead this deconstruction of a technology which engineers blessed and ecologists cursed. Reality was more complex, accommodating, as it did, both good dams and bad dams, to put it simply. As Asmal (2001: 3) puts it, 'Instead of my archetype I saw: dams praised by ecologists and dams despised by engineers ... dams boosting fisheries, dams causing deadly floods ... dams by-passing thirsty adjacent communities, ... dams creating wetlands and work.' In the event this message was perhaps too subtle. The World Bank, which had sponsored the study, withdrew its support and China embarked on an ambitious programme of loans and concessions to construct large dams in Africa. The 'anti-dam' international non-governmental organization (INGO) was bound to lose against Southern elites articulating an economic development discourse.

The Water Decade (1980s) came after the Second Development Decade (1970s) and sought to implement the ideology and practice of developmentalism in the field of water and sanitation. The International Decade for Clean Water and Sanitation, to give it its full title, was launched in a mood of great confidence, committed to the 'eminently achievable' goal of 'safe water and sanitation for all by 1990'. Only one person in five in the developing world had access to clean water so some progress at least seemed possible. However, from the very start, it was unclear what actual funding would be committed to this initiative. Nor was it clear whether developing-country governments would see it as a priority. What organizational and financial model would be deployed to make this vision materialize? Would rapid economic growth and urbanization – not to mention the rapidly rising populations – not overwhelm the efforts at improving existing water facilities?

There was a clear tendency for the water provision backlog to remain more or less in place for all these reasons, despite all the glowing statistics. The basic statistical picture is shown in Table 1.1.

TABLE 1.1 Percentage increase in delivery of water and of population benefited in developing countries

	1970–80	%	1980–90	%	1990–2000	%
Urban	66	67	108	75	35	95
Rural	217	14	109	29	24	66
Total	100	29	130	43	29	79

Source: Jolly (2003)

What we note, then, is a considerable increase in urban area provision and population covered between 1970 and 1990 and, from a much lower baseline, a doubling of rural area coverage in the 1970s, 1980s and 1990s, but still only reaching two-thirds of the population.

The balance sheet of the Water Decade is highly contested, not least from the perspective of the free market approach which followed. Officially it was a success insofar as rural water supply average in the developing world increased from 30 to 50 per cent overall. However, even in the course of its implementation, serious problems had been identified. Not least it is entirely unclear how much was actually invested worldwide in water infrastructure. Much of the improvement in terms of increased access was achieved simply through the repair of existing facilities. The main problem, however, was that the global slowdown had already led to 'structural conditionality' for international loans, and strict cost recovery in the operation and maintenance of water facilities was overwhelming the developmentalist mission. Smaller-scale initiatives on the ground were able to succeed and that was perhaps one positive lesson learned by those in the wider professional world.

Overall, we might agree with David Hemson (Hemson et al. 2008: 21), who argues that 'despite the very evident failures [of the

Water Decade] it has become very important to reclaim the 1980s as a time of reactive progress to keep up a sense of momentum'. From a post-neoliberal perspective it is now possible to reassess this era both critically and more realistically. When there is a paradigm shift (as neoliberalism was) then what went before – such as developmentalism based on import-substitution industrialization and large state-led projects – is simply obliterated. In this regard, in relation to water we should consider the verdict of the World Health Organization, for which 'The 1980s were not a lost decade for water; it had been declared a water decade. During that time more people had gotten access to water than ever before ... The challenge is to remobilize the commitment to global action on water' (WHO/UNICEF 2000:17).

Market miracles

The developmentalist model found paradigmatic expression in the famous Brandt Report, which sought to generate a 'new international economic order' to the benefit of both the North and the South. This was very much a reformist project which called for greater investment in the South to secure an expanding global economy by encouraging consumption therein. Northern risks of recession would be staved off by expanding consumer markets in the South. The Brandt Commission also recognized the links between economic crisis and weak or failing government, thus reinforcing the need for reform of the international development regime. While this programme was rational it was also utopian in the real-world context, and in the early 1980s a new development paradigm, based on the promise of free-market-led development, moved into a dominant position.

While the Pinochet dictatorship in Chile from 1973 onwards pioneered the new 'market miracle' paradigm, it was Thatcherism and Reaganism in the 1980s which made it into a dominant global model. Its basic tenets were quite simple: the market should work unimpeded to allow for the determination of prices, the state should withdraw from regulatory functions, the national economy should be opened up to international trade, and both the capital and labour markets should be deregulated. These principles became codified in what was known as the Washington Consensus, which rapidly attained global paradigm status. The neoliberal solution to problems in the water sector was to make a decisive move towards privatization. Water should be recognized as an economic good like any other, with its price set by free market mechanisms. The commodification of water was part of a drive to convert knowledge, people and life itself (DNA) into commodities which could be bought and sold. This was, at the time, part of the new common sense at a global level with all contrary discourses derided and disallowed.

The turn to the market involved a dramatic discursive operation. Whereas in the past 'reform' in a development context might signal land redistribution (agrarian reform) or greater education access (educational reform), it was now subverted to simply mean a greater role for market forces. There was a great emphasis on consumer 'demand' in relation to water, but what that meant in practice was simply an 'ability to pay'. Now clearly social need or demand regarding water cannot be equated with or only expressed through an ability to pay. To cap it all, the term 'sustainability' was rolled in, still clothed in the respectable environmental garb, to now signify profitability. Thus, for water to be sustainable it would have to be profitable. Gradually a societal reaction to this wave of deregulation and unbridled freedom for market forces contested the commodification of water and reinstated its status as a basic social need if not human right.

The move towards the commodification and destatization of water was codified in the 1992 Dublin Principles resulting from an influential gathering of water professionals and policy-makers. These principles were designed to learn from the lessons of the Water Decade and to chart a way forward for water provision. Water scarcity was an overriding theme, as was also the economic value of water. The term 'demand responsiveness' meant more than just funding people and communities which demanded water but also targeted those who were able or willing to pay for it. This would clearly impact most severely in rural areas where infrastructure was weak or non-existent. The principle was that water has an economic value (or one that can be generated) and that competing users (say commercial farmers and the poor) should be subject to market supply and demand forces. While destatization could mean a return to traditional community control, in practice it mainly led to privatization and the hard-headed logic of 'cost recovery'.

There have been many case studies on how the commercialization of water services worked out in practice. We may first take one case study of urban water services in Zambia entitled 'Waiting for miracles' (Dagdeviren 2008) as an example. The structural adjustment programmes imposed on the global South by the international financial institutions had led to a severe curtailment in government infrastructure investment. Privatization was to lead to improved efficiency, service quality and greater access. But, as 'Waiting for miracles' found, a heavy reliance on tariff rationalization without paying attention to investment and maintenance was bound to lead to problems. In the end, after a decade or more of privatization, it was found that this was 'a poor policy prescription, involving "spectacular failures" in the words of the United Nations Development Programme (UNDP)' (ibid.: 102). Whatever the intentions of the Dublin Principles, privatization quite simply did not deliver greater access to water for the poor.

From a broad perspective, neoliberalism was about freeing the market from state domination but also, supposedly, about liberating civil society as the overbearing state was rolled back. What was then predicted to emerge was a new form of 'governance' (as distinct from traditional state-based government) which would be both more efficient and more democratic. The non-governmental organizations (NGOs) would fill the gap in terms of service delivery as the national state was forced to retreat. The NGOs would also, somehow, represent the grass roots and establish a direct dialogue with the World Bank and others. But, in practice, as Ferguson (2006: 38) has noted, 'this "rolling back" of the state provoked or exacerbated a far-reaching political crisis'. Privatization led, more or less inevitably, to criminalization as the predictable 'state failure' ensued. The poor pay the price, as usual, for this failed Western initiative.

The neoliberal water model placed governance at the centre. There was a focus on state failure in relation, for example, to corruption by officials or on the poacher/gamekeeper dilemma, whereby the state is both supplier and regulator. Karen Bakker and colleagues have pointed to problems in terms of a top-down culture of governance, such as lack of clear property rights, lack of skills and cultural beliefs regarding appropriate water treatment protocols (Bakker at al. 2008: 1895). Some of these issues, however, would be present in both private and public provision of water services. The main problem in relation to governance probably lies elsewhere. Even supporters of privatization such as Water Aid now acknowledge that a weakened state cannot hope to have the capacity for regulation of the water sector or, for that matter, promote local community participation and the enforcement of entitlements.

The neoliberal period also saw a renewed emphasis on the role of women with regard to water. Previously a welfare approach had prevailed with women and children seen as the main beneficiaries of improved water supplies. With the neoliberal emphasis on the efficiency and effectiveness of water supplies, women entered the high-level discourse as agents who could improve the management or governance of water. From 2000 onwards, in particular through the 2000 Third World Water Forum in Kyoto, there was a commitment to 'good governance', community-based approaches and 'due regard to pro-poor and gender perspectives in water polices' (UN 2005: 3). In practice this was a reprise of the 1970s women and development perspective, which entailed enlisting women in the officially sanctioned – and ineffective – development effort. Most often the emphasis was on women as potential economic agents, who might be encouraged to access microcredit to build wells for their communities, all within a framework where demand was equated with ability to pay.

There is today a general consensus across the water sector that privatization has failed both in its own terms and as a sustainable water management system. A dramatic turning point in the rise and fall of privatization was the Water Wars episode in Bolivia in the late 1990s/early 2000s. The World Bank had made it a condition of a large loan for refinancing of water services in the Cochabamba region that management and delivery of the public water service be ceded to the private sector. The single bid from a subsidiary of the transnational Bechtel Corporation duly won the contract. Within months it had doubled the price of water, making its cost equivalent to half of a monthly minimum wage. The World Bank had stipulated that some of the loan would be used to subsidize water access for the poor but that did not occur. A massive regional revolt occurred, mobilizing the indigenous communities in particular, which changed the course of Bolivian history and brought a dramatic end to privatization when the government was inevitably forced to intervene (see Barlow 2001). Since then, the raw power of the corporations has been somewhat tempered by national governments which realize the profoundly destabilizing effects which fundamentalist free market ideologies can have.

In the early 2000s the corporate sector (especially the transnational corporations) began to retreat from the water sector, having realized 'the difficulties of extracting profit delivering water to indigent communities' (Lane 2012: 17). And so water privatization has lost its clear hegemonic position, but the discourse is still quite prevalent. While the 'market miracle' with regard to water turned out to be a mirage there is still a lingering economism present in dominant water paradigms, as we will see in the next sections. There is also a more positive legacy of this period with regard to a new-found emphasis on governance, gender and sustainability. These can, of course, become simple political slogans attached to a dominant economic driver, but they do at least open the door to a more participatory and engaged community perspective on water provision and access.

Soft solutions

From the late 1990s onwards, the 'market miracle' had turned into a mirage. The collapse of Argentina's economic miracle in 2001 sealed its fate and by the time the 2007–09 global crisis hit, the Washington Consensus was already being reconfigured. The likes of George Soros – one-time financial speculator – were now calling for a 'Third Way' in politics to save global capitalism from itself. Joseph Stiglitz, chief economist at the World Bank, also turned into a critic of the model and advocated a Polanyian approach, whereby the market is tempered by social control mechanisms. A somewhat incoherent post-Washington Consensus was to emerge which rejected full capital market liberalization, brought back a role for the state in economic development, and called for an effective regime of 'global governance' to compensate for the market miracle which had not materialized.

But the post-Washington Consensus was nowhere near as coherent as its predecessor, and even the 2007–09 global recession did not lead to a simple 'death of neoliberalism'. Rather there emerged a hybrid or mixed mode in which the new paradigm still sought to maintain the key principles of the old regime, while dealing with the contradictions it generated through some reforms. The

Blair Commission for Africa reflected this new order and (in a pale reflection of the Brandt Commission) sought to reconcile the interests of the rich North and the poor South. For example, it argued that water was both a right and a basic need, the meeting of which would benefit the productivity of the poor. It emphasized the need for greater investment and a sector-wide coordination for water, but this call, predictably, was lost in the now pre-eminent 'war against terrorism' after 2001.

The 'hard path' to adequate water supplies stressed the importance of large-scale, centralized and capital-intensive initiatives. It was, in short, a technological fix for water problems. Once it was recognized that supply management was not the only issue at stake, a more nuanced 'soft path' emerged after 2000. It was more low-tech than high-tech, more of a social fix than a technological fix. Decentralized solutions – for example, avoiding the piping of water over long distances – clearly make sense. A whole range of appropriate technologies – such as solar distillation, rainfall capture or green roofs – also make sense. From a broader viewpoint, however, the dominant market perspective may be perfectly capable of co-opting this thinking and presenting the neoliberal model in a more decentralized bottom-up and pro-poor guise.

As Larry Swatuk (2008: 26) notes, 'the rise of IWRM to the centre of global water management is nothing short of remarkable'. It was shaped and promoted widely as a normative blueprint for sustainable water management by a coalition of international development policy actors. It was very much part of the new global governance paradigm, designed to compensate for the effects of raw tooth-and-nail free market fundamentalism. Global water governance sought to promote the coordination of water resources in a more equitable and ecologically sustainable manner, while keeping much of the pro-market impetus alive (see Conca 2006). As a discourse it was presented by the international policy-maker and INGO communities as somehow 'above politics', but, of course, it was a clearly political project and its management is political as well. For now we deal with the main effects.

Essentially the IWRM paradigm saw a shift from the 'hardware' approach of the modernization era (dams and other large-scale projects) to one which emphasized 'software' – by that meaning the social dimension, which included community, gender and governance as key factors. As Jeffrey Wade (2012: 215) puts it, 'the emerging "soft path" approach tends to look at water not as an end-product, but as a means to accomplish certain tasks'. Thus in agriculture the demand is not for water per se but for it as a means to increase agricultural productivity. The soft approach seeks to match provision with user needs. Thus, for example, higher-quality water might be reserved for domestic consumers. But also water markets and pricing are used to encourage more efficient water use. Small-scale, more decentralized, water systems are encouraged as well as water reuse and reclamation. Collaboration between agencies and engagement with communities can produce a more sustainable water management system.

Good governance of water – in the sense of allocative and regulatory politics – is central to the IWRM approach. This can be readily interpreted within a community power perspective which promotes the enablement of community resources and voice. The political disenfranchisement of the poor is a common characteristic across the developing world and the governance approach is seen as a way of addressing this deficit. Citizen entitlement to the bare necessities of life – which includes water, of course – can be very much part of a radical governance agenda. However, this is not likely to succeed if governance is perceived as part of the World Bank agenda, designed to disenfranchise national states, when these are necessarily key agents in national democratic development and political participation around water and every other conflictual issue in society.

The move towards an integrative 'shift' approach to water occurred at the same time that the overarching 'good governance' paradigm came into question. It had been launched as part of a righteous ethnocentric Western lesson to developing countries on what democracy meant. It was also explicitly linked to economic reform, for which read free market policies. After 2000 it was widely recognized that 'good governance provides an inadequate agenda for Africa' and that it would be better to 'make use of indigenous institutional creativity' and practices 'rooted in their sociocultural context' (Booth 2011: 2). Rather than coming in with rigid institutional blueprints, Northern aid agencies and financial institutions were asked to try 'working with the grain' in terms of adapting to local political practices. As yet it is not clear what this paradigm shift might mean in relation to water governance, but it should signal a more flexible and possibly more bottom-up approach.

It is probably too early to evaluate the success of the IWRM approach insofar as it is very much a work in progress. What is clear, however, is that it is stronger as an international discourse than as a national practice (in Africa, for example). Longer-standing commitments to the 'hydraulic mission' there mean the ecocentric approach is not quite as clearly commonsense as it might be in the North. Nor does acceptance by the 'great and the good' at international conferences of policy-makers and INGOs translate so readily into concrete support on the ground. IWRM has become institutionalized as part of the Global Water Governance project, but it still lacks validation in terms of tangible achievements. While it constitutes a powerful epistemic community, especially at the transnational level, there is still very much a legitimacy gap when it comes to assessing its success or otherwise.

What has become quite clear over the last decade or so is that the national state needs to resume a central role in water provision. It is not a role that local communities can play or that international NGOs should play. While the World Bank has, for some time, recognized the need to 'bring back' the state, there is now a much more robust argument emerging on the need for a democratic developmental state in southern Africa (see Edigheji 2010). Put at its simplest, the economic miracle of China could not have been achieved without a developmental state. Such a state can work with societal actors to enhance capacity and build strong pro-development, pro-poor state–society linkages. A stronger, but also fundamentally reformed, democratic state is the only entity capable of addressing the needs of the poor for sustainable access to safe water.

The global economic crisis unleashed by the US banking collapse in 2008 has reopened the debate on development models. Clearly the old neoliberal hegemonic model is no longer viable but no alternative has yet gained dominance. What is clear is that the larger economies of the South, less linked into the global financial system, came out better from the crisis. One clear difference between those which succumbed to the Northern-induced turmoil and those that did not (to the same degree), such as China, India and Brazil, has been the presence of a developmental state. The twenty-first-century developmental state will be different from that of the mid-twentieth century with more synergistic state–society relations and a greater emphasis on democratic institutions (Evans 2010). If water is taken as a basic social need, and one that has not been met by the unregulated market policies which collapsed in 2008, then it may be opportune for the developmental state to take a more central and leading role in ensuring adequate and safe water supplies for the population.

Ways forward

The main thing we need to recognize when engaging with the water and development debate is the complexity of the issues – for example, around the pluses and minuses of dams. This is hardly unique to the water and development problematic but reflects wider changes in global knowledge power dynamics since the end of what we might call organized capitalism. We can no longer treat national societies as self-sufficient bounded entities given the dramatically increased tempo of internationalization in the 1990s, commonly known as 'globalization'. We moved from a society dominated by structures to one where flows dominate, be they capital, labour, finance or ideas. Whether we call the emerging order 'liquid modernity' (Bauman), 'network society' (Castells) or something else is not important. What is essential is recognition that the water and development problematic is not a simple or unilinear one, amenable to various 'fixes', but rather reflects a complex relationship between local, national and global dynamics and between power networks and the fluid network of social relationships.

For a better or more nuanced understanding of water and development issues we might posit a distinction between 'practical water needs' and 'strategic water needs', building loosely on the practical/strategic gender needs debate of the 1980s (see Moser 1989). Practical water needs can be defined in terms of the adequate supply and distribution of water to communities in need. A new approach would be a multi-sectoral one defined to enlist the maximum partners but with an overall commitment to the primacy of the market model of water provision. Strategic water needs, on the other hand, would place an overarching emphasis on social needs with regard to water, would have a more restricted popular-sector base for its demands and would articulate a decommodification or social control over the overall market philosophy. To be sure, these models do not present themselves in such stark terms but they might allow us to deconstruct critically the complex dynamics of water and development politics and conflicts.

In pragmatic terms, to address practical water needs we would probably have to 'go with what works'. There is a growing consensus across the political spectrum that pragmatism should prevail over all dogmatisms. The previous waves of water and development orthodoxies and critiques have given way to a new mood of flexibility and an acceptance that no one has all the answers. Thus Synne Movik and Lyla Mehta, in an influential post-paradigm 'going with the flow' perspective manifesto, argue that there are no 'silver bullets' in terms of water and sanitation, that we need innovative thinking in terms of institution frameworks and that we should look at how 'innovative technologies [can] be made to "go with the flow" rather than be pushed, to stimulate and nurture more diversity and innovative ways' (Movik and Mehta 2010: 12). This approach mirrors the rethinking of the African governance debate in terms of 'working with the grain' (Booth 2011), where the emphasis lies in working with indigenous power dynamics and institutional frameworks.

If, however, we are addressing the strategic water needs of the poor, dispossessed and disenfranchised in the global South we might take a different approach. The 'high politics' of water, as a global issue, works at a rarefied level, which simply ignores the politics of power on the ground. Even when left-of-centre governments are in office – as across much of Latin America – there is a noticeable gap between the rhetoric and the reality of pursing the strategic water interests of the poor. While water politics have been transformed by the rhetorical shift against the earlier neoliberal recipes, the democratization of water resource management still lies far behind. Inevitably the pressure of social movement is weighed against the perceived interests of national development and those of the multinational corporations that still play a pivotal role. One analysis of water reform in Latin America concludes that mass mobilization is a prerequisite for advancing water rights and that an alliance is forged with the state, municipalities and the community to reduce capitalist dependency and respect the autonomy of the people (Terhorst et al. 2013: 67).

One certainty, going forward, is that water will remain a critical issue on the international development agenda. The World Bank (2010) posits a crisis for the human race with the need for water likely to rise by nearly 50 per cent over the next two decades. Water scarcity is set to become an ever-deepening issue across the developing world and, in particular, for sub-Saharan Africa. The influential Camdessus Report had already warned that 'It is impossible to escape the conclusion that the global water sector in its many forms is in a disastrous condition. Water is not being sufficiently developed and conserved ... Sector management is deficient, services are deteriorating and deficits growing ... the financial situation has been getting worse ... and the sector shows no signs of generating funds to meet future service standards' (Winpenny 2003: 8).

Another conclusion I would draw from the analysis above is that water is essentially a political, as much as, or more than, a technical issue. The global governance of water seeks out transnational solutions to a conflictual issue, aiming to stabilize the status quo on a sustainable basis. Those whom Riccardo Petrella (2001) calls the 'water lords' derive political power from the ownership and control of water. The nation-states of the developing world – hollowed out by neoliberalism – consider ways in which they might regain control of a national asset now largely governed by transnational actors. And in urban and rural communities across the global South there are ongoing struggles with and against all of the above groups for access to safe water as a basic human right.

UN-Water has now advanced a proposal for a post-2015 Global Goal for Water, supported by a coherent, cohesive and mutually reinforcing set of targets. The aim is to have a global goal that is universally applicable while responding to specific national circumstances. Clearly any coherent aspiration for poverty reduction will need to address current deficits in terms of the management of water and the provision of water-related services. However, from the perspective developed in this chapter, we might be wary of MDG-type strategies. It seems clear that these targets do not add up to a development strategy in, and of, themselves and that they are subordinated to a global strategy dominated by the large financial and corporate organizations. Thus, water for all will need to be taken up in a more organic, even 'bottom-up', manner at national and particularly regional levels if it is to be an integral element for an empowering development process.

References

Allan, A. J. (2003) 'IWRM/IWRAM: a new sanctioned discourse', Occasional Paper no. 50, SOAS Water Issues Study Group, University of London.

Arrighi, G., B. Silver and B. Brewer (2003) 'Industrial convergence, globalization and the resistance of the North–South divide', *Studies in Comparative International Development*, 38(1): 3–31.

Asmal, K. (2001) 'Introduction: World Commission on Dams Report, Dams and Development', *American University International Law Review*, 16(6): 1411–33.

Bakker, K., M. Kooy, N. E. Shofiani and E. J. Martijn (2008) 'Governance failure: rethinking the institutional dimensions of urban water supply to poor households', *World Development*, 36(10): 1891–1915.

Barlow, M. (2001) *Blue Gold: The Global Water Crisis and the Commodification of the World's Water Supply*, San Francisco, CA: Committee on the Globalization of Water, International Forum on Globalization.

Biswas, A. K. (2004) 'Integrated Water Resources Management: a reassessment', *Water International*, 29(2): 248–56.

Booth, D. (2011) 'Introduction: Working with the grain? The Africa Power and Politics Programme', *IDS Bulletin*, 42(2): 1–10.

Conca, K. (2006) *Governing Water: Contentious Transnational Politics and Global Institution Building*, Cambridge, MA: MIT Press.

Conway, G. and J. Waage (2010) *Science and Innovation for Development*, London: UK CDS.

Dagdeviren, H. (2008) 'Waiting for miracles: the commercialization of urban water services in Zambia', *Development and Change*, 39(1): 101–21.

Edigheji, O. (ed.) (2010) *Constructing a Democratic Developmental State in South Africa*, Cape Town: HSRC Press.

Evans, P. (2010) 'Constructing the 21st century developmental state: potentialities and pitfalls', in O. Edigheji (ed.), *Constructing a Democratic Developmental State in South Africa*, Cape Town: HSRC Press.

Ferguson, J. (2006) *Global Shadows, Africa in the Neoliberal World Order*, Durham, NC, and London: Duke University Press.

Finger, M. and J. Allouche (2002) *Water Privatisation: Transnational Corporations and the Re-regulation of the Global Water Industry*, London: Taylor and Francis.

Ghosh, G. (2012) 'Some for all rather than more for some: a myth or a reality?', *IDS Bulletin Special Issue: 'Some for All': Politics and Pathways in Water and Sanitation*, 43(2): 10–12.

Hemson, D., K. Kulindwa, H. Lein and A. Mascarenhas (eds) (2008) *Poverty and Water: Explorations of the Reciprocal Relationship*, London: Zed Books.

Jolly, R. (2003) *Evaluating and Monitoring the Access to Water Supply and Sanitation*, Report of the third World Water Forum, Kyoto: WSSC.

Kansiime, F. (2002) 'Water and development-ensuring equity and efficiency', *Physics and Chemistry of the Earth*, 27(11/12): 801–3.

Lane, J. (2012) 'Barriers and opportunities for sanitation and water for all, as envisaged by the New Delhi Statement', *IDS Bulletin*, 43(2): 13–40.

Moser, C. O. N. (1989) 'Gender planning in the third world: meeting practical and strategic gender needs', *World Development*, 17(11): 1799–825.

Movik, S. and L. Mehta (2010) *Liquid Dynamics*, Brighton: IDS.

Nicol, A., L. Mehta and J. Allouche (eds) (2012) 'Some for all? Politics and pathways in water and sanitation', *IDS Bulletin*, 43(2).

Petrella, R. (2001) *The Water Manifesto: Arguments for a World Water Contract*, London: Zed Books.

Showers, K. (2002) 'Water scarcity and urban Africa: an overview of urban rural water linkages', *World Development*, 30(4): 621–48.

Swatuk, L. (2008) 'A political economy of water in southern Africa', *Water Alternatives*, 1(1): 24–47.

Terhorst, P., O. Marcela and A. Dwinell (2013) 'Social movements, left governments, and the limits of water sector reform in Latin America's left turn', *Latin American Perspectives*, 40(4): 55–69.

UN (2005) *Women and Water*, Geneva: Department of Economic and Social Affairs, United Nations.

Wade, J. (2012) 'The future of urban water services in Latin America', *Bulletin of Latin American Research*, 31(2): 207–21.

WHO/UNICEF (2000) *Global Water Supply and Sanitation Assessment 2000 Report*, Geneva: WHO/UNICEF Joint Monitoring Programme for Water Supply and Sanitation.

Winpenny, J. (2003) *Financing Water for All, Report of the World Panel on Financing Water Infrastructure*, World Water Council.

Wittfogel, K. A. (1957) *Oriental Despotism: A Comparative Study of Total Power*, New Haven, CT: Yale University Press.

World Bank (2010) *World Development Indicators*, Washington, DC: Development Data Group, World Bank.

2 | LIQUID DYNAMICS: CHALLENGES FOR SUSTAINABILITY IN THE WATER DOMAIN

Lyla Mehta and Synne Movik

Introduction

Water is pivotal to survival, human well-being and productivity, but water resources are under pressure in many parts of the globe in an uncertain climate – from human needs and environmental requirements, from agriculture, from mining and industry and burgeoning urban areas. Thus a key challenge is managing our limited water resources in a sustainable way. A further challenge is to ensure that adequate, safe and affordable water services are provided universally to all in a way that is equitable and endures over time. In March 2012, it was announced that in 2010 the world had met the water Millennium Development Goals (MDGs) of halving the proportion of people without sustainable access to safe drinking water, well in advance of the MDG 2015 deadline. Between 1990 and 2010, over two billion people gained access to improved drinking water sources, such as piped supplies and protected wells, a reduction of 25 per cent in absolute numbers (WHO 2012). However, 768 million people still use unimproved sources of drinking water and 40 per cent of these live in sub-Saharan Africa. Largely, rural dwellers and the poorest of the poor have been bypassed in the achievement of this goal. Also achieving gender equality, social equity and sustainability have tended to be overlooked and, as we outline below, are only now getting attention in the post-2015 MDG discussions. The picture is bleaker for sanitation – 2.4 billion people still lack access to basic sanitation (WHO and UNICEF 2013). We recognize that sanitation and water issues are highly interlinked. Still, because they have different logics, politics and disciplinary underpinnings, this chapter will only focus on sustainability issues in the water domain.

We argue that debates about access have so far paid insufficient attention to the long-term sustainability of systems and services for accessing water. They have also somewhat neglected issues concerning uncertainty and social, environmental and technological dynamics – particularly through addressing power imbalances and enhancing equity. Also, global debates and policies usually fail to address water problems in ways that are sustainable and meet the needs of poorer and marginalized people. Among many possible reasons for these failures, we highlight two pervasive tendencies. First, policy debates and the often generalized, globalized arguments that underpin them tend to remain disconnected from the everyday experiences of poor and marginalized women and men. In other words, the framings – or understandings and representations – of water systems that dominate policy debates are frequently at odds with the perceptions, knowledges and experiences of the lived realities of local water users, so that issues central to poorer people's perspectives and priorities are neglected. Secondly, current approaches sometimes fall short of the task of addressing emergent challenges associated with contemporary dynamics in water systems, which we refer to as 'liquid dynamics'. 'Liquid dynamics' are the patterns of complexity and interaction between the social, technological and ecological/hydrological dimensions of water systems (and here we also include service provision). These involve rapid changes and interactions across multiple, interlocking scales, affected by processes such as climate change and rapid urbanization. The result is a variety of possible pathways within water systems. Yet most analytical and policy debates in relation to water have not sufficiently appreciated such dynamics. A sustainable water system can be understood as one that maintains a level of service provision over the long term by adapting and coping with these dynamic components and contexts.

We begin by outlining key strands in the current debate, emphasizing the dominance of approaches based on global water assessments, technological fixes and universalized notions of water scarcity. Each has generated important critiques, giving rise to major fault-lines in analysis and policy. Next we introduce a simple framework for thinking about such dynamic systems and for considering the implications for pathways to sustainability. We then turn to the political and institutional relationships that shape debates and action and argue for the need to move from narrow, technically focused approaches such as cost–benefit analysis, towards broader appraisals that allow a wider range of perspectives to inform policy and political discourse. Water issues in this chapter encompass both what is commonly known as water supply/services and water resources management, or, as the 2006 *Human Development Report* puts it, 'water for life' and 'water for production' (UNDP 2006). Water for life refers to water for drinking and domestic purposes and is considered key for human survival. Water for production refers to water in irrigation, industry and small-scale entrepreneurial activities as well as for the production of food for subsistence. This distinction, however, is highly problematic from the perspective of local users whose daily activities encompass both the domestic and productive elements of water and for whom there is little sense in separating water for drinking and washing and water for small-scale productive activities so crucial for survival.

Current debates: examining the fault-lines and beyond

Who is shaping the debate? Water is a multifaceted resource whose state is variable across time and space (Mehta 2003). It fluctuates in availability and is not easily controlled, and it cannot be produced in the true sense of the word. It has different faces and meanings in the everyday contexts within which people live their lives. It can be simultaneously perceived as a free, social, economic, cultural or symbolic resource, and access to water reflects power asymmetries and socio-economic inequalities.

However, official discourses tend to focus on certain aspects of water, often dominated by economic and engineering aspects. Dominant debates and related policy approaches are largely framed by a few major global players such as the World Bank, the Global Water Partnership, UNICEF, the World Health Organization, the World Water Council and the Joint Monitoring Programme (JMP) which gives rise to a set of approaches that emphasize universalized notions more than local and contextual ones, and technical issues more than social ones, and even when the social and gender dimensions are acknowledged, questions of power and political economy may be neglected. We explore these emphases and fault-lines in contemporary debates, moving from those around global water assessments, to those around technological fixes to water problems, to those around water scarcity and access.

Global assessments and their problems There are many recent examples of global assessments of the water 'crisis'. However, there is a range of problems with the ways such assessments are framed, and the assumptions they make. First, their portrayals of scarcity largely focus on the physical and volumetric aspects of water, as opposed to considering disparities in distribution. Secondly, there has largely been a primacy of 'First World' definitions which make it difficult to monitor sustainability of use and impacts on the poorest at local and national levels. Thirdly, much is missed by the way global agencies define both water targets and indicators for assessing progress. Take the MDGs.

Water is an MDG target rather than a goal in itself – the goal is MDG7 to ensure environmental sustainability, while the target 7.C is to halve, by 2015, the proportion of the population without sustainable access to safe drinking water and basic sanitation. The Global Analysis and Assessment of Sanitation and Drinking Water (GLAAS) and the WHO/UNICEF JMP for Water Supply and Sanitation are the two official UN mechanisms to monitor progress towards the MDG target 7.C. Even though the water MDG has been met, recent analyses are highlighting several problems around sustainability, equity and water safety in global monitoring systems (UNICEF and WHO 2011). MDG progress until now has largely been measured by averages, which say little about regional variations and variations between socio-economic groups or by gender. Peri-urban and slum areas, which are some of the fastest-growing areas in the world, have not been included in these statistics (Allen 2010). Issues concerning equity and discrimination have been overlooked as a result of focusing on the quasi-'low hanging fruit' and the areas in which it is easy to extend coverage (Allen and Bell 2011). It is important to note that General Comment No. 15 on the human right to water by the Committee on Economic, Social and Cultural Rights was produced only in 2002, and thus had no influence on the formulation of the original MDG in 2000.

JMP definitions of 'improved' water sources have been contested and controversial because they do not take into account cultural and local perceptions of what works and what doesn't. Katharina Welle's research has demonstrated that there is a big gap between the ways global agencies and national agencies both define and measure water access. In Ethiopia, for example, water access is measured through the hardware constructed and reported on by sector staff rather than by following JMP standards concerning actual use of water structures and surveys employing a range of metrics (Welle 2013). Most of the time, the setting of national targets and their measurement are political exercises and may not match on-the-ground realities, where local notions of access depend on issues such as the quality and taste of water provided and the power games around how the scheme is managed on a day-to-day basis.

The MDG indicator 'use of an improved drinking water source' has not included measuring issues concerning drinking water safety or sustainable access. This means that actual numbers of people around the globe with safe and sustainable access to water will be much lower than what is currently estimated by the JMP (UNICEF and WHO 2011). A handbook for 'rapid assessment of drinking water quality' (RADWQ) has recently been put together, but it remains to be seen to what extent the guidelines provided in the handbook will be followed by national governments (WHO and UNICEF 2012).

The MDG definition of 'improved' sources does not take into account the time spent or distance walked in collecting water. Owing to cultural norms, women and girls can spend between three minutes and three hours per day collecting water. In twenty-five countries, it is estimated that women spend a combined total of at least 16 million hours each day collecting drinking water (Mehta 2013). The MDG definition also does nothing to address the naturalization of women's and girls' water collection activities – the acceptable distance used to be up to one kilometre, which poses the question: should rural women and girls be spending so much time collecting water in the twenty-first century? There has also been little comparable international data on gender indicators and most of the agencies lack proper sex-disaggregated data, making it impossible to monitor progress or devise gender-sensitive policies. However, there have recently been some improvements. The JMP post-2015 consultation has emphasized issues of Equity, Equality and Non-Discrimination (END) which can overcome some of the issues outlined above (JMP 2012). For instance, it has been proposed that intra-household inequality should be addressed through disaggregating data by age, gender, health, disability and so on. How these issues will be taken up in the post-2015 agenda remains to be seen, but they do constitute progress in the desired direction.

Finally, there has been a tendency to ignore critical issues concerning the social, institutional and financial sustainability of water services. The hardware or project-oriented approach has led to the lack of focus on the sustainable provision of a service, issues we deal with in detail in this chapter.

In sum, despite some recent developments, global assessments have tended largely to be framed in particular ways that obscure questions of equity, sustainability, distribution and access. They also show little evidence of reflexivity, i.e. an awareness of how such assessments reflect, at least in part, the social, economic and political positions of the individuals and organizations that produce them. Not surprisingly, then, water is a site for contentious politics and this struggle is over both access and meaning. Both are key in determining whether water debates and policies lead to sustainability and social justice.

Scarcity, technology, rights and access It is estimated that, by 2025, 1.8 billion people will be living in countries or regions with absolute water scarcity, and two-thirds of the world population could be under stress conditions. Moreover, conflicts and growing competition over water allocation are expected to lead to 'water wars'. But what is scarcity? How has it been conceptualized? Does the way the 'problem' is constructed shape the proposed solutions? And do global or theoretical portrayals of scarcity match up to the way the issue is experienced locally or is there sometimes a disconnect between global and local solutions?

While the term water 'shortage' refers to the actual physical amounts of water available, water 'scarcity' is usually moulded by social and political dimensions and can be a social construct or the result of affluence, lifestyle choices and expectations (Lankford 2010; Mehta 2010). Much of the work on scarcity tends to focus on volumetric approaches or classifies countries according to a 'water stress index' on the basis of their annual water resources and population (Shiklomanov 1998; Falkenmark and Widstrand 1992). However, the focus has been broadened to acknowledge that there are different 'orders' of scarcity, ranging from physical (first-order) to socio-economic (second-order) scarcity, which refers to the lack of ability to adapt to the problem of physical scarcity and to the socio-political, technological and cultural changes that a society must undertake to deal with scarcity (third-order scarcity) (Allan 1998; Ohlsson and Turton 1999; Wolfe and Brooks 2003). But even these debates fail to distinguish adequately between the socially constructed and biophysical aspects of scarcity. They tend not to disaggregate users and their entitlements or to look at the politics of distribution. Nor do they focus up front on the social relations underlying how technology choices are made. Finally, most global portrayals of water scarcity see it as something natural and inevitable, instead of something that is either exacerbated, or caused, by socio-political processes. Instead, much work has demonstrated that water 'crises' are more often the result of struggles over access to, and control over, water resources rather than a natural condition (UNDP 2006; Mehta 2005). Simplistic notions of scarcity often lead to simplistic solutions which can intensify problems of access and exclusion. These range from enhancing water supplies, increasing and improving existing infrastructure and technologies, to bringing in markets through cost-recovery principles and privatizing scarce water supplies.

Often technology is evoked to solve problems of water scarcity. In the water domain, recent 'technological optimist' policies range from the search for the new 'blue revolution' and more irrigation systems for Africa (Movik et al. 2005) and the crop biotechnology revolution, to – at their most far fetched – expansion into space to mine Mars for water. There is no doubt that technologies have key roles to play in addressing water problems. Yet driven by conventional engineering paradigms, technological choices in water are often portrayed as existing outside politics, with technology expected to provide solutions that transcend politics. However, technologies and techniques are of course often deeply political and culturally embedded. Contestations around technological solutions, be they large dams or India's fantastical river interlinking project, have become sites of politics, with questions about both their cultural and material implications. Furthermore, the relationships between technology and sociocultural issues are often overlooked. Necessity is not always the mother of invention. Instead, culture and meaning can also drive a society's technological development (Pfaffenberger 1992). For example, large water structures embody power and prestige in many ancient hydraulic societies (Mosse 2003). Pumps in villages break down, owing not just to technological issues, but also to intra-village conflicts and local politics. Thus, it is necessary to understand the dynamic interplay between society, technology and ecology – something which rarely comes to the fore in conventional analyses.

In the past decade, rights-based approaches and notions of entitlement to water have been evoked as ways to enhance access. The human right to water was the result of decades of intense global struggle and lobbying, as it was initially resisted by powerful players in the water domain and countries such as Canada and the USA. It was not explicitly recognized in the 1948 Universal Declaration of Human Rights. However, in July 2010 the UN General Assembly and later, in September 2010, the UN Human Rights Council finally recognized access to clean water as a human right. This official recognition was a great victory for the global water justice movement and has been used as a powerful mobilizing tool for water struggles all around the world. South Africa, Ecuador, Bolivia, Gambia, Tanzania, Uruguay and others have recognized the right to water, which means committing to not undermining this right – for example, by ensuring access to safe and affordable services (Sultana and Loftus 2012).

But globally there has been a considerable gap between rights talk and rights practice, and governments are usually constrained by their financial commitments to achieving universal access to water, and may not prioritize their national governments' global commitments. Bolivia, for example, has been at the forefront of international campaigns to recognize the human right to water. Yet domestically the progressive Morales government has been criticized for pursuing economic development policies based on industrialization and extractive industry expansion that are elite-driven and can violate local people's rights to water (Bustamante et al. 2012). South Africa was the first country to provide constitutional recognition to the right to water, and in 2001 the Free Basic Water Policy was introduced, which provided a basic supply of water to all households free of charge. At the same time, the South African government's water policies were also informed by several dominant framings in water management which include an emphasis on cost recovery, user fees for water and controversial cut-offs which have often violated poor people's basic rights to water (McDonald and Ruiters 2005). There is also a considerable gap in the ways in which local women and men interpret this right and how it is legally defined. The focus on the right to safe drinking water (i.e. consumption) has had a limiting effect on water resource management, neglecting the need for productive uses of water. In South Africa and beyond, there have been passionate debates about whether the right to water should go beyond mere domestic supplies to also cover livelihood issues, which are crucial for the family's survival, where women often play a significant role – e.g. in providing water for productive purposes in women's home gardens. Given that poor and marginalized people's rights to water are violated owing to the actions of powerful players who often contaminate, appropriate or reallocate water resources to suit their own interests (known as 'water grabbing'), there have also been calls to expand the scope of the human right to water to engage with issues concerning water resource management and waste water (Franco et al. 2013).

Debating sustainability in water We have so far demonstrated how different approaches to conceptualizing scarcity, access and rights are part of the framing of international and national debates around water. Despite the continued prevalence of approaches focused on technical aspects of water supply, there have been important moves towards a greater recognition of distributional issues. For example, the need to share limited water resources equitably is the logic behind the water allocation reform processes under way in many parts of the world such as in South Africa (Movik 2012).

But merely enhancing access is not enough. There is also a need to look at what we might term the 'functionality' of water access, i.e. the particular services that people derive from water and how these are rooted in their livelihoods and in particular social and cultural contexts. This calls for greater attention to diverse local settings and to the meanings and values that people attach to water in their everyday lives than is found in much contemporary analysis and policy discourse. At the same time, the sustainability of that functionality is key, referring to the extent to which water access enables people, communities and regions to use water services in a way that is resilient and robust over time and in the face of shocks and stresses and in ways that go beyond mere survival. As discussed, our concern in this chapter is to stress that sustainability should be achieved in an inclusive and socially just way.

In water-related processes and interventions, analysts have argued that it has not been easy to assess whether something is sustainable or not, owing to the difficulty of defining sustainability in operational and quantitative terms (Figueres et al. 2003). In part this is due to questions concerning the adequacy of assessments and designs to gauge social and environmental costs. These could include: natural resource depletion; compensation to future generations for social and cultural costs as well as the depletion of natural resources; impacts on health, or financial and institutional costs. Engineers such as Mihelcic et al. have stressed the importance of bringing together three dimensions when viewing sustainability in water (2003). These include societal sustainability (social justice, equity), environmental sustainability (human and ecosystem health, natural resource protection and restoration) and economic sustainability (productivity, employment, growth, etc.). Watkins et al. (2004) build on these to identify and explore several metrics for water use sustainability. These include: (1) the ratio of water withdrawal to total supply; (2) the percentage of income spent on water; (3) the incidence of waterborne diseases; and (4) the indices related to a managed system's ability to cope with extreme events. They also consider the temporal and spatial scales over which such metrics can be calculated. Those who are primarily interested in service delivery would not necessarily look at tension between development and the environment. Instead, they would focus more narrowly on service delivery in the context of water supply. While recognizing that the natural resource base must be protected and maintained to ensure a durable supply, the focus here would be on ensuring that the service providing water works over time and that both the quality and the quantity of the water continue to be available for the period for which it was designed (Abrams et al. 2001).

Within the water, sanitation and hygiene (WASH) sector, there are multiple emergent and emerging initiatives that set out to address sustainability in a variety of ways. One example is the Rural Water Supply Network, which treats sustainability mainly from an 'appropriate technology' point of view, through developing tools that gauge the applicability and ease of introduction of different technologies in specific contexts (Olschewski and Casey 2012).

UNICEF has 'sustainability compacts' with national governments, as well as a sustainability checklist for institutional, social, technical and financial indicators of rural water supply projects, but it does not have an explicit focus on environmental sustainability. The key focus revolves around whether technologies are appropriate and durable, whether the projects are financially viable, etc. Other examples include NGOs, such as WaterAid (2011), which have developed their own frameworks for sustainability, emphasizing the need to address three key dimensions of sustainability – the lack of capacity, the scarcity of funds, and the fragmentary nature of past approaches. In 2013 there was the WASH Sustainability Forum, hosted by the World Bank, which focused on the role of collaboration – particularly with national governments – in order to provide lasting water services. The strengths of these initiatives lie in their explicit recognition of the need to look beyond simple delivery, supported by the statistics of the increasing numbers of people having access to improved water services, and to understand that delivery provision is not a one-off event but a long-term process. All these initiatives address the idea of 'sustainability' to varying degrees, and provide contextual understanding. However, in many of them, the main focus of concern is the sustainability and appropriateness of technologies and of the projects themselves. While this is certainly important, we argue that more attention should be paid to the social dynamics – including power relations and differing perspectives of the value of services – that exist in such contexts, which form part of the basis for whether or not particular initiatives will be sustainable in the long run. Current approaches lack adequate criteria to judge sustainability or pro-poor development in water (Figueres et al. 2003). An approach is needed that takes account of the interaction of social, technological and ecological dimensions of complex, dynamic water systems, and addresses whether they are sustainable in terms that poorer and marginalized people value and which enable them to exercise agency in water services provision.

Addressing sustainability in dynamic water systems

In today's dynamic world, water systems involve rapidly changing social, technical and ecological processes. In this section, we discuss these liquid dynamics and introduce a perspective on sustainability that takes them into account. We suggest that how water systems

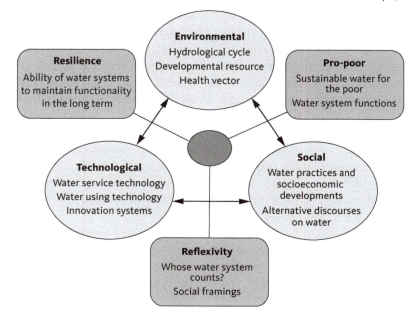

2.1 A heuristic for understanding liquid dynamics

are understood, or 'framed', differs according to the individual or group concerned and their social, political or disciplinary positioning. Particular framings in turn justify particular approaches to water governance. We are interested in the interaction between how water systems are framed, the interventions that result, and their outcomes.

Figure 2.1 illustrates these concerns in a simple diagram of a water system in its environment. The system's context includes the multiple framings of the system's dynamics, and what values different groups – hydrologists, engineers, state agencies, NGOs, well-off or poor people, men or women – attach to structures and functions. As authors, our own 'meta-framing' of this analysis is shaped by our interest in the resilience of these systems in relation to the functions valued by poor people, and a concern for greater reflexivity. As pointed out earlier, the functionality that people derive from water systems is determined by the interactions between complex social, technological and environmental processes. While each of these is discussed in turn below, it is important to bear in mind that all of these three are deeply interconnected. For example, social activities do not simply impact upon the physical flows and operation of hydrological cycles (Oki and Kanae 2006). Rather, the meaning societies invest in water, both culturally and economically, influences how they frame and understand hydrological cycles, interpret data, read in between gaps in the data, and as such socially construct water cycles. This can subsequently lead to interventions that affect the water system and its services for the poor (sometimes in unanticipated ways). Conversely, it could also be argued that debates on water are increasingly articulating uncertainties derived from climate change and variability, yet still failing to acknowledge other uncertainty dimensions that do not just refer to observable processes of biophysical change.

Social, cultural, technological and environmental dynamics Social *processes* include demographic change, the concentration of populations in urban centres, patterns of agricultural practice, socio-economic development, and changes in livelihoods and lifestyles that affect demands on water services and resources. For example, rising norms of 'cleanliness' in affluent societies are leading to changes in water practices, while in terms of food consumption, the growing presence of meat in daily diets is also impacting heavily on water demand (Shove 2003). Secondly, social and cultural processes and relations around caste, gender, ethnicity, race and so on often shape who gains access to water services and whose perspective counts when allocating 'scarce' resources. There are also culturally embedded reasons that dictate local people's preferences and knowledges regarding water. For example, a village woman may prefer to collect water for drinking from a hole in the river bed rather than government-supplied water from a tanker. The river bed is farther away from her home, but she may value the outing and also prefer the taste, and its quality may also be better than water provided in the tanker, which counts as an 'improved' source. Thirdly, social processes underpin the development of governance arrangements for meeting demand and arbitrating between conflicting demands. A final set of social processes influencing water systems and their functionality are relations of power and knowledge. These in turn shape the interventions made into hydrological cycles, their material effects, and the consequent form those cycles take. In mundane terms, these affect decisions regarding where water schemes are built and who is allowed legitimate access. There are also inevitably knowledge gaps and uncertainties (e.g. the impacts of climate change on water availability) (IPCC 2011). Yet powerful institutions rarely admit to such uncertainties and knowledge gaps and it is easier to operate on assumptions of a more stable, certain water world that they can shape in predictable ways – even though in practice such views often prove illusory.

Technologies play an important mediating role between the social and the environmental dimensions of systems. Societies in the global North have long-established and standard water technologies, in many cases little altered from the capital-intensive, hydraulic civil engineering technologies first introduced by the Victorians (Hamlin 1992). This is the technological paradigm that most utility companies entering into developing-country markets inhabit. But such capital- and resource-intensive technologies can be ill suited to other environmental contexts, such as rapidly growing peri-urban areas (Mehta et al. 2013; Allen et al. 2006). The dominant technological paradigm has been the reliance on inter-basin transfer of water through large irrigation projects, large dams and so on. While benefits have accrued, there have also been major social and environmental costs as well as unintended consequences such as disease outbreaks (WCD 2000). This has resulted in a renewed interest in alternative and/or updated traditional technologies more appropriate for specific situations, to complement or replace traditional civil engineering solutions such as rainwater harvesting, especially in peri-urban areas which tend to be avoided by conventional service providers. But here too there may be unintended ecological impacts. Also there are challenges concerning equity and scale – can these systems serve large populations? – as well as questions around productivity and markets in a context where these are often isolated small-scale initiatives amid globally connected food and industrial systems. Some therefore argue that there is a 'crisis of innovation' in the water industry, and troubling complacency around current, long-standing technology solutions that simply will not work for the majority of the world (Thomas and Ford 2005). In other cases, strong arguments are being made for greater attention to finding ways to go to scale with quality, sustainability and equity (Mehta and Movik 2011).

Thus different technological developments have different implications for the long-term sustainability of water systems and services, and for the livelihoods and well-being of the poor. This raises crucial questions in liquid dynamics: which trajectories of technology development improve resilience in ways that suit the poor, and which undermine it? How far, in different settings, are the technology strategies of donors, governments and global utility companies inclined towards appropriate water service technology solutions for the poor, and where is more attention needed to develop more pro-poor innovation systems, especially in difficult-to-reach environments such as the peri-urban interface?

With reference to *environmental dynamics*, geo-hydrological conditions are an obvious and key factor in water systems. It is estimated that people around the world withdraw, in aggregate, around 3,800 cubic kilometres of circulating renewable freshwater resources, or about 10 per cent of the maximum available yield globally (Oki and Kanae 2006). However, this masks stark distributional inequalities and high stress in specific regions (UNDP 2006). Climate change is introducing new uncertainties to these flows, as is the growing recognition of environmental requirements (IPCC 2011). Many hydrologists accept that the social is a major intervening factor. And not just at local or regional scales, but across the global scale too. For example, Oki and Kanae (2006: 1069) have argued that: '… it no longer makes sense to study only natural hydrological cycles. For this reason, some studies have started to consider the impact of human interventions on the hydrological cycles, thereby simulating more realistically the hydrological cycles on a global scale.'

While the integration of social impacts into hydrological studies has been widely accepted for some time now, much of the work continues to be based on an equilibrium model of water systems. Thus, water users' social practices are understood as intervening in and disrupting hydrological cycles, and as needing to be brought back in line to restore hydrological balance. Such narratives often justify policy processes aimed at restoring such balance. However, such notions overlook the more dynamic, sometimes non-equilibrial, ways that social and hydrological processes interact.

Addressing sustainability In multiple ways, then, dynamic environmental, social and technological processes co-construct water systems and the functions that people derive from them. Shifting demographics, technological innovation, economic development, land-use patterns, climate change, prevailing social values, new institutional arrangements, and other factors obviously affect the operation of water systems and services. Some factors can be internal to the water system itself and others may be more contextual. A sustainable water system can be understood as one that can maintain a level of service provision over the long term by adapting and coping with these dynamic components and contexts. Yet while sustainability refers to maintaining services in a general sense, the concept of sustainability needs to take account of the fact that services are valued differently by different social groups (such as the poor), and that what is sustainable will also depend on normatively defined goals such as poverty reduction or the achievement of greater social justice. We thus would argue that a sustainable water system should both maintain itself over time and promote human well-being as well as social and gender equality.

Properties contributing to sustainability are stability, durability, robustness and resilience. Depending on the sustainability goals in question, these properties – and the possible trade-offs between them – may be valued in different ways. The *stability* of a water system relates to its ability to withstand shocks internal to the system, such as engineering failures, financial shocks, switches in ownership or governance, and so on. The *durability* of the system rests on its ability to maintain service provision even when conditions within the system change, inducing stresses, such as declining aquifer levels, periods of drought, or growing numbers of households, agricultural or industrial connections/users. Relatively rapid changes in context can also challenge the system, and the ability of water services to cope with these exogenous shocks is a product of system resilience. Examples of such external shocks include disasters such as floods, pollution incidents, rapid urbanization, disease outbreaks, and sudden shifts in land-use patterns, such as deforestation. Finally, the *robustness* of the system is the exogenous correlate of its durability, in the sense that it is the ability of the system to adapt to more gradual contextual developments, such as climate change, demographic change, agricultural intensification and industrialization. These factors also link to technological and environmental sustainability, in the sense that particular technologies might serve to enhance stability and durability – for instance, through paying sufficient attention to contextual factors to avoid unnecessary breakdown of engineering structures, or the presence of adequate infrastructure and storage to cope with droughts and floods, and thereby also mitigate potential environmental disasters.

In practice, the way different, interacting and complex processes influence the provision of water services may not fall so neatly on either side of the spatial boundary of the system (internal or exogenous) or the temporal boundary (sudden shocks or slower trends). To a large extent, this depends upon how we decide to analyse and organize these real-world complexities, by defining system boundaries and classifying real-world processes and events in certain ways and not others. These are questions about how water stakeholders negotiate and interpret water systems – how the system is socially constructed or framed. Of course, questions of scale matter tremendously in issues concerning sustainability of water systems and services. How should the boundaries be set for studies concerning sustainability and resilience? Obvious physical or hydrological boundaries such as watersheds are complicated by territorial jurisdictions, and intersected by socio-technical networks whose webs of interaction make boundary-setting more difficult. Should we be looking at the impacts on distant river sources of urban water systems and services in assessing sustainability? Which relations should be privileged in analyses? In short, whose water 'system' counts?

One example of an approach that treats water issues as part of an integrated social-technological-ecological system geared towards equitable sustainability is Integrated Water Resource Management (IWRM). The core point of IWRM is *integrated management* of sectoral and aggregate *demand* to ensure that activities impacting on a water body are coordinated, taking into account synergies and cumulative effects of actions (Shah and Van Koppen 2006). The notion of integration provides a framework that seeks to avoid fragmented and piecemeal approaches to water supply, water management and waste-water treatment. Based on the four Dublin Principles of managing water in a holistic way, in a participatory manner, acknowledging the importance of women and recognizing the economic value of water in competing uses, IWRM's pivotal importance in water development has been confirmed in global water fora such as the triennial World Water Forum, first held in 1997.

However, IWRM has been criticized for being a vague and fuzzy concept, and for being difficult to implement in a practicable fashion (Biswas 2004; Molle 2008). For instance, agreeing on what 'integration' means in practice is open to a variety of interpretations. The most straightforward form involves the systematic consideration of the various dimensions of water and their interdependence (e.g. quality and quantity; surface water and groundwater). The task here is to ensure adequate linkages between various water management functions, such as water supply, waste-water disposal and flood protection. A second, more comprehensive interpretation of integrated water management addresses the interactions between water, land and the environment. In this case, the management tasks cross sectoral boundaries between land and water use – for example, in flood-plain management, the reduction of diffuse-source pollution or the preservation of water-dependent habitats. The third, most far-reaching form of integration looks beyond physical impacts to the interaction between water and economic and social development. This approach is rooted in the debate on sustainable development and addresses, in addition to the above, the role of water in, for instance, electricity generation, transportation or recreation (Mitchell 1990). Other forms refer to the integration of analytical perspectives and the fact that the organization of knowledge production tends to be along disciplinary and sectoral lines. Water management is also integrated with ecosystem services, ecological sustainability, economic growth, poverty alleviation, gender equity, employment generation, quality of life; in short, human development (Bolding et al. 2000). It is often overlooked that integration is also a political process, and we need to ask who is doing the integrating and whose interests are being represented, and how should contested interests be contained. Moreover, Jairath (2010) argues that while IWRM recognizes inequity in access and control over water resources, this is conceptualized as a management distortion and not as derived from an imbalance in power relations between those with differential access to water benefits. Thus while productivity and efficiency gains may be possible through better-organized/coordinated activity, the same cannot be said of the sharing of the benefits thus generated, unless access to these benefits is ensured through political rearrangements.

The framework outlined in this section shares some important features with the IWRM approach, in its concern with sustainability, including a better appreciation of the integrated social-technological-environmental systems and equity. However, our framework attempts to go farther, in specifying the sustainability goals of poorer and marginalized people and the systems properties that contribute to them and in addressing the relationship between systems dynamics and their framing by different groups. This, we hope, offers the potential for a more systematic and operational approach to water sustainability, while also addressing explicit normative goals of poverty reduction and the promotion of social and gender justice.

Meeting governance challenges in water

Water management and provision take place through a range of institutional arrangements, either formal or informal. Usually there is a mix of institutional types and arrangements which transcend these divides and tend to be messy, overlapping and power-ridden (Cleaver 2012). The increasing dynamism and multiple framings that characterize water systems pose many challenges for policies and institutions aiming to address contemporary problems. Water management and service provision have evolved considerably from the command-and-control 'hydraulic imperatives' and supply-driven approaches that dominated in the 1950s to the 1970s, when engineering perspectives dominated over social ones. Today there are trends in multi-scale, polycentric and participatory governance which recognizes the need of a large number of stakeholders and the need to combine different knowledges for social learning. However, in both cases (whether command-and-control or participatory), power is intertwined with institutions and social/political interests (Mollinga 2007). Water interventions (small and large) then invariably end up with winners and losers and a range of material effects. There have been some key moves in political, institutional and management approaches to water issues: from an emphasis on centralized to decentralized systems, recognizing the role of local institutions and community management; from supply-driven approaches to an emphasis on demand and rights; and from state-based approaches to those including global governance and market-based mechanisms. We discuss these themes below, starting with the rise of 'global governance'.

Water is increasingly conceptualized as a global governance issue. Policy documents and big international events often produce statements such as 'the global water crisis must be tackled' or 'global water resources are growing scarcer'. Yet, as Roth et al. (2005) argue, this overlooks more contextualized understandings of what water management problems actually are. Thus, aggregated and simplistic representations risk impoverishing the debate and hampering the search for effective solutions to problems faced by water users in local settings. Moreover, though there is an increasing focus on global water issues, there is no consensus on whether water should be treated as a separate sector, or whether it should be a cross-cutting issue. One perspective is to separate global water governance into five fragmented areas – water law (which includes trans-boundary water and legal conventions), water policy, hybrid (public–private) policy-making, the framing of water as an economic good, and the positioning of water within the human rights arena (Gupta et al. 2013).

With respect to the field of water law and policy, there have been major shifts in thinking. Many countries were busy reforming their water legislation during the 1990s and early 2000s, concentrating to a large extent on crafting water rights regimes in response to what is perceived as an increasing scarcity of water (Saleth and Dinar 2000; Burchi 2004). Water rights are seen as creating better security and facilitating allocation to promote efficiency of use as well as opening up opportunities for more equitable distribution. As the literature on legal pluralism acknowledges, the 'rules of the game' that structure access to water in practice involve in-formal rules and norms, as well as formal ones (Meinzen-Dick and Bruns 1999; Roth et al. 2005). Often, local norms, rules and values may partially merge with formalized rules and regulations, creating 'morphed' institutions that are fluid and adaptive in their nature. Acknowledging such complexity is part of a general trend in analyses of resource exploitation that increasingly recognizes that resource governance is more than just the adherence to a set of specific rules; it is characterized by contingency, ambivalence and conflict. Using legal pluralism as a lens to explore the fluidity and hybridization of rules, norms and values thus may help in gaining a more thorough understanding of how institutions respond adaptively to the dynamics of water management systems.

Closely linked to water law are the trends in the water policy field, long dominated by IWRM, which is abuzz with new concepts and ideas. Terms such as adaptive management (Pahl-Wostl et al. 2010), water security (Cook and Bakker 2012) and 'nexus' thinking, such as water-food-energy or water-land-climate and similar constellations, are increasingly gaining ground (Hoff 2011). Making sense of the plethora of concepts being bandied about and how they relate to one another is a challenge. For instance, some argue that adaptive management is a supplement to IWRM thinking while others hold that advocating a 'nexus' approach is a simplified version of IWRM. Hitherto, by far the most dominant discourse has been IWRM, and an important principle of this approach has been the concept of subsidiarity, and devolving management to the lowest possible level (Kemper et al. 2007). However, while such efforts are laudable, a parallel process of greater recentralization is also observed, driven in part by alarm concerning scarcity and mistrust on the part of policy-makers and managers of local communities' ability to handle water management issues in a sustainable manner (Movik 2010). This quest for control is reinforced by the discourse of water security, which emphasizes the need for countries to secure their water supplies in the face of increasing uncertainties and potential threats. Such recentralization processes (through the emphasis on licences and permits, for example) risk partly cancelling out the efforts of decentralization, as seems to be the case in South Africa, for instance (ibid.; Movik and De Jong 2012). These processes can also marginalize the rights of women and invisible users of water, who lack formal rights and gain access through informal means (Van Koppen 2007).

With respect to hybrid governance (public/private), framing water as an economic good and as a human rights issue (see above), there are long-standing debates. There is now an emerging consensus that international public sector reform in irrigation and water management arose from transnational pressure for structural adjustment and liberalization (Castro 2008; Swyngedouw 2009). Devolution – like privatization – responds to global economic ideas that markets, and local governments, should take on more of the tasks hitherto performed by large, inefficient, central state machineries (Crook and Manor 1998; Finger and Allouche 2002). The debates have often tended to centre around dichotomies such as public/private, human right/economic good, and citizen/consumer. Bakker (2007) argues that such binary positions conflate several separate issues of resource rights and governance. She highlights that water is subject to multiple market *and* state failures, and that the most promising approach seems to be one that embraces a twofold tactic, reforming rather than abolishing state governance, while fostering and sharing alternative local models of resource governance. Further, it needs to be recognized that there is no one model of community governance that can be imposed; rather they need to build on local uses and norms. It might be helpful, then, to draw on the concept of 'polycentrism', which recognizes that it is not a question of 'either-or' (Ostrom 1990). The challenge is to incorporate and appraise the different framings of sustainability that arise in such polycentric settings.

Amid contemporary liquid dynamics, charting pathways to sustainability that work for the poor will require greater attention to the politics of knowledge and decision-making. This may require more attention to participatory approaches and also greater reflexivity from powerful institutions, in order to recognize how their framings of water problems are only some views among many. Furthermore, scale remains an issue, with multilevel, networked governance arrangements being an important complement to both global-level and local approaches. Knowledge politics, issues concerning a wider political economy and the politics of framing need to come to the fore in water governance debates. This implies a significant shift from the current situation, in which most dominant governance approaches emphasize the universality of knowledge and consistently ignore the plurality of perspectives and local practices.

Designing appraisal of water systems and services

The debates concerning water governance are also reflected in the social processes through which knowledges are gathered and produced to inform decision-making and wider institutional commitments. Change of appraisal practices has followed a trajectory from closed and narrow forms of appraisal design, epitomized in the use of cost–benefit analysis to appraise large dams, through to those that better allow for complexity, negotiation of perspectives, and sensitivity to power relations, to include poorer people's voice and agency, and to link appraisal with pathways to sustainability. One such trajectory has been the move towards multi-stakeholder forums, such as the World Commission on Dams (WCD). It emerged in 2000 as a response to protest movements which had questioned conventional approaches to dam-building and appraisal since the late 1980s. It involved a unique multi-stakeholder dialogue initiated by the World Bank, the International Union for Conservation of Nature (IUCN), donors and activist groups. And it concluded that, while dams have made a considerable contribution to human development, in too many cases unacceptable costs have been borne in social and environmental terms (WCD 2000). The WCD stands out as a global initiative that sought to tip the balance between the so-called winners in large dam projects and the losers, who are, more often than not, poor and powerless people. However, its conclusions were rejected by the World Bank and dam-building nations such as Turkey and India, and its principles have not been integrated to any great extent into ongoing best practice around the world.

There are also tensions around risk assessments in water. Such assessments continue to be very technocratic and top-down, and to emphasize narrow notions of risk rather than the broad range of uncertainties that tend to be at play in dynamic systems. In response to critiques concerning the narrow, top-down nature of many appraisal processes, as well as to the challenges of dealing with complex dynamic systems, there was a growth in interest in appraisal approaches that emphasize participatory action research, learning and reflexivity. In recent decades, however, there has been a shift from 'getting rid of uncertainty' to new concepts and practices such as 'adaptive management practices' which embrace uncertainty through scenario planning and social learning (Brugnach et al. 2008; Pahl-Wostl et al. 2007). But there is still reluctance to embrace uncertainty in hydrological and hydraulic systems (Pappenberger and Beven 2006). This is because there is an assumption that it cannot be understood by policy-makers and the public or that uncertainty boundaries are too wide to be useful in decision-making. Action learning and social learning can provide a vehicle to open up reflexivity among the various partners involved, concerning their own knowledge and understandings of systems, and other possible knowledges that might be excluded. Reflexive institutions thus offer potential for generating and critiquing knowledge and discourse, providing a forum and mechanism for assessing and implementing public policy in ways that avoid many of the problems of dominating discourses and social exclusion discussed in this chapter. Nevertheless, critiques directed to the Habermasian notion of deliberative democracy also apply in the water domain. These critiques question the assumption that citizen dialogue and debate can build consensus based entirely on reason and rational communication. Rather, social groups may have incommensurable worldviews that cannot be reconciled with deliberation and reason alone (Mouffe 1999). There are invariably going to be tensions and trade-offs between meeting ecological goals and those around gender and social equity in water management. For example, urban river conservation programmes often end up displacing poor slum dwellers who live by the river, and that displacement may not take into account their rights to livelihood and water. Thus, ecological sustainability, democracy and social justice may not necessarily be compatible (Dobson 1998). Furthermore, straight Habermasian communicative rationality may in fact run counter to environmental objectives in instances where 'local' knowledge does not include sufficient appreciation of environmental dynamics and long-term environmental risks and uncertainties, especially where these are due to climate change. In short, it is a significant challenge to marry perspectives on sustainability that reflect the priorities of the poor, while also taking account of biophysical complexities and uncertainties. It is one which will require approaches that emphasize new learning alliances and partnerships across places and disciplines.

Conclusions: ways forward for research and practice

In this chapter we have argued that despite growing global attention to water issues, there often remains a major disconnect between globalized assessments and policy debates, and the needs and priorities of poor and marginalized people as they live with liquid dynamics. Approaches to defining water problems and designing solutions often rest on an image of a more stable, controllable world. Also, views that see water problems in aggregate, technical terms and ignore the sociocultural, political and distributional issues that can underlie what constitutes access often result in policies and interventions that promote singular views of 'progress' in water. Yet such progress often fails to address sustainability and meet goals of poverty reduction and social justice.

We have also argued that it is important to be aware of the multiple, divergent understandings or framings of system dynamics and aims held by different people and groups, whether local water users, development agencies, scientists or engineers. Just as these multiple framings interplay with the liquid dynamics of water systems, so there are many possible pathways to sustainability. These can be directed towards different goals, and emphasize different dimensions of systems properties as key to achieving these. Which pathways unfold over time depends heavily on power relations and institutional arrangements. We have outlined instances in which approaches taken are not geared in any way to meet the interests of poorer groups, whether in cases where political and commercial interests drive the development of large dams that displace people without adequate settlement or compensation policies, or where global water governance is geared to universalized notions of scarcity that fail to reflect people's livelihood priorities. In other instances, governance is aimed at supporting local users – for instance, through community-based approaches – yet in ways that overlook intra-community and gendered power relations. Alongside presenting adaptive forms of governance that can respond flexibly to dynamics and uncertainties, we have underscored a need for attention to power relations across all scales as a central feature of any analysis. This needs to be complemented strongly by reflexivity in analysis and governance, whereby those involved recognize more fully how their social and political positions shape the ways they understand water systems, and how this in turn shapes their management interventions.

Building pathways to pro-poor, equitable sustainability in water will inevitably involve a plurality of approaches. Mapping what works when, where and how will need to involve detailed case studies, urban as well as rural, in ways that attempt to break down conventional silos between water supply and services, water management and waste-water issues (Van Koppen et al. 2014). In each case, it will be important to pay particular attention to the interests and priorities of marginalized and poor women and men. Learning through such case studies, in turn, should help further develop an approach to sustainability that embraces equity, pro-poor agency, power and resilience.

We end with a few concluding thoughts regarding policy and practice. First, human rights approaches to water, while absolutely necessary, also need to embrace some of the liquid dynamics outlined in this paper. To realize rights to water for all, the resource base does matter and this means paying attention to issues such as environmental integrity, water management, contamination, etc. Further, if rights to water are rolled out in parallel with market-friendly, macroeconomic policies as they currently are in several countries, they can end up violating poor people's rights to water. This means that the right to water needs to embrace both a strong social and environmental justice perspective in order to really be meaningful for poor people around the world.

While we welcome some of the new global initiatives which are seeking to address issues around sustainability and equity, especially in the post-2015 era, these initiatives have tended to be Northern and expert-driven and have not necessarily taken on board local and Southern voices. Whether the focus on human rights, universality and equity will indeed be taken up in the post-MDG agenda remains to be seen. This is because target- and goal-setting is intensely political and many good intentions may not be pursued because issues such as equity and rights are difficult to quantify. Finally, these initiatives could pay more attention to issues concerning power relations, cultural politics, structural inequalities and political economy. For it is these issues which determine whether water systems or services will be sustainable ultimately.

Note

An earlier version of this chapter was published in *Wiley Interdisciplinary Reviews: Water*, 1(4): 369–84, July–August 2014. We thank past and present colleagues in the STEPS Centre (www.steps-centre.org) for their help and inspiration. In particular we thank Adrian Smith for drawing our attention to important debates around sustainability. We also thank Beth Mudford for helping with the copy-editing of this article.

References

Abrams, O., L. Palmer and I. Hart (2001) *Sustainability Management Guidelines for Water Supply in Developing Countries*, Department of Water Affairs and Forestry, South Africa.

Allan, A. J. (1998) 'Moving water to satisfy uneven global needs: "trading" water as an alternative to engineering it', *ICID Journal*, 47(2): 1–8.

Allen, A. (2010) 'Neither rural, nor urban: service delivery options that work for the peri-urban poor', in M. Kurian and P. McCarney (eds), *Peri-urban Water and Sanitation Services: Policy, Planning and Method*, London: Springer, pp. 27–61.

Allen, A. and S. Bell (2011) 'Glass half empty? Urban water poverty halfway through the Decade of Water for Life', *International Journal of Urban Sustainable Development*, 3(1): 1–7.

Allen, A., J. Dávila and P. Hofmann (2006) 'The peri-urban water poor: citizens or consumers?', *Environment and Urbanization*, 18(2): 333–51.

Bakker, K. (2007) 'The "commons" versus

the "commodity": alter-globalization, anti-privatization and the human right to water in the global South', *Antipode*, 39(3): 430–55.

Biswas, A. K. (2004) 'Integrated Water Resources Management: a reassessment', *Water International*, 29(2): 248–56.

Bolding, A., P. P. Mollinga and M. Zwarteveen (2000) 'Interdisciplinarity in research on integrated water resource management: pitfalls and challenges', Paper presented at the Unesco-Wotro international working conference on 'Water for Society', 8–10 November, Delft.

Brugnach, M., A. Dewulf, C. Pahl-Wostl and T. Taillieu (2008) 'Toward a relational concept of uncertainty: about knowing too little, knowing too differently, and accepting not to know', *Ecology and Society*, 13(2): 30.

Burchi, S. (2004) 'Water laws for water security in the twenty-first century', in J. Trottier and P. Slack (eds), *Managing Water Resources: Past and Present*, Oxford: Oxford University Press, pp. 117–29.

Bustamante, R., C. Crespo and A. M. Walnycki (2012) 'Seeing through the concept of water as a human right in Bolivia', in F. Sultana and A. Loftus (eds), *The Right to Water: Politics, Governance and Social Struggles*, Earthscan Water Text Series, London and New York: Routledge, pp. 223–40.

Castro, J. E. (2008) 'Neoliberal water and sanitation policies as a failed development strategy: lessons from developing countries', *Progress in Development Studies*, Special Issue on 'GATS and development: the case of the water sector', 8(1): 63–83.

Cleaver, F. (2012) *Development through Bricolage: Rethinking institutions for natural resource management*, London: Routledge.

Cook, C. and K. Bakker (2012) 'Water security: debating an emerging paradigm', *Global Environmental Change*, 22(1): 94–102.

Crook, R. C. and J. Manor (1998) *Democracy and Decentralisation in South Asia and West Africa: Participation, Accountability and Performance*, Cambridge: Cambridge University Press.

Dobson, A. (1998) *Justice and the Environment*, Oxford: Oxford University Press.

Falkenmark, M. and C. Widstrand (1992) 'Population and water resources: a delicate balance', *Population Bulletin*, 47(3): 1–36.

Figueres, C., J. Rockstrom and C. Tortajada (eds) (2003) *Rethinking Water Management: Innovative Approaches to Contemporary Issues*, London: Earthscan.

Finger, M. and J. Allouche (2002) *Water Privatisation: Trans-national corporations and the re-regulation of the water industry*, London: Spon Press.

Franco, J., L. Mehta and G. J. Veldwisch (2013) 'The global politics of water grabbing', *Third World Quarterly*, 34(9): 1651–75.

Gupta, J., A. Akhmouch, W. Cosgrove, Z. Hurwitz, J. Maestu and O Ünver (2013) 'Policymakers' reflections on water governance issues', *Ecology and Society*, 18(1), art. 35.

Hamlin, C. (1992) 'Edwin Chadwick and the engineers, 1842–1854: systems and anti-systems in the pipe and brick sewers war', *Technology & Culture*, 33(4): 680–709.

Hoff, H. (2011) 'Understanding the nexus', Background paper for the Bonn 2011 Nexus Conference 'The water, energy and food security nexus', Stockholm Environment Institute (SEI), Stockholm.

IPCC (2011) *Special Report: Managing the Risks of Extreme Events and Disasters to Advance Climate Change Adapta-*

tion (SREX), ipcc-wg2.gov/SREX/, accessed 23 November 2011.

Jairath, J. (2010) 'Advocacy of water scarcity: leakages in the argument', in L. Mehta (ed.), The Limits to Scarcity: Contesting the Politics of Allocation, London: Earthscan, pp. 215–38.

JMP (2012) JMP Working Group on Equity and Non-Discrimination Final Report, UNICEF–WHO Joint Monitoring Programme

Kemper, K. E., W. A. Blomquist and A. Dinar (2007) Integrated River Basin Management through Decentralization, Berlin: Springer.

Lankford, B. (2010) 'A share response to water scarcity: moving beyond the volumetric', in L. Mehta (ed.), The Limits to Scarcity: Contesting the Politics of Allocation, London: Earthscan, pp. 211–30.

McDonald, D. and G. Ruiters (eds) (2005) The Age of Commodity: Water Privatization in Southern Africa, London, Earthscan.

Mehta, L. (2003) 'Problems of publicness and access rights: perspectives from the water domain', in I. Kaul, P. Conceição, K. Le Goulven and R. U. Mendoza (eds), Providing Global Public Goods: Managing Globalization, Oxford: Oxford University Press.

— (2005) The Politics and Poetics of Water: The Naturalisation of Scarcity in Western India, New Delhi: Orient Longman.

— (2010) The Limits to Scarcity: Contesting the Politics of Allocation, London: Earthscan,

— (2013) 'Ensuring rights to water and sanitation for women and girls', Paper to the United Nations Commission on the Status of Women, 57th session, New York, 4–15 March.

Mehta, L. and S. Movik (2011) Shit Matters: The Potential of Community-led Total Sanitation, London: Practical Action.

Mehta, L., J. Allouche, A. Nicol and A. Walnycki (2013) 'Global environmental justice and the right to water: the case of peri-urban Cochabamba and Delhi', Geoforum.

Mehta, L., F. Marshall, S. Movik, A. Sterling, E. Shah, A. Smith and J. Thompson (2007) 'Liquid dynamics: challenges for sustainability in water and sanitation', STEPS Working Paper 6, Brighton: STEPS Centre.

Meinzen-Dick, R. S. and B. Bruns (1999) Negotiating Water Rights, London: Intermediate Technology Press.

Mihelcic, J. R., J. C. Crittenden, M. J. Small, D. R. Shonnard, D. R. Hokanson, Q. Zhang, H. Chen, S. A. Sorby, V. U. James, J. W. Sutherland and J. L. Schnoor (2003) 'Sustainability science and engineering: emergence of a new metadiscipline', Environmental Science & Technology, 37(23): 5314–24.

Mitchell, B. (1990) Integrated Water Management: International experiences and perspectives, London: Belhaven Press.

Molle, F. (2008) 'Nirvana concepts, narratives and policy models: insight from the water sector', Water Alternatives, 1(1): 131–56.

Mollinga, P. (2007) 'Beyond benevolence? Looking for the politics of social transformation in the Human Development Report 2006 on water', Development and Change, 38(6): 1235–43.

Mosse, D. (2003) The Rule of Water. Statecraft, Ecology and Collective Action in South India, New Delhi: Oxford University Press.

Mouffe, C. (1999) 'Deliberative democracy or agonistic pluralism?', Social Research, 66(3): 745–58.

Movik, S. (2010) 'Return of the Leviathan? Hydropolitics in the developing world revisited', Water Policy, 12(5): 641–53.

— (2012) *Fluid Rights: South Africa's Water Allocation Reform*, Cape Town: HSRC Press.

Movik, S. and F. de Jong (2012) 'Licence to control: implications of introducing administrative water use rights in South Africa', *Law, Environment and Development Journal*, 7(2): 66, www.lead-journal.org/content/11066.pdf.

Movik, S., L. Mehta, S. Mtisi and A. Nicol (2005) 'A blue revolution for African agriculture?', *IDS Bulletin*, 36(2): 41–6.

Ohlsson, L. and A. R. Turton (1999) 'The turning of a screw: social resource scarcity as a bottleneck in adaptation to water scarcity', Occasional Paper Series, School of Oriental and Asian Studies Water Study Group, University of London.

Oki, T. and S. Kanae (2006) 'Global hydrological cycles and world water resources', *Science*, 313: 1068–72.

Olschewski, A. and V. Casey (2012) 'Processes for strengthening the sustainability and scalability of WASH services: development of the Technology Applicability Framework and Guidance for Technology Introduction – research report', WASHTech Project.

Ostrom, E. (1990) *Governing the Commons: The Evolution of Institutions for Collective Action*, Cambridge: Cambridge University Press.

Pahl-Wostl, C., M. Hare and J. Sendzimir (2007) 'The implications of complexity for integrated resources management – the second biannual meeting of the International Environmental Modelling and Software Society: complexity and integrated resources management', Special Issue, *Environmental Modelling and Software*, 22(5): 559–60.

Pahl-Wostl C., P. Kabat and J. Möltgen (2010) *Adaptive and Integrated Water Management: Coping with Complexity and Uncertainty*, Berlin: Springer.

Pappenberger, F. and K. J. Beven (2006) 'Ignorance is bliss: or seven reasons not to use uncertainty analysis', *Water Resources Research*, 42(5): 1–8.

Pfaffenberger, B. (1992) 'Social anthropology of technology', *Annual Review of Anthropology*, 21: 491–516.

Roth, D., R. Boelens and M. Zwarteveen (eds) (2005) *Liquid Relations: Contested Water Rights and Legal Complexity*, New Brunswick, NJ, and London: Rutgers University Press.

Saleth, R. M. and A. Dinar (2000) 'Institutional changes in global water sector: trends, patterns, and implications', *Water Policy*, 2: 175–99.

Shah, T. and B. van Koppen (2006) 'Is India ripe for the Integrated Water Resources Management? Fitting water policy to national development context', *Economic and Political Weekly*, 41(31): 3413–21.

Shiklomanov, I. A. (1998) *World Water Resources: A new appraisal and assessment for the 21st century*, Paris: UNESCO.

Shove, E. (2003) *Comfort, Cleanliness and Convenience: The Social Organisation of Normality*, Oxford: Berg.

Sultana, F. and A. Loftus (2012) *The Right to Water: Politics, Governance and Social Struggles*, Earthscan Water Text Series, London and New York: Routledge.

Swyngedouw, E. (2009) 'Troubled waters: the political economy of essential public services', in J. Castro and L. Heller (eds), *Water and Sanitation Services: Public Policy and Management*, London: Earthscan, pp. 38–55.

Thomas, D. A. and R. R. Ford (2005) *The Crisis of Innovation in Water and Wastewater*, Cheltenham: Edward Elgar.

UNDP (United Nations Development

Programme) (2006) *The Human Development Report 2006: Beyond Scarcity: Power, poverty and the global water crisis*, Basingstoke: Palgrave Macmillan.

UNICEF and WHO (2011) *Drinking Water. Equity, Safety and Sustainability*, JMP thematic report on drinking water, UNICEF and WHO.

Van Koppen, B. (2007) 'Dispossession at the interface of community-based water law and permit systems', in B. van Koppen, M. Giordano and J. Butterworth (eds), *Community-based Water Law and Water Resource Management Reform in Developing Countries*, Oxfordshire: CABI, pp. 46–64.

Van Koppen, B., S. Smits, C. R. del Rio and J. Thomas (2014) *Scaling-up Multiple Use Water Services: Accountability in the Water Sector*, Warwickshire: Practical Action Publishing.

WaterAid (2011) *Sustainability Framework*, WaterAid.

Watkins, D. W., J. McConville and B. Barkdoll (2004) 'Metrics for sustainable water use', Proceedings of the EWRI World Water and Environmental Resources Congress 2004, Salt Lake City, UT.

WCD (2000) *Dams and Development: A New Framework for Decision-making*, London: World Commission on Dams/Earthscan.

Welle, K. (2013) 'Monitoring performance or performing monitoring: the case of rural water access in Ethiopia', Unpublished PhD Dissertation, University of Sussex.

WHO (2012) 'Millennium Development Goal drinking water target met', www.who.int/mediacentre/news/releases/2012/drinking_water -20120 306/en/index.html, accessed 1 March 2013.

WHO and UNICEF (2012) *Rapid Assessment of Drinking-water Quality: A handbook for implementation*, Geneva: WHO Press.

— (2013) *Progress on Drinking Water and Sanitation – 2013 update*, Geneva: WHO Press.

Wolfe, S. and D. B. Brooks (2003) 'Water scarcity: an alternative view and its implications for policy and capacity building', *Natural Resources Forum*, 27: 99–107.

3 | CAN IWRM FLOAT ON A SEA OF UNDER-DEVELOPMENT? REFLECTIONS ON TWENTY-PLUS YEARS OF 'REFORM' IN SUB-SAHARAN AFRICA

Larry A. Swatuk

Introduction

More than a decade ago, at the second World Water Forum in The Hague, the Netherlands' then Prince of Orange, and now newly crowned king, declared that the world water crisis was 'a crisis of governance'. Scholars and development practitioners rallied around this phrase, further arguing that there was, in fact, no 'water crisis' at all, but a 'crisis of water management'. Taken together, these two positions helped foster a series of frameworks, programmes, projects and networks devoted to 'solving' the so-called water crisis. The dominant paradigm simultaneously emerging from, framing and reflecting these activities is Integrated Water Resource Management (IWRM) (Allan 2003; Conca 2006; Swatuk 2008). The logic informing IWRM seems impeccable: the problems with water derive from fragmentation across government sectors, divisive approaches and understandings of the resource across the watershed, and narrow understandings of what water is (i.e. blue[1]) and for (i.e. humans and (agro)-industry). Most recently, within the context of global warming, no less an august body than the World Economic Forum has weighed in with the need to consider water governance and management within the context of 'the water, energy, food and climate security nexus' (WEF 2011). To this end, both the Department for International Development (DfID) in the UK and the Deutsche Gesellschaft für Internationale Zusammenarbeit (German Federal Enterprise for International Cooperation) (GIZ) in Germany have begun to filter their development assistance through the 'nexus' framework (see, for example, r4d.dfid.gov.uk/Output/189277/Default.aspx).

It is difficult to be 'against' either IWRM or a nexus approach: both policy and programming benefit from these integrated and holistic perspectives. But one wonders at the way in which such useful frameworks rather quickly turn into contextual spaces, wherein a wide array of 'stakeholders' use the discursive space created by IWRM (and likely now 'nexus') to foster their own parochial and non-integrative agenda. So for many minor government actors IWRM becomes another means to supplement income through per diems 'earned' through an endless series of meetings, workshops and trainings (see www.cap-net.org for a sense of some of this activity). For many major government actors, IWRM becomes the justification for often poorly considered mega-projects. In the trans-boundary setting, these projects are often justified as means to build peace and foster trust between, and among, otherwise fractured states (Earle et al. 2010; Swatuk and Wirkus 2009). For the private sector, IWRM provides the entry point for profit-oriented water delivery systems; and for civil society organizations, IWRM is 'a licence to drill boreholes' across rural landscapes (see www.wateraid.org/uk/ for an indication of some of these activities). Taken together, in my view, all of this IWRM-fostered activity reveals, and in many cases reinforces, the disintegrated and divisive nature of water resource access, use and management across the Third World landscape (Swatuk 2010; MacDonald and Ruiters 2005). In the words of Lewis Jonker, 'scarcity is really about access' (personal communication, 2010) (see also Noemdoe et al. 2006; Mehta 2007, 2001).

Eminent world water scholar Asit Biswas (2008) has argued that part of the problem is the broad generality of the concept of IWRM. Some scholars have argued for an opportunistic 'low hanging fruit' approach (Moriarty et al. 2004). Others suggest we put it into the background, as a general way of thinking, but take a much more specific approach, such as water for poverty alleviation in rural areas (Merrey 2008). Scholars and practitioners on the political left see all of this 'fiddling with management' as a way of diverting attention away from the deep structural flaws in a system where inequitable access to water and sanitation mirrors Gini coefficients of income inequality (Bond 2002; Ruiters 2015; Cullis and Van Koppen 2009). In other words, these scholars are doubtful of the possibility of floating IWRM on a sea of underdevelopment.

In this chapter, I provide a cursory survey of the landscape of IWRM project-related outcomes in Africa and set these activities within the socio-political and theoretical context of the African state form. The chapter aims to facilitate a better understanding of the challenges and opportunities presented by IWRM. It uses IWRM's stated goals of social equity, economic efficiency and environmental sustainability as the organizational framework to discuss water resources access, use and management in both rural and urban contexts. It uses Conca's (2006) framing of the challenges of governance and management through the organizational understanding of territory, authority and knowledge as its theoretical point of departure.

Somewhere between the 'is' and the 'ought'

In his important study *Governing Water*, Ken Conca (ibid.) traces the course of, and critically reflects upon, the long march towards global water governance. While it is a relatively straightforward march along a linear path from the 1972 Stockholm meeting on Man and the Biosphere (which created among other things the United Nations Environment Programme, UNEP), to the Earth Summits at Rio de Janeiro (1992), Johannesburg (2002) and back to Rio (2012); and while it is equally straightforward to trace the course of global thinking, policy and strategy as it relates to water management and governance – from Mar del Plata to Dublin to Bonn – what are not so straightforward are the actors, forces and factors at play. Because water is not an ordinary good,[2] a diverse array of stakeholders, with a diverse array of needs and interests, are ineluctably drawn together to discuss how best to allocate this shared resource. Conca argues that the goal of global water governance is to embed these often contentious and conflicting interests and needs within 'institutional configurations and orientations' – in other words, to create an institutional structure and process for dealing with multiple interests regarding a shared resource so as to minimize negative outcomes and to maximize shared benefits.

A global water architecture has emerged to facilitate this exercise, with the recently ratified United Nations Convention on Non-Navigational Uses of Shared Watercourses (henceforth the UN Convention) acting as a meta-normative anchor informing and shaping processes at every scale, from the global to the regional to the national and on down to the individual stream or water point. Discursive spaces have been opened up by way of new associations, journals and meeting places (see Conca ibid. for details).

The European Union's Water Framework Directive (WFD) is an important piece of legislation regarding sustainable management of trans-boundary EU waters (Kallis and Butler 2001; Hering et al. 2010). Given the significant involvement of the EU in developing countries and regions, the impact of the WFD is to be felt worldwide as it shapes EU development policy, projects and programmes in Africa, Asia and Latin America.

In the twenty-plus years since the creation of the Dublin Principles, African states have reshaped their water laws, policies and procedures to be in line with these emergent global norms (see Solanes and Gonzalez-Villareal 1999). Pan-African organization (e.g. the African Union African Ministerial Council on Water – AMCOW) and regional organizations (e.g. the Southern African Development Community, SADC, the Common Market for Eastern and Southern Africa, COMESA, the Economic Community of West African States, ECOWAS) function as discursive nodal points whereby member states, globally (e.g. the World Bank; the Global Water Partnership) and regionally (e.g. the African Development Bank, AfDB; the Development Bank of South Africa, DBSA), influential actors, along with donor states (e.g. DfID, GIZ, EU, USAID), private companies and (international) NGOs hammer out the particularities of turning policy into practice (see Conca 2006; Swatuk 2002; Swatuk and Mazvimavi 2010 for details).

In 2000, the second World Water Forum declared that the world 'water crisis' was a crisis of governance – not one of absolute physical scarcity. This statement opened the door for a re-examination of the ways and means of governing and managing the world's water. Conca (2006: 116) describes the common pathway (the way things are; things as 'is') as follows:

> the sovereign state is the territorial reference point for water governance and management; the state (as represented by its government) is the acknowledged authority for decisions regarding access, use and management of water resources; decisions regarding access, use and management derive from expert/specialist knowledge deployed by the state in service of the national interest.

Such an approach to water governance and management has been common throughout the ages (Solomon 2010), especially during the high modern/industrial period when states, generally in competition with each other, engaged in a concerted 'hydraulic mission' to capture water resources in the interests of political and economic power (Allan 2003; Solomon 2010; Swatuk 2010 for a South African case study). This tendency to govern and manage a fugitive resource in terms of the needs of a spatially static state, a shared resource in terms of partial, 'national' interests (as determined by elites), and a resource essential to the functioning of a complex system in terms of highly specific expert knowledge designed to put a river 'to work', is now widely regarded as the source of environmentally unsustainable, socially inequitable and economically inefficient maldevelopment. These three, the 'triple E', comprise the rallying cry of Integrated Water Resources Management:

- Environmental sustainability
- Economic efficiency
- social Equity

The Dublin Principles also articulated, among other things, the need for better governance, meaning, *inter alia*, participation of all stakeholders within a river basin. Thus, in direct response to the perceived negative cycle of unsustainability set in motion by the 'is', IWRM and good governance emerged as the twin meta-norms shaping the way water resource governance and management 'ought to be' (Allan 2003; Conca 2006). Not only is the global literature on IWRM and good water governance replete with the so-called 'triple E', it also adopts without question the ideas that: (i) the appropriate territorial space is not the sovereign state, but the river basin; (ii) the appropriate governing/managing authority is the stakeholder group (which includes the state as only one, albeit centrally important, actor); and (iii) that decisions regarding resource access, use and management should be taken on the basis of inclusive forms of knowledge derived from stakeholders (e.g. indigenous knowledge and/or so-called 'citizen science'), wherein 'expert science' would constitute only one part of the knowledge tree.

Shaping the global water governance and management agenda in terms of the 'ought' immediately opened a Pandora's box of problems and challenges, almost all of which stem from present beneficiaries' perceptions regarding anticipated future losses to be incurred through the new institutional configurations and orientations. Put simply: water is power, and to revise and rearticulate water institutions is to challenge existing forms and bases of power. Homer-Dixon's (1991) 'resource capture/ecological marginalization dynamic' is an elegant heuristic. It accurately describes the dynamics surrounding a scramble for resources due to one or a combination of supply-side, demand-side and structural pressures. In the context of the new water architecture, moving from the 'is' to the 'ought' aims to fundamentally alter extant structural conditions across the water world, so challenging in many cases the existing relations between states, the private sector and civil society. The socio-political reverberations have been felt globally, but they resonate particularly strongly in the context of the African state form, which will be discussed later in the chapter.

The march towards global water governance exists within, and reflects the dynamics of, local and global political economy. So while expert networks have been articulating an 'ought' for water, the 'is' has become further entrenched in many parts of the world, owing largely to the greater dynamics of neoliberal globalization. Every aspect of the 'ought' is being contested: by states such as China, Ethiopia and India, all hell-bent on high modern hydraulic missions that accept neither the river basin as territory, nor basin-wide stakeholders as authority, nor anything but hydraulic engineering and speculative politico-economic benefit modelling as valid knowledge; by governments and private companies that 'inform' citizens as 'customers' regarding various aspects of treating water not as part of a system, but as a commodity. Yet, as with partial implementation of structural adjustment conditionalities, governments across the global South have taken aboard the 'water as commodity' and 'user-pay' narratives, all the while backsliding from these positions in practice as citizens protest, sometimes violently (Mottiar 2013; Bond 2013; Bond and Mottiar 2013; Goldin 2010).

The results, after twenty years of implementing water reforms in light of IWRM, present a very mixed picture. While some scholars chalk up the shortfalls to 'poor governance', or a 'lack of capacity', or the essential explain-all phrase 'a lack of political will', I feel it to be more instructive to see the situation as an interregnum in the Gramscian sense, whereby 'the old is dying, but the new is not yet born'. We know that historical practices and systems lead to unsustainable, inequitable and uneconomic outcomes, but the constellation of social forces within and across states remains in favour of these practices. Indeed, meddling at the margins with new forms of management and governance, privatized forms of service delivery and public–private partnerships on mega-projects is actually good for the dominant actors in business and politics and among the global 5 per cent.[3]

The African state form

Today, the popular press and certain academic and policy circles are quick to claim that 'Africa is rising', or that 'Africa is open for business' (assuming that to be part of the 'rising' is a 'good thing'), in some ways offsetting the hitherto dominant narrative of the 'resource curse', the 'paradox of plenty', failed or failing states and so on. According to Moseley (2014: 56), 'African economic expansion over the past 12 years [i.e. since 2000] has outpaced that of the world over the same period, as well as its own growth in the previous two decades'. Much of this is fuelled by (mainly Chinese) demand for basic commodities and precious minerals and metals, particularly gold, which continues to fetch extraordinarily high prices on world markets owing to unflagging socio-political instability across great swaths of the (Arab) world. Moseley (ibid.) presents a quite sophisticated analysis of the political economies of African states, showing there to be a good deal of economic diversification under way on the continent, but still a heavy reliance on primary commodity production for export. There are two important points to draw out here in relation to water resources governance and management. The first relates to access to water and sanitation. African economies revolve around the principal city as the nodal point for imports, exports and virtually all aspects of the formal economy. Whatever is grown or made in a particular country emanates from or flows to or through the principal city. Yet tens, if not hundreds, of millions of residents in African cities lack access to improved sanitation and potable water supplies at a level one would reasonably expect to be available to an average citizen living in a capital and/or principal city. From Lagos to Luanda, Kinshasa to Kampala, Cape Town to Dar es Salaam, and Harare to Durban via Gaborone and Johannesburg, the state of basic water and sanitation services is abysmal. Indeed, when one considers the amount of (global) effort that has gone into 'UN decades for this or that', national, regional and continental plan-

TABLE 3.1 Selected country access to improved sanitation and improved water supply (%)

Country	Improved sanitation 2009	Improved sanitation 2012	Improved water, rural 2012	Improved water, urban 2012
Angola	56	60	34	68
Botswana	63	64	93	99
South Africa	72	74	88	99
Gambia	60	60	84	94
Cameroon	44	45	52	94
Nigeria	29	28	49	79
Senegal	50	52	60	93
Kenya	29	30	55	82
Uganda	33	34	71	95
Tanzania	11	12	44	78
Mauritius	90	91	100	100

Sources: data.worldbank.org/indicator/SH.STA.ACSN/countries?display=default and wdi.worldbank.org/table/3.5

ning, donor state support, NGO activity, global proclamations at various world water fora – be they mainstream or 'alternative' – it is embarrassing to see people queue for hours at a user-pay kiosk in a central business district (CBD), or to see 'flying toilets' being tossed over back fences into waste-strewn public spaces. Perhaps most telling of all is the fact that where freshwater availability is greatest across the African continent – i.e. Central Africa (with 48 per cent of total continental run-off) and the Gulf of Guinea (with 24 per cent of total continental run-off) – people in these regions (in terms of percentage of people per country) have the least access to potable water and sanitation on the African continent (see Tables 3.1 and 3.2).

Tony Allan (2003) describes domestic water supply as 'small water', and argues that where sustainable water management is concerned the focus must be on 'big water', i.e. that used for crop production. Huub Savenije (2000) laments the common misinterpretation of an absence of adequate domestic water as a problem of physical scarcity. What these scholars are illustrating is that shortages of domestic water of acceptable quality and

TABLE 3.2 Surface water resources in the sub-regions of Africa

Region	Area (km²)	Run-off km²/year	% of total run-off	Run-off (mm/ year)	Water/ capita/ year
Central Africa	5,328,660	1,912	48	359	21,849
Eastern Africa	2,924,970	260	7	89	1,567
Gulf of Guinea	2,119,270	952	24	449	5,388
Indian Ocean islands	594,270	345	9	581	18,533
Northern Africa	5,752,890	50	1	9	346
Southern Africa	4,738,520	271	7	57	2,653
Sudano-Sahelian	8,587,030	160	4	19	1,609
Africa	30,045,610	3,950	100	131	4,979

Source: FAO (2003)

quantity reflect social and political problems, not a shortage of the resource itself. In the African context, the availability of domestic water reflects the persistent socio-economic inequalities typical of primary commodity-dependent political economies: in addition to their spatial separation (guarded and gated communities for the few; crowded and crime-ridden slums for the many), those at the commanding heights have well-watered gardens, swimming pools, continuous supply (either self-supplied through boreholes or municipality-supplied through an articulated system, more often a combination of both), often of a potable quality; the rest have to make do with buying water from kiosks or vendors, or having it run intermittently from an on-plot or community standpipe, or have it piped into the house up to a predetermined daily amount that will automatically cut off should they reach that government-determined limit before midnight. As far as sanitation is concerned, the disparities are far starker: with multiple in-house flush toilets for the few and a shocking variety of options – all not only inadequate but rife with race, class, gender and ethnicity pathological dimensions – for the many. It is my contention that, far from a 'capacity' issue, this is the visible face of structural inequalities – call it 'structural violence' if you will.

The second point concerns 'big water', and resource capture on the scale of the sovereign state (by states and corporations) and the watershed (by private companies, other states and powerful individuals). If 'Africa is rising', it is rising on the back of existing political economic practices where (shadow) states and (multinational) corporations command a greater percentage of blue and green water (the latter through land-grabbing exercises) for cash crop production and resource extraction for export. If there is enough of a domestic outcry, elites may be pressured to onshore a diamond polishing house or two, as is the case with Debswana in Botswana. If the first 'scramble for Africa' shaped the systems of access, use and management of the continent's water and related resources to reflect the extra-continental needs of colonial and imperial powers, then the so-called 'second scramble for Africa's resources' has deepened rather than disrupted these resource flows, serving the interests of criminals and carpet-baggers found everywhere, from Africa's state houses and swanky suburbs (the comprador elite), to the factory floors, front rooms, foyers and five-star restaurants serving a global elite in the world's metropolises, new and old. Resource-extractive economies are notoriously unequal, with very high Gini coefficients of income inequality. Research by Cullis and Van Koppen (2009) showed in a study of the Olifants river basin in South Africa that a Gini coefficient of water inequality, when adjusted for indirect benefits from water through, for example, employment, mirrored almost exactly South Africa's high income inequality coefficient of 0.64. As states and multinational corporations scramble for re-sources across sub-Saharan Africa, the relative equalities that exist in largely agrarian states, such as Malawi, Tanzania and Uganda, are likely to take on the highly unequal character of their resource-extractive counterparts such as Namibia, Botswana, South Africa and Zimbabwe.

Signs of 'the ought'

The negative side needs no further elaboration. If you are in an African city, just walk around the block to see what I mean. If you are in a smallholder-dominated rural area, the evidence is there as soon as you open your eyes. As described below, there are elements of positive water resource development, use and manage-ment, though they less reflect the ideals of IWRM and good water governance (the 'ought') than they do a modified sort of 'is', where governments in the name of the state act, seeking direct benefits for themselves and, tangentially, state power, employing or deploying expert (World Bank, FAO – Food and Agriculture Organization of the United Nations – DfID, consultants) knowledge in the search for these benefits.

We should not be so misguided as to think that win-win sorts of outcomes result from 'proper management', whereas failed projects and programmes or zero-sum outcomes result from 'mismanagement', or 'lack of capacity' and so on. Perhaps these are contributing factors, but they too are symptomatic of a deeper structural problem, i.e. the constellation of social forces in the African state form. Given the abiding tendency to centralize power and to channel economic decision-making regarding the formal economy through central government – be it five-year plans, or tenders for services, commodity marketing boards or educational book suppliers – and given the centrality of water to wealth creation, leaders of African states are loath to relinquish any authority to entities and people they cannot control. This means that power over resource access, use and allocation rarely if ever devolves to actors beyond the state and investments are never undertaken unless immediately and obviously in the interest of state power (the 'is').

Where there are signs of 'the ought', these positive outcomes seem to me to be a function of one of five dynamics regarding the sovereign state: (i) states[4] see direct benefits, such as through large-scale infrastructure development exercises; (ii) states are pressured from below, primarily in urban areas; (iii) states are pressured by their 'peers', i.e. other states within regional, continental and global constellations of social forces; (iv) states are enticed by an irresistible setting; and (v) states are not bothered by either the process or the outcome, most often concerning small water provision in rural and urban areas.

(i) States as beneficiaries

IWRM argues that for good water governance to exist, all relevant stakeholders in a river basin must be meaningfully involved in decision-making, and that these decisions must be taken based on the best available knowledge. In the context of a shared resource (and there are many shared river basins in Africa; see a representative number in Table 3.3), sovereign states have shown a willingness since independence to strike mutually beneficial binding agreements on specific aspects of blue water (see Conca 2006 for details). For example, spurred on by a desire for flow regulation for drought/flood control and large-scale irrigation of the Senegal river, the riparian states there entered into an agreement to create the Organisation pour la Mise en Valeur du fleuve Senegal – the Senegal River Basin Development Authority (OMVS) (Alam et al. 2009). On the Zambezi, Zambia and Zimbabwe created the Zambezi River Authority, a bilateral entity designed to manage the Kariba dam for hydropower production along the middle of the river. There are numerous specific agreements, generalized organizations and technical/knowledge and data-sharing committees across sub-Saharan Africa. So, where sovereign states are the 'stakeholder', they have shown a general willingness to trade off some of their independence for shared benefits in specific instances, with the latest agreement being that signed between South Africa and the Democratic Republic of the Congo on the provision of funding for the Inga III hydroelectric dam project. While environmental NGOs show a propensity to critique these agreements at every opportunity, it should be noted that such benefit-sharing exercises that go 'beyond the river' (Sadoff and Grey 2002) are generally highly regarded and considered a necessary step towards environmental peace-making for regional peace and security (Conca and Dabelko 2002). While the knowledge brought to bear remains expert-oriented and exclusive of civil society groups as meaningful stakeholders, governments perform on the assumption that they have the right to act in the name of their citizens in relation to their own state's and the other riparian state's expressed interests, and often widen the circle of knowledge creation by assembling teams of experts from all basin states. Litfin (1998) describes this process as a 'sovereignty bargain'.

In direct response to the global trends towards 'institutional orientation and configuration' as the necessary means for IWRM and good governance in shared waters, the majority of Africa's major surface waters are now subject to basin-wide agreements, be they commissions, initiatives, authorities or 'joint permanent technical committees'.[5] There is a general tendency to regard the creation of these commissions as necessary, important and high-water marks in regional cooperation. Where there are persistent and increasingly serious problems, such as those between Egypt and the upper riparian countries on the blue and white Nile, most

TABLE 3.3 Selected trans-boundary rivers in Africa

River/lake name	Number of countries sharing the basin	Remarks	Management structures
Nile	10	Africa's longest river at 6,700 km; basin covers 3 million km²	Permanent joint technical committee; Nile Basin Initiative
Niger	10	4,100 km in length; basin area 1.47 million km²	Niger Basin Authority
Congo	9	3,100 km in length; basin area 3.7 km². Receives 30% of Africa's total rainfall	
Zambezi	8	3,000 km in length; Kariba and Cahora Bassa dams important for hydropower generation in southern Africa	Zambezi River Authority; Zambezi Watercourse Commission
Senegal	4	1,050 km in length; basin area is 0.5 million km²	Senegal River Development Organization

especially Ethiopia, the presence of regional organizations, such as the Nile Basin Initiative, helps to set these disagreements within a broader (beyond the river, benefit-sharing) context and to give a formal shape (institutional orientation and configuration) to what could disintegrate into a single-issue, bilateral conflict. Even the presence of a hotly disputed legal document such as the 1959 Treaty, which allocated the entire flow of the Nile river to Sudan and Egypt, is regarded as a valuable focal point for discussion and therefore better than no treaty at all.

Evidence collected by Conca, Wu and Neukirchen (in Conca 2006) shows that governments, acting as state authorities, enter into cooperative agreements with other states when and where direct and demonstrable benefits are to be had. Aaron Wolf and his colleagues have demonstrated that states in trans-boundary basins generally conflict and cooperate on the same suite of issues – water quantity and the infrastructure necessary to manage it (Wolf 1998; Wolf et al. 2003; Wolf et al. 2005; De Stefano et al. 2010), so conflict often leads to cooperation, with the OMVS as a trenchant case study.

Mirumachi and her colleagues have demonstrated that conflict and cooperation coexist and coevolve in shared river basins (Mirumachi 2015; Mirumachi and Van Wyk 2010; Zeitoun and Mirumachi 2008), with states entering into benefit-sharing arrangements (such as the Lesotho Highlands Water Project, LHWP) where major gains for elites and national economies create significant losses for locally affected communities. Basin-wide organizations are meant to guide resource use on to and along an 'ought' pathway, in part to avoid the (economically) partial and (socially and environmentally) suboptimal outcomes of bilateral projects such as the LHWP, or treaties such as those setting the contested boundaries between Malawi and Tanzania on Lake Malawi/Nyasi, South Africa and Namibia on the Lower Orange, and the highly contested allocation of waters on the Nile.

In terms of the 'ought', river basin organizations at both national and trans-boundary levels are designed to become supranational authorities, generating their own revenues and master plans, and making allocative decisions independent of state authorities. State authorities are envisioned as playing a regulatory role, setting out the governance and management framework for these organizations. Given Africa's inheritance of nonsensical colonial boundaries, these basin organizations are seen by many as a first step towards continental integration and hence economic and socio-political reinvigoration. However, it is clear that river basin organizations in the African context do not come anywhere near to replacing state authorities as a supranational authority. Rather, the tendency is to utilize regional organizations as data-gathering, knowledge-generating and agenda-shaping ('horse-trading') entities. State actors bypass regional organizations in the name of 'sovereignty' if it is in their perceived interest to do so. For example, Malawi is the only state to have failed to ratify the Zambezi Watercourse Commission agreement. Recent research by Fatch and Swatuk (2014) shows that Malawi treats its share of the Zambezi basin as four separate entities with each piece of the overall basin subject to specific bilateral behaviours, actions and/or agreements: e.g. the Songwe River Basin Development Plan with Tanzania, to be made operational through the Joint Permanent Commission of Cooperation, forms the basis for significant cooperation; but the international border (established through treaty) along Tanzania's shore continues to be a matter of contention, though amicable use of the shared waters continues by stakeholders there; Malawi and Mozambique have cooperative agreements on particular aspects of resource access, use and management on both Lake Malawi and the Shire/Zambezi river. Malawi and Mozambique established a Joint Watercourse Commission in 2003 to help shape their interactions.[6] The government of Malawi regards the Zambezi watercourse commission, not as a desirable supranational entity, but as a possible threat to Malawi's sovereignty (ibid.). This is but one of many similar cases across sub-Saharan Africa, from Lake Chad to Lake Victoria, and from the Limpopo river to the Volta river.

The SADC Protocol on Shared Watercourses is a unique document on the African continent. Shaped in terms of the UN Convention, it is a legally binding document that commits SADC member states to the pursuit of 'equitable and reasonable use' of the region's shared watercourses. It is widely regarded by regional policy-makers and water experts as a fundamentally important document that has made joint planning and cooperation on the region's shared watercourses possible (Swatuk and Fatch 2013). In line with the predominance of sovereignty, however, member states reserve the right to act in their 'national interest', agreements made prior to the enforcement of the Protocol are exempt from the Protocol, and members may opt out of the agreement if they so wish (though peer pressure is likely, in my view, to keep them in line). Member states regularly invoke the Protocol when entering into bilateral or trilateral arrangements, while bypassing the relevant watercourse commission of which they are a member. Granted, the commission shapes water and related resource use decisions within the context of the basin, but the basin organization rarely if ever determines the feasibility of these activities. Indeed, in the context of the Orange-Senqu river basin commission, South Africa sidesteps 'the basin' by dealing with Lesotho separately (upper Orange) from its relations with Namibia (lower Orange). Botswana, as a non-water-contributing member, participates in joint studies and so on, but the day-to-day hard bargaining excludes it – which doesn't concern it unduly, since all SADC states tend to behave in the same way: where national interests are likely to be affected, they will approach the relevant riparian state actor at that time.

While quite a large literature has emerged on the back of these organizations in terms of benefit-sharing (Klaphake and Scheumann 2009; Alam et al. 2009), a critical literature has also emerged questioning the extent of benefits and beneficiaries in interstate agreements on shared waters (Kistin and Ashton 2008; Swatuk and Wirkus 2009). What this literature shows is the extent to which trans-boundary waters depart from the 'ought', reflecting the centrality of water in wealth creation and state power in Africa.

(ii) Pressure from below

Africa is well into its third decade of post-Cold War experimentation with democracy. What can be more democratic than a public drinking fountain, well-maintained public toilets and equal dignity in equitable access to potable drink and private defecation? The general statistics show some improvements towards meeting the Millennium Development Goals for access to potable water and improved sanitation. Where civil society is strong, such as in South Africa, there has been significant movement not only in terms of shaping laws, policies and procedures towards 'some water for all forever', but also in delivering the real services (L. Thompson 2014). Granted, there are endless problems with delivery, and, following delivery, with operation and maintenance of these systems of supply.

According to data from the World Bank, only fourteen sub-Saharan African states have been able to provide access to improved water supplies (a very broad category that varies from in-house taps to community boreholes, tubewells and 'protected springs') for 70 per cent or more of their rural populations, with five of the fourteen claiming more than 90 per cent coverage (four small island states and Botswana, a rich country with a small rural population). States have fared much better in terms of urban water supply, with only nine states having less than 80 per cent coverage, and none lower than 63 per cent (South Sudan) of their urban populations having access to an improved water supply (see a representative selection of states in Table 3.1 above). Access to improved sanitation (which is also a broad category that goes from in-house flush toilets to chemical toilets, pit latrines and mobile toilets) reveals a much more desperate situation. Only eight sub-Saharan African states report more than 60 per cent of their total population having access to improved sanitation (four small island states and Angola, Botswana, Gambia, Rwanda). At the other end of the scale, with very low levels of access, lie South Sudan and Niger (both 9 per cent), Malawi (10 per cent), Chad and Tanzania (both 12 per cent), as well as Sierra Leone (13 per cent).

It seems to me that the evidence and statistics from South Africa present the possibilities for better access for all: despite rapid urban population increase, and a large overall population (relative to much of the rest of Africa), a great percentage of which is poor, overall coverage of water and sanitation continues to improve in percentage terms, suggesting absolute overall improvements. Granted, sanitation roll-out remains fraught with problems (Bond and Mottiar 2013) and South African townships are topsy-turvy with citizen group protests. But this is the point: South African citizens are engaging with the state and while their methods may be crude, they have the backing of the post-apartheid Constitution. Two decades of 'democracy' across sub-Saharan Africa have yielded few demonstrable benefits for the average citizen. Most often, the dual economy meets only once in a while, at the ballot box. More often than not, African citizens prefer to practise exit rather than voice, finding their own ways towards water and sanitation security, buying bagged water, flinging bagged faeces, and remaining distrustful of governments they largely regard as kleptocracies with revolving seats of power. Can anyone blame them for such an attitude? The lesson from South Africa is clear, however: voice matters.

(iii) 'Peer pressure'

As the Arab Spring continues to demonstrate, there are extreme perils to be faced when the populace confronts its government. Sub-Saharan African peoples have shown a willingness to engage in organized violence in the name of overthrowing the state or shaping a state of one's own. Poor service delivery has never proved to be a catalyst for civil war. However, resource capture in the form of state-sanctioned 'land grabs' may yet prove to be such a catalyst. The dangers to be associated with poor urban/national governance continue to shape the global governance landscape, now filtering through the lens of 'climate change and national/regional/global insecurity'. Thus, sub-Saharan African states are fully engaged with their state-system peers in a wide variety of activities intended to head off the worst aspects of another 'Arab Spring'. The MDGs and the IWRM/good (global) water governance agendas shape interstate and related actor engagement. Each of these narratives provides resources to states in exchange for particular practices and behaviours. As articulated above, the water governance and management landscape is dominated by donor states, international organizations, international financial institutions and powerful international NGOs, all of which are pressing their own agendas as they reflect their preferred interpretation of, for example, the Dublin Principles or approaches to climate change adaptation.

So International Rivers or Conservation International emphasize 'stakeholder participation', 'environmental sustainability' and 'river basins' as the appropriate geography for action; USAID and DfID press for gender equity, market-based solutions and increased institutional capacity; international financial institutions (IFIs) demand transparency and accountability and other aspects of good corporate governance; multilateral agencies (the EU, Nordics) and international organizations such as the FAO, UNESCO and the International Water Management Institute (IWMI) provide knowledge-gathering and dissemination with a particular emphasis on food security and poverty alleviation, so hoping to shape state policies by shaping agendas. Much of this overlaps and adds up, so that when you participate at a regional meeting, such as the biannual meeting of the SADC River Basin Organizations, or one of the many training sessions provided through the Nile Basin Initiative (gender mainstreaming, conflict resolution, IWRM, good governance, water for health, Water and Sanitation – WATSAN – etc.), a select array of individuals from each of these organizations is usually present. Indeed, they are omnipresent. In my view, there is value here, though much of this activity smacks of patrimonialism ('do as I say, not as I do') and neocolonialism (i.e. Africa as ongoing social science experiment). The values are several: one is that the language of 'the ought' is infused throughout sub-Saharan Africa by what Keck and Sikkink (1998) label 'norm entrepreneurs', so people are increasingly used to thinking 'beyond the state' where water resource access, use and management are concerned. A second value is that all of this activity gathers important and valuable information regarding access to resources, amounts of resources and so on, and in an increasingly transparent way. Websites of governments, and various agencies, willingly offer up information that was hitherto guarded jealously by states. A third value concerns the involvement of 'stakeholders' and the ever-present 'capacity-building' aspect of water management – i.e. an entirely new generation of young people is being trained, not only within states but across regions (through, for example, the SADC/WaterNet regional MSc programme in IWRM) and the continent (through the New Partnership for Africa's Development – NEPAD – and the AU's African Ministerial Council on Water), thus being exposed to new ideas, people and things. A fourth very important value is that peer pressure around democracy, participation and good governance creates important space for the interests and issues of previously marginalized groups and people to begin to be addressed – not merely ignored or directly repressed.

Of course, we should not be naive about the potential of these activities, particularly in the short term, to shift water resources governance and management away from the 'is' and over to the 'ought'. One persistent problem, it seems to me, is the way the commodification of the resource and the privatization of service delivery have crept in on cats' paws, so that they are not just part of the conversation but the rarely contested primary means of realizing water security for IWRM. Citizen self-help is recast as 'entrepreneurism' and lumped together with other desirable 'job-creating' aspects of service delivery: you want it, you must pay for it.

(iv) The irresistible setting

Sometimes states deliver because they get caught up in the moment, the moment usually being a global forum of some kind where 'the ought' takes centre stage, and state actors, wanting to be good global citizens, sign up to something they later wish they had ignored: e.g. environmental and social impact assessments for dam development. Conca (2006) shows how water-related treaties and agreements have tended to follow in the wake of major world meet-ings. The deals struck at Rio in 1992, Kyoto in 1997, Johannesburg in 2002 and Bonn in 2010 helped move the global ideals forward. Granted they are ignored as often as they are attended to, but these international meetings have played an important role in setting a shared agenda. The post-2015 agenda, which will determine a set of Sustainable Development Goals, will no doubt keep the pressure upon states to sign up to a wide variety of necessary things – such as water and sanitation – they really do not care about.

(v) Out of sight, out of mind

As stated at the outset, water is not an ordinary good. Indeed, irrespective of the scale, how water is accessed, used, developed and managed reflects the character and content of the social relations of production (urban/rural/national/regional/global), both past and present. Of course, what we know is that more than 80 per cent of world income accrues to fewer than 20 per cent of the world's population, with staggering figures regarding how the world's eighty-five billionaires command more resources than the poorest 3,000 million (V. Thompson 2014). Thus, IWRM and good water governance are designed to change these facts by changing our practices. Are we foolish to expect good water governance or IWRM, then, when confronted with the fact that water mirrors the way things are? Admittedly, this is a rhetorical question. But this out-of-the-ordinary good is used in many different ways and sometimes people left to their own devices can manage it very well indeed. These people are usually to be found far from the state houses and nodal points of national and global power: in the deep rural areas; in the squatter settlements; in places where cooperation is necessary for sustainable livelihoods. Van der Zaag and Bolding (2009), writing in the context of stream-level water management in rural Mozambique, wonder how we might 'scale up' the sustainable, equitable and efficient management practices of local people. Left to their own devices, people living in squatter settlements develop their own systems of waste management and water delivery. These often exist parallel to – like a city within a city – formal systems of urban waste management and water services. McKague et al. (2011) describe the myriad ways people around the world are engaged in community-scale practices that are innovative, creative and sustainable. They also illustrate how, in some instances, state actors can partner with local communities to deliver sustainable services and build social capital.[7]

Granted, in the context of neoliberal globalization, state actors tend to leave the needs of the urban and rural poor to local and global NGOs and the private sector. Claiming 'lack of capacity', this is equivalent to a 'get out of jail free' card. The problem, in my view, is that an absent state can never build the type of social capital necessary for either good water governance or IWRM to thrive. It has been said that Africans get the states they deserve, and that civil society reflects the character of the state: a weak and predatory state reflects a weak, disunited and 'exit-oriented' civil society.

Conclusion

For more than twenty years I have argued that water can function as the means towards better state–civil society relations in Africa. I have believed unquestioningly in IWRM. Having looked dispassionately at the evidence, and reflecting on numerous case studies, it seems to me highly unlikely that IWRM can float in an African sea of underdevelopment. As the 86 per cent of Beninois or the 85 per cent of Congolese without access to improved sanitation will attest: captured resources will stay captured. Perhaps it is time to let IWRM sink anyway, and to take Merrey's (2008) advice and approach the specific question of how to provide water for poverty alleviation head-on. In other words, confront the forces in support of the 'is', and think clinically about what is achievable in the immediate term for people with the most abiding needs.

Notes

1 'Blue water' is the amount of rainfall that enters lakes, rivers and groundwater; 'green water' is the amount of rainfall that is either intercepted by vegetation or enters the soil and is picked up by plants and evapotranspired back into the atmosphere.

2 Savenije (2002) highlights eight reasons why water is profoundly different from other resources. It is: essential; scarce; fugitive; indivisible; bulky; nonsubstitutable; not freely tradable; and complex (being a public good, location-bound, having high mobilization costs, satisfying a heterogenous market, showing macroeconomic interdependencies; being prone to market failure; and having high merit value).

3 Research published in 2012 by Edward N. Wolf and the Pew Research Center showed that the top 5 per cent of US households owned 63.1 per cent of all US wealth (as reported in the print edition of the *Mail & Guardian*, 26 September–2 October 2014, p. 26).

4 When I say 'states', I mean those authoritative actors within government acting in the name of the state.

5 See www.transboundarywaters. orst.edu/research/RBO/RBO Africa. html for details.

6 According to a former student of mine, who was present at the negotiations, 'the whole thing took about five minutes'. I asked about stakeholder involvement and his answer was, 'There was no consultation; a decision was taken by the two governments, they met, agreed and that was it' (personal communication).

7 See the numerous case studies available at www.growinginclusivemarkets.org/.

References

Alam, U., O. Dione and P. Jeffery (2009) 'The benefit-sharing principle: implementing sovereignty bargains on water', *Political Geography*, 28: 90–100.

Allan, A. J. (2003) 'IWRM/IWRAM: a new sanctioned discourse?', Discussion paper no. 58, Water Issues Study Group, University of London.

Biswas, A. K. (2008) 'Integrated water resources management: is it working?', *Water Resources Development*, 24(1): 5–22.

Bond, P. (2002) *Unsustainable South Africa*, Pietermaritzburg: UKZN Press.

— (2013) 'Water rights, commons and advocacy narratives', *South African Journal of Human Rights*, 29(1): 126–44.

Bond, P. and S. Mottiar (2013) 'Movements, protests and a massacre in South Africa', *Journal of Contemporary African Studies*, 3(2): 283–302.

Conca, K. (2006) *Governing Water: Contentious Transnational Politics and Global Institution Building*, Cambridge, MA: MIT Press.

Conca, K. and G. D. Dabelko (eds) (2002) *Environmental Peacemaking*, Washington, DC: Johns Hopkins University Press.

Cullis, J. and B. van Koppen (2009) 'Applying the Gini Coefficient to measure inequality of water use in the Olifants River water management area, South Africa', in L. A. Swatuk and L. Wirkus (eds), *Transboundary Water Governance in Southern Africa: Examining underexplored dimensions*, Baden-Baden: Nomos, pp. 91–110.

De Stefano, L., P. Edwards, L. de Silva and A. T. Wolf (2010) 'Tracking cooperation and conflict in international basins: historic and recent trends', *Water Policy*, 12: 871–84.

Earle, A., A. Jagerskog and J. Ojendal (eds) (2010) *Transboundary Water Management: Principles and practice*, London: Earthscan.

FAO (2003) *Statistical Yearbook, World Food and Agriculture*, Rome: Food and Agriculture Organization of the United Nations.

Fatch, J. and L. A. Swatuk (2014) 'Transboundary water politics in the Zambezi Basin: Malawi and its "neighbors"', Paper presented at the annual meeting of SADC/GWP/ WaterNet, 29–31 October, Lilongwe, Malawi.

Goldin, J. (2010) 'Water policy in South Africa: trust and knowledge as obstacles to reform', *Review of Radical Political Economics*, 42(2): 195–212.

Hering, D., A. Borja, J. Carstensen, L. Carvalho, M. Elliott, C. K. Feld, A.-S. Heiskanen, R. K. Johnson, J. Moe, D. Pont, A. L. Solheim and W. van de Bund (2010) 'The European Water Framework Directive at the age of 10: a critical review of the achievements with recommendations for the future', *Science of the Total Environment*, 408(19): 4007–19.

Homer-Dixon, T. F. (1991) 'On the threshold: environmental changes as causes of acute conflict', *International Security*, 16(2): 76–116.

Kallis, G. and D. Butler (2001) 'The EU water framework directive: measures and implications', *Water Policy*, 3(2): 125–42.

Keck, M. and K. Sikkink (1998) *Activists beyond Borders*, New York: Cornell University Press.

Kistin, E. and P. J. Ashton (2008) 'Adapting to change in transboundary rivers: an analysis of treaty flexibility on the Orange-Senqu River basin', *International Journal of Water Resources Development*, 24(3): 385–400.

Klaphake, A. and W. Scheumann (2009) 'Understanding transboundary water cooperation: evidence from Sub-Saharan Africa', in L. A. Swatuk and L. Wirkus (eds), *Transboundary Water Governance in Southern Africa: Examining underexplored dimensions*, Baden-Baden: Nomos, pp. 47–72.

Litfin, K. (1998) *The Greening of Sovereignty in World Politics*, Cambridge, MA: MIT Press.

MacDonald, D. and G. Ruiters (eds) (2005) *The Age of Commodity: Water* and *Privatization in Southern Africa*, London: Earthscan.

McKague, K., D. Wheeler, C. Cash, J. Comeault and E. Ray (2011) 'Introduction to the special issue on growing inclusive markets', *Journal of Enterprising Communities*, 5(1).

Mehta, L. (2001) 'The manufacture of popular perceptions of scarcity: dams and water-related narratives in Gujarat, India', *World Development*, 29(12): 2025–41.

— (2007) 'Whose scarcity? Whose property? The case of water in western India', *Land Use Policy*, 24(4): 654–63.

Merrey, D. (2008) 'Is normative integrated water resources management implementable? Charting a practical course with lessons from Southern Africa', *Physics and Chemistry of the Earth*, 33: 899–905.

Mirumachi, N. (2015) *Transboundary Water Politics in the Developing World*, London: Routledge.

Mirumachi, N. and E. van Wyk (2010) 'Cooperation at different scales: challenges for local and international water resource governance in South Africa', *Geographical Journal*, 176(1): 25–38.

Moriarty, P., J. Butterworth and C. Batchelor (2004) *Integrated Water Resources Management*, Delft: IRC.

Moseley, W. G. (2014) 'Structured transformation and natural resources management in Africa', in K. T. Hanson, C. D'Alessandro and F. Owusu (eds), *Capacity Development and Natural Resource Management in Africa*, Palgrave Macmillan.

Mottiar, S. (2013) 'From "Popcorn" to "Occupy": protest in Durban, South Africa', *Development and Change*, 44(3): 603–19.

Noemdoe, S., L. Jonker and L. A. Swatuk (2006) 'Perceptions of water scarcity: Genadendal and outstations', *Physics and Chemistry of the Earth*, 31: 771–8.

Ruiters, G. (2015, forthcoming) 'Reclaiming the City: Recent developments in trade union–community alliances and citizenship in post-alliance South Africa, 2010-2014', *Politikon*.

Sadoff, C. W. and D. Grey (2002) 'Beyond the river: the benefits of cooperation on international rivers', *Water Policy*, 4: 389–403.

Savenije, H. H. G. (2000) 'Water scarcity indicators; the deception of the numbers', *Physics and Chemistry of the Earth*, 25: 199–204.

— (2002) 'Why water is not an ordinary economic good, or why the girl is special', *Physics and Chemistry of the Earth*, 27: 741–4.

Solanes, M. and F. Gonzalez-Villarreal (1999) 'The Dublin Principles for water as reflected in a comparative assessment of institutional and legal arrangements for Integrated Water Resources Management', TAC Background Paper no. 3, Stockholm: GWP/SIDA.

Solomon, S. (2010) *Water: The epic struggle for wealth, power and civilization*, New York: HarperCollins.

Swatuk, L. A. (2002) 'The new water architecture in southern Africa: reflections on current trends in the light of "Rio +10"', *International Affairs*, 78(3): 507–30.

— (2008) 'A political economy of water in southern Africa', *Water Alternatives*, 1(1): 24–47.

— (2010) 'The state and water resources development through the lens of history: a South African case study', *Water Alternatives*, 3(3): 521–36.

Swatuk, L. A. and J. Fatch (2013) 'Water resources management and governance in southern Africa: toward regional integration for peace and prosperity', *Global Dialogue*, 15(2), online only, www.worlddialogue.org.

Swatuk, L. A. and D. Mazvimavi (2010) 'Water and human security in Africa', in M. Schnurr and L. A. Swatuk (eds), *Critical Environmental Security. Rethinking the links between natural resources and political violence*, New Issues in Security no. 5, Halifax, NS: Centre for Foreign Policy Studies Monograph Series.

Swatuk, L. A. and L. Wirkus (eds) (2009) *Transboundary Water Governance in Southern Africa: Examining Under-explored Dimensions*, Baden-Baden: Nomos.

Thompson, L. (2014) 'Agency and action: perceptions of governance and service delivery among the urban poor in Cape Town', *Politikon*, 41(1): 39–58.

Thompson, V. (2014) 'The world's 85 richest people are as wealthy as the poorest 3 billion. What exactly does that mean?', *The Atlantic*, 21 January, www.theatlantic.com/business/archive/2014/01/the-worlds-85-richest-people-are-as-wealthy-as-the-poorest-3-billion/283206/, accessed 30 September 2014.

Van der Zaag, P. and A. Bolding (2009) 'Water governance in the Pungwe River Basin: institutional limits to the upscaling of hydraulic infrastructure', in L. A. Swatuk and L. Wirkus (eds), *Transboundary Water Governance in Southern Africa: Examining Under-explored Dimensions*, Baden-Baden: Nomos, pp. 163–77.

WEF (World Economic Forum) (2011) *Water Security: The water, energy, food and climate security nexus*, Washington, DC: Island Press.

Wolf, A. (1998) 'Cooperation and conflict along international waterways', *Water Policy*, 1(2): 251–65.

Wolf, A., A. Kramer, A. Carius and G. D. Dabelko (2005) 'Managing water conflict and cooperation', in *Worldwatch Institute, State of the World 2005: Global Security*, London: Earthscan.

Wolf, A., T. Shira, B. Yoffe and M. Giordano (2003) 'International waters: identifying basins at risk', *Water Policy*, 5: 29–60.

Zeitoun, M. and N. Mirumachi (2008) 'Transboundary water interaction I: reconsidering conflict and cooperation', *International Environmental Agreements: Politics, Law and Economics*, 8(4): 297–316.

4 | WATER POLITICS IN EASTERN AND SOUTHERN AFRICA

Sobona Mtisi and Alan Nicol

Introduction

The 1990s witnessed radical transformations in the governance and development of water resources in East and southern Africa, driven in part by the outcome of the Earth Summit in 1992 and a drive for resource management under Agenda 21, and due to the 'new politics' that emerged after the end of the Cold War stasis.

Central to this transformation was the wide-scale adoption and implementation of Integrated Water Resource Management (IWRM) principles in national and regional water policy frameworks. The IWRM approach sought to promote the coordinated management of water, land and related resources in order to maximize the resultant economic and social welfare in an equitable manner, without compromising the sustainability of vital ecosystems (GWP 2000; Calder 1998). At the core of the IWRM concept is the emphasis on managing water within its natural hydrological boundaries, decentralization of water management, stakeholder participation, and the user-pays principle, which were stated to provide an effective framework for water management that leads to effective allocation of water for poverty reduction and livelihood improvement (GWP 2000; WWAP 2003; Soussaan 2006). IWRM-type approaches sought to accelerate the devolution of responsibilities to water users and build transparent and accountable mechanisms of resource allocation (GWP 2000: 30), building on the emphasis under Agenda 21 of local solutions and management at the lowest appropriate level. To achieve this, IWRM focused on a mix of policy, institutional and legal reforms at national and regional level based upon the following key characteristics:

• A decentralized and accountable structure that is coherent and consistent at each layer of administration, from the local and regional to the national, as well as from the sub-catchment to the river basin levels.

- Self-management of independent bodies and self-financing at user and higher levels of activity, according to user's ability to pay.
- Market mechanisms as integral to water allocation, determining the value of water between sectors, the value to the management agency and to the user.
- Government as enabler rather than controller, with key responsibilities for capital investment, supporting legislation, data collection and processing, and support for basic technical research and development.
- Achievement of comprehensive and consistent legal codes which define water rights and responsibilities of individuals, groups, agencies and government bodies. A set of procedures for *de jure* and extralegal arbitration of disputes and established enforceable penalties for misuse and degradation of water resources (Turral 1998: 5).

The idea of institutional restructuring central to the concept of IWRM was viewed on the basis of the importance of institutions as constraining and enabling structures in people's livelihoods (see IFAD 2001). In short, institutions were viewed as critical channels through which people's livelihood strategies are shaped and mediated to the extent that decentralized institutions of water management were seen as providing the necessary structures for enabling poor people to secure access to water for their livelihoods. The machinery of IWRM, in essence, was (and, to an extent, still is) seen as inherently *developmental*.

In addition, decentralization of water management was seen as a means to provide an institutional forum for promoting participation and representation of different water users, particularly the poor, in water resources management (Ribot 2002), closely allied to the ideas of democratic decentralization that were prevalent in the 1990s. Proponents of IWRM argued that, because of the dominant role water played in rural livelihoods, a decentralized framework of water management would enable users, particularly the poor, to participate, and have a voice and leverage in decisions over water resources that they depend on for their livelihoods (UNDP and IFAD 2005). This idea of 'citizen stakeholder' presupposed a more or less benign resource environment in which individuals would freely engage in 'managed contestation' over access to key resources within new institutions established under IWRM. Little understanding existed – or at least was factored in – of entrenched elite (and other) interests over resource management that might bar this kind of democratic exercise.

In tandem with the institutional architecture that emerged – and linked to it – were arguments for treatment of water as an economic good, which came to the fore through the Dublin Principles. These were expressed in particular through the user-pays principle, representing a construct of 'efficiency' and self-financing of decentralized institutions of water management, with a simple concept of financing based on payment for water access rights and volumetric use. This, it was argued, would eventually lead to a situation in which fees for water more accurately reflected the 'true economic value' of water, resulting, so the reasoning went, in more efficient allocation and use of water. Price would become an incentive for water users to use water more efficiently, and for responsible authorities, mainly commercial entities, to efficiently allocate water to different water users (Serageldin 1995). These notions were based on economic principles of efficient and transparent markets, effective institutional environments and the capacity for all users to work within such environments to the best of their 'rational' economic interests.

It is mainly through the above-stated theoretical justifications of the concept of IWRM and its strong links to poverty reduction and livelihood improvement that IWRM principles were widely promoted and adopted in East and southern Africa from the early 1990s onwards. Indeed, as a result, since the late 1990s, many East and southern African countries have embodied IWRM principles in sector policies and strategies, and have embarked on water sector reform processes. These have been supported directly by donors (e.g. Gesellschaft für Technische Zusammenarbeit – GTZ, now GIZ – the Swedish International Development Agency – SIDA – the US Department of State, the EU, DfID, the Danish International Development Agency – Danida – and Austrian Aid) and more obliquely (but often by the same funders) via regional networks such as the Global Water Partnership (GWP) and Country Water Partnerships (CWPs). Further, the water sector reform process was endorsed by regional and continental bodies such as SADC, the

African Development Bank and the Africa Water Task Force through the Accra Declaration of Africa Regional Stakeholder Conference for Priority Setting in 2002.

South Africa South Africa and Zimbabwe were quick to adopt and implement IWRM-based water sector reforms in southern Africa. The government of South Africa wrote several policy documents, culminating in the passing of various pieces of water legislation. Key policy documents include the Water Law Principles (DWAF 1996), and the Resource Pricing Policy for South Africa (DWAF 1997a). These were quickly followed by the White Paper on a National Water Policy (DWAF 1997b) and the Pricing Strategy for Raw Water Use Charges (DWAF 1999). These policy documents provided the basis upon which the Water Services Act (1997) and the National Water Act (1998) were passed. The National Water Act (1998) introduced the concept of a strategic reserve with which to meet environmental sustainability objectives and the guaranteeing of basic human needs. It also called for the right to use water to be granted to users, who should be registered and licensed, and should pay for water. Essentially, the legislative and policy changes reflected the embodiment of the concepts of IWRM, and led to the creation of catchment management agencies (CMAs). The CMAs provided not only a decentralized and integrated management of water, but also an institutional platform for the broad-based participation of water users in decision-making processes related to water. The core purpose of CMAs was to ensure the sustainable use of water resources in their areas of operation, in line with the aims of the Act, the National Water Resource strategy, and with a Catchment Management Strategy. Nineteen Water Management Areas were demarcated countrywide. Several pilot CMAs were established, with facilitation and supervision activities being undertaken by regional offices of the Department of Water Affairs and Forestry (DWAF) and contracted consultants. Below the CMAs were Water User Associations (WUAs), which operated at a local level and were effectively 'cooperative associations of individual water users who wished to undertake water-related activities for their mutual benefit' (Brown and Woodhouse 2004: 24). Invariably, Irrigation Boards, which were previously established to manage water resources at the local level on behalf of commercial interests in agriculture and industry, were to be transformed into WUAs by including the previously excluded water users. In South Africa's homelands, where blacks were settled, Water User Associations could be established among smallholder farmers to manage their particular scheme.

However, the rolling out of this type of management structure was often slow and uneven, owing largely to the complexity of the task, the political-economic histories of the communities in which catchments were based (i.e. the wider 'problem sheds' in which watersheds were situated) and the enormous shift represented in allocation priorities by the inclusion of new stakeholders in the CMAs. In 2004, after six years of the reform, only one Water Management Area (WMA), the Inkomati, had been launched, which was widely acknowledged as being at an advanced stage of implementation. One of the key issues that undermined the successful establishment of CMAs in the eighteen WMAs was the lack of institutional capacity to carry forward the process of reform, and the obstacles to recruiting stakeholders to support their establishment. Much of this challenge was based in the legacies of apartheid and the disempowerment of the black majority.

Zimbabwe Similarly, Zimbabwe embarked on its own water sector reform process in the mid-1990s, which mirrored the water reforms in South Africa. A key policy document entitled 'Towards an Integrated Water Resources Management Process in Zimbabwe' provides policy guidelines and principles for a new approach to water resources management. The Water Act and the Zimbabwe National Water Authority Act, both of 1998, paved the way for a decentralized and catchment-based system of water management and associated allocation of, and payment for, water.

After testing the key principles of IWRM in two areas, seven catchment areas were delineated on the basis of the major hydrological zones in Zimbabwe. Each catchment area was managed by a Catchment Council, composed of representatives of the various water users within the catchment. The main responsibilities of a Catchment Council included preparing catchment outline plans for their respective river system, determining applications and granting water permits, regulating and supervising the use of water and dealing with conflicts over water (Mtsi 2008).

Below the Catchment Councils, there are Sub-Catchment

Councils, which form a lower-tier water management institution responsible for the management of a sub-catchment area. Sub-Catchment Councils comprise representatives from different water user groups that exist within a particular sub-catchment area. Parallel to Catchment and Sub-Catchment Councils is the Zimbabwe National Water Authority (ZINWA), an institution responsible for advising the minister responsible for water resources on the formulation of national policies and standards on dam safety, borehole drilling, water pricing, water resources planning, management and development. At sub-national level, ZINWA provides technical assistance to the Catchment and Sub-Catchment Councils, and has the exclusive responsibility for the management, supply and development of 'agreement water' (ibid.).

Uganda and Ethopia Similarly, both Uganda and Ethiopia adopted IWRM principles in their approach to water resources management. In Ethiopia IWRM principles were enshrined in key policy documents (e.g. the National Water Resources Management Policy), water legislation, and the institutional architecture for water management. Specifically, the National Water Resources Management Policy was focused on enhancing and promoting efforts towards efficient, equitable and optimal utilization of water resources that would contribute to the country's socio-economic development on a sustainable basis. This was complemented by the country's five-year national development plan, the Plan for Accelerated Sustainable Development to End Poverty (PASDEP) (2005/06–2009/10), which attached high priority to water development and water sector reform based on IWRM principles.

The Ethiopia Country Water Partnership (ECWP), under the auspices of the Global Water Partnership (GWP), was launched in December 2003 with a mandate to promote and implement IWRM principles in Ethiopia's water sector. Its broad-based membership was drawn from, *inter alia*, the federal and regional government agencies, local and international NGOs, donors, research and academic institutions, women and the private sector. In 2005, the ECWP established two pilot watershed management schemes in Berki in Tigray region (northern Ethiopia) and Messena in Amhara region (north-east Ethiopia). Funding for these two pilot schemes was provided by the United States Department of State. The main objective of the schemes was to put IWRM principles into practice through establishing watershed-based management schemes and putting in place an institutional framework for broader stakeholder participation and decentralized water management. To this end, Water Partnerships were established at regional, catchment, administrative district and station levels, composed of stakeholders drawn from government agencies, NGOs, universities and agricultural research institutes. The Regional Water Partnership was supported by a regional technical team that was responsible for conducting technical and socio-economic assessments for the watershed.

In Uganda, the major impetus came in the time following the Earth Summit period when Uganda was selected as a priority country for IWRM in Africa. The Water Action Plan (WAP) of 1994 provided the basis for sustainable water resources development and management, based on IWRM principles. It set priorities for water resources development and management, and a structure for their management at national and sub-national levels. Stemming from WAP, the government of Uganda enacted a Water Statute in 1995, and announced a National Water Policy in 1999, thus instituting a legal and institutional framework for IWRM. From 2003 to 2005, Uganda conducted the Water Resources Management Reform Study, which led to the preparation of a WRM reform strategy. Its key recommendation was a shift from centralized to catchment-based WRM, structured in a three-tier institutional framework (i.e. Water Management Zone; catchment; and district level). The cornerstone of the strategy of the Ministry of Water and the Environment (MWE) was to devolve planning and water management to the catchment level within the institutional and geographical framework of Water Management Zones (WMZs). WMZs were largely delineated along the country's major hydrologic catchments, with adjustments in delineation made to ensure that a district was not located in more than one WMZ (World Bank 2011). As a result, Uganda's water management has been organized into four WMZs, namely Upper Nile in the north, Lake Kyoga in the east, Lake Victoria in the south, and Albert Nile in the west and south-west. Therefore, each WMZ comprises different catchments which can be either national catchments (e.g. Lake George) or trans-boundary (e.g. Kagera).

The WMZs constitute the platform for participatory and integrated water resources planning, management and development at the catchment and WMZ level. They are responsible for the planning, coordination and implementation of IWRM activities, in collaboration with other stakeholders; support the catchment management committee (CMC) in preparing and implementing IWRM Plans in the Catchment Management Organization (CMO); and support CMC in monitoring and enforcing relevant by-laws, guidelines, regulations, permits, plans and standards. The WMZ is composed of a team of senior staff from the Ministry of Water and the Environment and other technical staff.

Below the WMZ are catchments, spread over several districts. Currently, there are seven catchment areas in Uganda, namely Sio-Malaba-Malakisi, Lake George, Lake Kyoga, Lake Albert, Katonga, Kagera and Rwizi. Each catchment area is managed by a CMO, composed of representatives from various water user groups, including district councils, officials from government departments found at local level, such as Environment and Natural Resources, NGOs and community-based organizations CBOs. The catchment is the level that provides a platform for involvement of key stakeholders, policy initiation, and review of relevant proposals. The CMO is supported by the WMZ team of DWRM (Directorate of Water Resource Management) and/or NGOs.

Each CMO has structures for stakeholder coordination that include a Stakeholder Forum, a CMC, a catchment technical committee (CTC) and a Catchment Secretariat. The activities in the catchments are driven by a CMC, which consists mainly of political leaders of the different districts within the catchment and representatives of other key stakeholders who ensure that activities are effectively implemented. The CTC is responsible for supporting the CMC in its decision-making processes and is therefore mainly composed of local technical staff of participating districts and key stakeholders within the basin. The Catchment Secretariat is responsible for:

- coordination of planning of WRM issues within the catchment area;
- coordination of preparation and implementation of the IWRM plan in the catchment, in liaison with local governments (LGs), relevant district officers, water users' associations and other stakeholders;
- coordination, implementation, monitoring and enforcement of

relevant acts, by-laws, guidelines, regulations, permits, plans and standards (Mwebembezi n.d.).

So far four CMOs have been set up in Uganda (Rwizi, Albert, Mpanga and Semliki), with six more planned in future. The district level constitutes the next tier of local-level water management, below the catchment level. This is where actual implementation of water management activities is carried out. The key institution at the district level is the Water User Association, composed of representatives of different water user groups. The main functions of the WUA are to coordinate and implement the activities decided in the stakeholder forum and CMC; assist the CMC in information dissemination, planning, regulation and enforcement of water resources and management activities; and make and implement by-laws.

Different meanings of the IWRM-based water sector reform

It is apparent from the foregoing that the IWRM concept has been widely incorporated into national policies and strategies across a number of states in East and southern Africa. This has come in various forms, reflecting the framing and articulation of different and divergent interests, sometimes at odds with national development priorities and rural people's livelihood concerns. In Zimbabwe and South Africa, there existed two strands that shaped the debate and subsequent adoption of the IWRM principles in national policy frameworks. These were the 'redistribution' and 'allocation' theses. At the core of the 'redistribution thesis' was the view that, for water sector reform to improve the livelihoods of rural people, it should redress structural inequalities in legislative and administrative frameworks of water management, frameworks that disempowered the poor, and undermined their productive uses of water. Within this debate, institutions of water management were supposed to be decentralized to bring them closer to water users, particularly the poor and the previously excluded, with the view that they could represent themselves and participate in the management and local-level decision-making processes on a resource that they depended upon for their livelihoods.

Underlying the call for water reforms was a need to redress colonial inequalities in access to water, a recognition of historical and customary rights of water access for rural people, and a requirement for the principles and objectives, as well as the legal and administrative framework, to take this into account (Mtisi 2008; Mohamed-Katerere 1998; Manzungu et al. 1999; Bolding 1999; Magadlela 1999; Matinenga 1999; Van der Zaag 1999; Magadzire 1995).

For international agencies and donors, and to a large extent governments, the debate on reforming Zimbabwe's water sector was largely framed in ways that sought to promote the adoption of IWRM principles and to link water reforms with the broader macroeconomic restructuring (Calder 1998; WRMS 1998). Differently put, the water reforms were intended to institute a technically efficient and administrative framework of water management, underpinned by stakeholder participation, decentralization, the user-pays principle and self-financing and poverty alleviation (Mtisi 2008). This can be referred to as the 'allocation thesis'. Within this perspective, the key route to the livelihood improvement of poor water users in rural areas lay in 'efficient' allocation of water among different water users, within a decentralized and participatory framework of water (ibid.).

Similarly, Brown and Woodhouse (2004), commenting on South Africa's water sector reform, noted that the Water Act of 1998 intended that allocation of water among users should be guided by social equity and economic efficiency goals. Actions to achieve each of these two goals need to be carefully managed if they are not to be conflicting. For example, steps towards the goal of greater equity would broaden the social base, across which benefits of water use were shared, by changing the allocation mechanisms that hitherto had skewed access to water resources towards a minority of the population. However, to achieve economic efficiency, water resources should be allocated so as to yield the greatest economic benefit per unit of water. Within South Africa, the concentration of water management expertise within white-dominated commercial agriculture meant that increasing water access for previously disadvantaged groups was likely, in the short term, to reduce efficiency.

Although Ethiopia, Uganda and South Africa have experienced sustained economic growth over the past twenty years, poverty is still significant among the majority of the population, particularly in rural farming communities. With reference to Zimbabwe, the past two decades have witnessed a significant increase in poverty levels among the population. In light of these realities, there are increasing calls, among some policy-makers and activists, for water development for domestic use, on-farm storage and large-scale dam construction for irrigation and hydropower. Proponents argue that water development and management is integral to achieving national and regional social and economic development goals.

Institutional change

It is apparent from the above that the implementation of the IWRM-based sector reforms has been slow and uneven across the four countries. While Zimbabwe has had some success in establishing functioning Catchment Councils throughout the country in the first two years of the reform, the Inkomati WMA in South Africa was widely acknowledged as the one at the most advanced stage of implementation, six years after reform began (ibid.). Ethiopia had two pilot watershed management schemes five years after the enactment of water legislation, while in Uganda two are currently functional, nearly a decade after legal and institutional reform. There are many issues that affect the establishment of water management institutions, their operations and, ultimately, achievement of the goals of water sector reforms. Key among them is the institutional complexity and lack of capacity to successfully implement and carry forward reforms.

Central to this is the challenge of financing capacity at national levels to sustain the water sector reform process. For instance, in Zimbabwe, after an initial period of donor funding of the water sector reform process (1998–2003), there was a withdrawal of donors, partly as a consequence of political fall-out with the government of Zimbabwe over fast-track land reforms. This severely undermined the effective implementation of a decentralized catchment-based water management approach as envisaged under IWRM. In some cases, the withdrawal of donor funds, post-2003, adversely affected the viability of Catchment and Sub-Catchment Councils.

Overlaying decentralized institutions of water management

Invariably, across the four countries, the creation of newly decentralized institutions of water management came immediately after earlier processes of decentralization of rural local governance. One process led to the establishment of local-level governance structures (such as district councils) as part of a wider local government reform. For instance, the Local Government Act of 1997 in Uganda, the 1984 Prime Minister's Directive in Zimbabwe, Ethiopia's 1995 Constitution and South Africa's Local Government Transition Act of 1993 all provided a basis for decentralization of local government, and the creation of local government and administration structures, namely villages, wards (*kebeles* in Ethiopia) and districts (*wereda* in Ethiopia). Such institutions were responsible for implementing and overseeing local-level development activities in all areas under their jurisdiction. In addition, district councils and sub-district institutions were meant to engender participation of rural people in rural development processes as they were the focal administrative points where different stakeholders met and discussed local-level development issues. Consequently, these have become the points where local populations engage to air their views on natural resource use.

In addition, another process of decentralization led to the transfer of responsibilities from central government departments to the local level for the implementation of national development objectives (i.e. deconcentration). This process saw the active involvement of representatives of government departments responsible for water, agriculture, environment and forestry at the local level. Thus, the continued role of deconcentrated government departments in the management of water, irrigation infrastructure, environment and agricultural extension has meant continued central government control of key aspects of water use and management. For instance, in Zimbabwe, the agricultural extension service (AGRITEX) was central in the management of water and crop production on two schemes and was restructured in 2003 to form the Department of Agricultural and Rural Extension (AREX). It is important to note that AGRITEX was the central government department through which communal irrigators on the two schemes liaised on issues pertaining to water management. However, its restructuring into AREX resulted in the department being relieved of its water management function, though it retained its responsibility to provide advice and extension services to irrigators on crop production. Similarly, in Uganda, the responsibility for water for agriculture is divided between representatives of the Ministry of Water and the Environment (bulk water supply) and the Ministry of Agriculture, Animal Industries and Fisheries (MAAIF) (on-farm development). Consequently, there is confusion over their respective roles and responsibilities, which has slowed progress on the development and management of water for agriculture (World Bank 2011). In Ethiopia, in each of the nine federal regions, there are specialized sector bureaus that implement sectoral policies and programmes in consultation with the regional executive. Although the Bureau of Water Development is the main institution responsible for the development and management of water resources, there are other bureaus with involvement in the area, such as health, agriculture, environment, pastoralists and finance.

The interrelationships between these decentralization processes has created a complex institutional landscape with confusion over roles and responsibilities, particularly given changes to the types of task undertaken by managers and local political actors. In Zimbabwe, responsibility for local-level development lies with the rural district councils, Ward Development Committees and Village Development Committees – a consequence of an earlier decentralization process in local governance. Yet within the context of the water sector reform, decentralized institutions of water management (i.e. ZINWA, Catchment and Sub-Catchment Councils) now have the responsibility for water development and management. This institutional division is not often clear among rural people, whom these two processes of decentralization are supposed to serve.

Invariably, in South Africa, Uganda and Zimbabwe, traditional institutions (chiefs, headmen and other channels of 'informal power') represent additional layers of local-level management of land and water resources. While in some places in rural Ethiopia land is officially allocated by peasant associations, traditional institutions play a central role in water allocation and management. For instance, among the Borana, where pastoralists rely on deep wells for water during the dry season, permission to use water from the wells is obtained with the consent of the *konfi*, or traditional leader, who manages the wells on behalf of the clan under the 'well council' (*cora ella*) (Flintan and Tamrat 2006: 265). Added to this are traditional authority structures, from headman to chief, which provide access to land, and therefore act as a medium for gaining access to water. Although the fact that traditional leaders have limited influence on water management has been demonstrated, the central role they play in land allocation shapes access to water and the subsequent participation in water management activities. In Uganda, land title (lack of) is fast emerging as one of the chief challenges to water reforms and catchment management and the relationship between land title and ownership over resources, including oil reserves, particularly in the country's Albertine Rift.

Water management plans must account for the geographic and social complexity of water and the need for adaptable, flexible and site-specific strategies, particularly given competition over resources other than water within the same shared landscapes of catchment and river basins. Water must be fairly allocated between competing uses, including hydropower, irrigation, industry and domestic water supply for smallholder cultivation and the watering of livestock. The rights and needs of both upstream and downstream users must be recognized and guaranteed to prevent conflict, which is possible only through scrupulous and unbiased ground assessments. It is critical to understand the sources underlying the onset and continuation of conflict.

The water reform and subsequent establishment of Lower Save East Sub-Catchment Council and ZINWA Middle Save has introduced another layer of decentralization to the rural landscape. The effect of these two broad processes of decentralization – one in local rural government, and the other in water management – both with independent developmental objectives, has led to the creation of an institutionally complex rural environment for different water users who wish to gain access to water, to understand and position themselves to effectively participate and play a role in water management within the Lower Save East Sub-Catchment Council.

Further, decentralized institutions of water management were superimposed on existing local government authorities, i.e. village development committees (VIDCOs), ward development committees (WADCOs) and rural district councils (RDCs), which had a mandate for participatory rural development activities. In view of this, the participation of new water users, mainly communal farmers, in decentralized water management processes has been attenuated by the decentralization processes in local government. Given that local government structures (i.e. VIDCOs, WADCOs and RDCs) are still used as the vehicle through which rural people represent their views, and participate in rural development projects, the Lower Save East Sub-Catchment Council represents another local-level participatory institutional structure, albeit constructed around water.

The decentralization in local government, introduced under

the 1984 Prime Minister's Directive, led to the creation of RDCs, WADCOs and VIDCOs, with a mandate to implement and oversee local-level development activities in all areas under their jurisdiction. In addition, RDCs, WADCOs and VIDCOs were meant to engender participation of rural people in rural development processes as the aforementioned institutions were the focal administrative points where different stakeholders met and discussed local-level development issues. Rural people channelled their development needs and concerns through VIDCOs up to the RDC. In Lower Save East Sub-Catchment Council, Chipinge Rural District Council was the central local authority accessed through the various VIDCOs, depending on the village where one lived, and then through the local ward councillor.

Within communal irrigation schemes, there exists another layer of deconcentrated government departments responsible for water management, such as water bailiffs, under the Department of Irrigation, and AREX officials, who are central in providing advice and extension services on crop production.

Parallel processes of decentralization

The construction of decentralized institutions of water management appears to reflect a parallel institutional process of decentralization within water reform, where, on the one hand, there is an array of ZINWA institutions while Catchment and Sub-Catchment Councils are on the other, albeit linked. Decentralization within Catchment and Sub-Catchment Councils can be viewed as 'devolution', partly on the basis that the councils are constituted by popularly elected officials from within the ranks of water users (i.e. those elected to the Sub-Catchment Council) and from within the ranks of representatives at sub-catchment and catchment level. However, an analysis of the institutional framework of decentralized water management, represented by ZINWA, can be characterized as deconcentration on account of the role the minister of water resources occupies within ZINWA structures and control of ZINWA by a national head office. ZINWA institutions can be stated to be non-participatory and accountable to the minister responsible for water. The former is clearly illustrated by the non-existence, at the local level, of an institutional forum for participation within the local ZINWA sub-office. Consequently, ZINWA sub-offices do not involve or engage users of 'agreement water' within a participatory framework, with a view to being responsive to, and reflecting, local water needs.

The formation of ZINWA Save Catchment and ZINWA Middle Save was legally based on the need to provide technical assistance and advice on the water legislation to Save Catchment Council and Lower Save East Sub-Catchment Council respectively. However, we have demonstrated that ZINWA and Catchment Councils appear to be parallel and contradictory institutional processes, embedded within the water reform. The establishment of Save Catchment Council, and Lower Save East Sub-Catchment, suggests the formation of devolved and participatory institutional frameworks for water management. On the other hand, the establishment of the ZINWA Save Catchment and ZINWA Middle Save represent a 'deconcentrated' system, aimed at the provision of technical assistance and advice to the Catchment and Sub-Catchment Councils. Yet the analysis has shown that ZINWA Save Catchment is vested with the overall responsibility for water management and decision-making within the catchment, which undermines the participatory process occurring at Save Catchment Council. Further, the catchment manager is not accountable to the Save Catchment Council in performing his duties. This further illustrates the usurpation of decentralized and participatory processes of water management by ZINWA Save Catchment.

Multiple decentralizations

This chapter has demonstrated that the institutional landscape within which participation in decentralized institutions of water management occurs is populated with a plethora of institutions of rural and water governance. One consequence of this has been the layering of decentralized institutions of water management over existing local institutions of water management, namely Block Committees, and Irrigation Management Committees in the Zimbabwe context. Within communal irrigation schemes, there exists another layer of deconcentrated government departments responsible for water management, such as water bailiffs, under the Department of Irrigation, and AREX officials, who are central in providing advice and extension services on crop production. To this end, the existence of the aforementioned institutions is militating against the effective participation of communal irrigators in decentralized water management processes.

In many cases, more generally across the Zimbabwe and Uganda examples in particular, there has been little coordination of activities between deconcentrated institutions. This is compounded by challenges to genuine participation. In Zimbabwe's Lower Save East sub-catchment area, for example, in spite of the fact that the Sub-Catchment Council was established partly as a result of the lobbying of commercial irrigators and, initially, based on the Water Committee of commercial irrigators, it appears that the formation of a substantive council involved communal farmers; communal, small-scale commercial irrigators; and commercial irrigators within the sub-catchment. Nonetheless, the election of the Sub-Catchment Council leadership was based on practical concerns for administrative capacity and need for office space for local-level water management to take place. This seems to confound notions of a popular vote embodied in participatory local-level water management, at least as regards the Sub-Catchment Council leadership.

Mismatch between rain-fed and wetland agriculture and participation

In Zimbabwe, the dependence of communal farmers on rain-fed agriculture made the whole water sector reform exercise and the establishment of Sub-Catchment and Catchment Councils of little relevance to their livelihood concerns. Since communal farmers in the sub-catchment area rely on rain-fed agriculture, and *matoro* (wetland) cultivation, the water sector reform exercise appears to effectively exclude the majority of them. A lack of water for productive agriculture among dryland farmers appears to have led to a lack of interest in participating in water management at Sub-Catchment Council level. This has been compounded by a perception that participation in water management activities at the Sub-Catchment Council is for irrigation schemes.

Lack of knowledge among representatives of new water users

Crucial in all four countries is the lack of knowledge and popularization of measures among existing and new water users. A lack of public information and knowledge about water reforms has been the norm. This has limited participation and added to the complexity of challenges, emanating from social, economic, political and historical factors that provide the broad context for reform implementation.

Within this policy landscape, policy and institutional processes that underpin water sector reforms in East and southern Africa are not benign and neutral, but are infused with power and politics, governing access to and management of water resources and the capacity to use water for productive purposes.

Decentralized institutions of water management, at basin and sub-basin level, are part of a wider array of institutions mediating access to water for different water users. Consequently, the creation of additional institutions of water governance, under the auspices of the water sector reforms, creates an even messier institutional context which different water users, particularly the poor, have to confront and negotiate when trying to gain access to water for their livelihoods.

Further, institutional arrangements that govern water and provide routes of access to water are power-laden, defining not only who is included and excluded in gaining access to water, but also selecting who can participate in decision-making processes on water. In many cases, and despite the prominence of new catchment-based institutions of water management, there is often a history of water governance and associated lines of authority and control, which reflect different perspectives, from customary, colonial and post-colonial influence.

By emphasizing management and efficient allocation of water among competing interests, water sector reforms within the region placed limited emphasis on the water development itself – i.e. the water pertaining to the institutional reform. That is despite the fact that dam-building for irrigation and hydropower development are central to trajectories of national economic development, agricultural development and poverty reduction in all four countries.

Although water development and water management are not exclusive categories, the IWRM approach does not provide sufficient guidance on water development and has been superimposed on development landscapes that are fast changing owing to other pressures – climate change, population growth, inward foreign direct investment and the impact of new infrastructure. Therefore, power relations, bureaucratic politics, interest groups, policy networks that tie the global and the local – all affect how water policy has been framed in practice, and how different actors' perspectives have been included or excluded, in East and southern Africa. The IWRM landscape of reform is in danger of becoming irrelevant unless it is able to co-evolve with the wider development contexts in both sub-regions.

A key argument for IWRM-based reform, built around poverty reduction and livelihood improvement, was widely criticized for being blind to historical context, past policies and political processes, and the dynamic changes over time. These were argued to be central to understanding the reasons for and circumstances of poverty (Mtisi 2008; Bracking 2003; Murray 2001) and therefore the relevance (or not) of IWRM plans. In other words, simply establishing decentralized and catchment-based institutional frameworks for water management, as the IWRM principles dictate, will not redress major structural causes of inequitable access to water that underpin poverty in East and southern Africa. A key point that has consistently emerged in both regions is that improving physical access to water for the poor for productive purposes is a prerequisite for successful poverty reduction interventions. The mere existence of institutions is not sufficient; rather the actions by institutions of water management to support the poor and privilege their access to resources are key. This is the next major challenge for water reforms in both regions.

References

Bolding, A. (1999) 'Caught in the catchment: past, present and future of Nyanyadzi water management', in E. Manzungu, A. Senzanje and P. van der Zaag (eds), *Water for Agriculture in Zimbabwe – Policy and Management Options for the Smallholder Sector*, Harare: UZP, pp. 123–52.

Bracking, S. (2003) 'The political economy of chronic poverty', Working Paper no. 23, IDPM, University of Manchester.

Brown, J. and P. Woodhouse (2004) 'Pioneering redistributive regulatory reform. A study of implementation of a catchment management agency for the Inkomati Water Management Area, South Africa', CRC Working Paper 89, www.competition-regulation.org.uk/publications/working_papers/.

Calder, I. R. (1998) *The Blue Revolution: Land Use and Integrated Water Resources Management*, London: Earthscan.

DWAF (1996) *Fundamental Principles and Objectives for a New Water Law for South Africa*, Pretoria.

— (1997a) *A Resource Pricing Policy for South African Water*, Pretoria: Water Research Commission.

— (1997b) *White Paper on a National Water Policy for South Africa*, Pretoria.

— (1999) 'How to establish a CMA', *National Water Act News*, November, pp. 2–3.

Flintan, F. and I. Tamrat (2006) 'Spilling blood over water? The case of Ethiopia', in J. Lund and K. Sturman (eds), *Scarcity and Surfeit. The Ecology of Africa's Conflicts*, Pretoria: Institute for Security Studies, pp. 243–319.

GWP (Global Water Partnership) (2000) 'Integrated Water Resources

Management', Background Paper no. 4, Technical Advisory Committee, Stockholm.

IFAD (International Fund for Agricultural Development) (2001) *Rural Poverty Report 2001: The Challenge of Ending Rural Poverty*, Oxford: Oxford University Press.

Magadlela, D. (1999) 'Irrigating lives: development intervention and dynamics of social relationships in an irrigation project', PhD thesis, Wageningen Agricultural University, Netherlands.

Magadzire, G. S. T. (1995) 'Water development for diversification within small holder farming sector – a ZFU perspective', in *Water Development for Diversification within Small Holder Farming Sector Conference Report*, Harare: ZFU/Friedrich Ebert Foundation.

Manzungu, E., A. Senzanje and P. van der Zaag (eds) (1999) *Water for Agriculture in Zimbabwe – Policy and Management Options for the Smallholder Sector*, Harare: UZP.

Matinenga, E. (1999) 'New Water Act for Zimbabwe?', in E. Manzungu, A. Senzanje and P. van der Zaag (eds), *Water for Agriculture in Zimbabwe – Policy and Management Options for the Smallholder Sector*, Harare: UZP, pp. 219–24.

Mohamed-Katerere, J. (1998) 'Access to water: right or privilege?', *Zimbabwe Law Review*, 12.

Mtisi, S. (2008) 'Zimbabwe's water reform and effects on local level water management processes and rural livelihoods: evidence from Lower Save East Sub-Catchment', PhD thesis, University of Manchester.

Murray, C. (2001) 'Livelihoods research: some conceptual and methodological issues', Chronic Poverty Research Centre Working Paper no. 5, University of Manchester.

Mwebembezi, L. (n.d.) *Status of Catchment Based Water Resources Management in Uganda*.

Ribot, J. C. (2002) *Democratic Decentralization of Natural Resources*, Washington, DC: World Resources Institute.

Serageldin, I. (1995) *Toward Sustainable Management of Water Resources*, Washington, DC: World Bank.

Soussaan, J. (2006) *Linking Poverty Reduction and Water Management*, Stockholm: Stockholm Environment Institute.

Turral, H. (1998) *Hydro Logic? Reform in Water Resources Management in Developed Countries with Major Agricultural Water Use: Lessons for Developing Countries*, London: Overseas Development Institute.

UNDP and IFAD (2005) *The Challenges of Water Governance*, New York: UNDP.

Van der Zaag, P. (1999) 'Water allocation principles in catchment areas', in E. Manzungu, A. Senzanje and P. van der Zaag (eds), *Water for Agriculture in Zimbabwe – Policy and Management Options for the Smallholder Sector*, Harare: UZP, pp. 168–78.

World Bank (2011) *Uganda Water Assistance Strategy: A Country Water Assistance Strategy for Uganda*, Washington, DC: World Bank.

WRMS (Water Resources Management Strategy) (1998) *Integrated Catchment Planning: A New Philosophy in Water Management in Zimbabwe*, WRMS Technical Secretariat and Ministry of Rural Resources and Water Development.

WWAP (2003) *Water for People, Water for Life*, United Nations World Water Assessment Programme, Paris: UNESCO.

PART TWO
CASE STUDY

5 | INTEGRATED WATER MANAGEMENT AND SOCIAL DEVELOPMENT IN UGANDA

Gloria Macri, Firminus Mugumya and Áine Rickard

Introduction

By 2000, it was estimated that one third of the world's population lived in countries that experience medium to high levels of water stress.[1] In the same year it was projected that this ratio would grow to two-thirds by 2025 if no action was taken to avert the situation (Agarwal et al. 2000). The 2006 UNDP *Human Development Report* also indicated that the global water problem was growing into a crisis which, if left unchecked, would derail progress towards attainment of the goals of the Millennium Declaration (UN 2000) by holding back advances in other areas of human development (UNDP 2006). Target 7c of the Millennium Development Goals (MDGs) (i.e. to reduce by half the proportion of people without sustainable access to safe drinking water and basic sanitation by 2015) and the 2003 UN proclamation of the period 2005–15 as the 'International Decade for Action "Water for Life"' constitute two examples of global efforts and commitments to address the problems associated with water scarcity.

The focus of the water decade was on ensuring implementation of water-related programmes and projects in order to facilitate attainment of the internationally agreed-upon water-related goals (UN 2009). While the MDG report of 2009 indicated that the world was on track to achieve the safe water target, it cautioned that 884 million people worldwide still used mainly surface water from unimproved water sources such as lakes, rivers, dams and unprotected dug wells or springs for drinking, cooking, bathing and other domestic activities. Of these people, 84 per cent (746 million) were estimated to be living in rural areas. The report emphasized that even using an improved water source was no guarantee that the water was safe, as test results from water samples obtained from many improved water sources did not meet the microbiological standards set by the World Health Organization (ibid.).

This chapter sets the national and historical context for rural safe water service delivery and development in Uganda and introduces the locale where all of the case studies research took place. It is enriched by the material drawn from an original survey, conducted in 2011, of a rural community (the study area parish) in central south Uganda which assessed the livelihoods, health, gender and water governance issues in the area. It is informed by both science/ technology and a social perspective and covers both water sourcing and water distribution/access. It provides a context and a backdrop for the chapters to follow by introducing some of the main issues that will be analysed and discussed.

Uganda's rural water supply sector in a historical perspective

The character of national policy design and implementation in sub-Saharan Africa, in terms of the socio-economic and political landscape, has been shaped by global and local development policy discourses. In Uganda specifically, the basic public service delivery trajectory has gone through various systems and regimes. Prior to the advent of colonial rule,[2] traditional communities, organized along clan lines, into chiefdoms or kingdoms, were able to provide for the basic needs of the people, largely through collective self-help efforts that combined participatory and partnership dynamics. Traditional leaders and elders successfully mobilized community members to participate in community self-help projects (Asingwire 2008). Trust and high levels of social cohesion and unity characterized and motivated communities to support each other. These dynamics significantly changed through the colonial and post-colonial eras to the present day, when more formal and bureaucratic service systems, based on new development paradigms such as the New Public Management (NPM) and network governance frameworks, predominate.

During the colonial period, safe water service delivery was largely the responsibility of local administration and kingdoms.[3] Before, and immediately after, independence in 1962, the British colonial government operated two systems of central–local government relations which existed alongside each other. The first was a system of devolution to federal and semi-federal systems (in kingdom areas) and the second was a system of district councils, which operated in areas without kingdoms. The major difference between the two systems of local government was that the kingdoms were allowed to collect their own taxes while the district councils relied on revenue from central administration (Muhangi 1996). Using their tax revenues, kingdoms could then finance the delivery of services to their subjects. These forms of local governments were constitutionally maintained after independence until 1967, when kingdoms were abolished and subdivided into districts. Subsequently, the Local Administration Act was enacted, which essentially centralized the powers of local administration district councils, thus creating a top-down approach to service delivery.

By the time of Ugandan independence about 18 per cent of rural areas, and more than 80 per cent of urban areas, had access to safe water, with good prospects for even greater improvement owing to good governance, stable economics and the new spirit of nationalism (ibid.). In the period after 1967, the supply-driven model of service delivery, inherited from the colonial administration, dominated the water sector (Asingwire 2008). The Water Development Department constructed boreholes all over the country and set up fifteen regionally based borehole maintenance units (BMUs) to take care of the maintenance. There was no role for the local communities in these arrangements. However, it did not take too long for these BMUs to be shown up as inefficient as they increasingly failed to respond to breakdowns in time. Over 70 per cent of the boreholes had broken down by the early 1970s with no hope of their being repaired (Muhangi 1996). From 1971 to the early 1980s political turmoil led to a significant collapse in most public services, including that of rural safe water supply. Poor maintenance of water sources resulted in a drastic reduction in safe water coverage in both rural and urban areas. By the early 1980s, rural safe water coverage had fallen from 18 per cent to less than 5 per cent. Efforts to fill service delivery gaps by non-government actors, including NGOs and bilateral and multilateral agencies, such as UNICEF, were undermined by war and political instability. Short-lived and highly centralized regimes overturned the economy and the country's planning and service delivery capacity for nearly two decades (1971–86).

When the current National Resistance Movement (NRM) government came into power in 1986, it put in place a strong system of participatory democracy and decentralized administration, allowing people from each geopolitically defined electoral area to elect their own leaders from village level up to district level (Asiimwe and

Musisi 2007). From this period onwards, greater efforts were made to improve, and speed up, the delivery of safe water through decentralized arrangements to local governments, especially in rural areas. New systems such as village-level operations and maintenance of water facilities were put in place. Together with the emergence and popularization of the structural adjustment programmes (SAPs), and public sector reforms of the 1980s and 1990s, a new set of actors, coordinated and regulated by the central government, emerged. As a result, in the 1990s a comprehensive legal, policy and institutional framework, for guiding all sector actors and their activities, was developed. Initially, the water sector was largely supported by non-government agencies, notably UNICEF, under its nationwide emergency programme. Government recovery programmes were also initiated countrywide with donor support. However, until the early 1990s, sector coordination and financial, human and technical capacity were all very weak, particularly at the local government level, which significantly affected progress in the sector. In 1990, an estimated 60 per cent of the population in rural areas still lacked access to safe drinking water (O'Meally 2011).

Since the early 1990s there have been efforts to improve sector coordination. These efforts culminated in the development of the National Water Policy (1999), which put in place supportive legal and institutional frameworks. These frameworks, together with increased sector funding coordination, have resulted in improved coverage of rural safe water services, though there is still some way to go (ibid.). According to the Joint Monitoring Programme (JMP), access to an improved water source in Uganda increased from 39 per cent in 1990 to 68 per cent in 2010 (UNICEF and WHO 2012). There are arguments that performance levels in increasing access to safe water in Uganda would have been much better if the community-based management system (CBMS) model of service delivery had been given appropriate attention by sector actors.[4]

Access to safe water in sub-Saharan Africa and the national picture in Uganda

Access to safe water is often determined by the number of people served by (or who collect water at) a particular improved water source. Despite reported global progress in access to improved water facilities, sub-Saharan African indicators have remained the

TABLE 5.1 Targets and achievements for rural safe water supply (2004–15) (%)

Indicator		Achievements/access					Targets		
		2004/05	2011/12	2012/13	2012/13	2013/14	2014/15		
Access: % of people within 1 km (rural) and 0.2 km (urban) of an improved source	Rural	61	64	64	66	67	77		
	Urban	67	69	70	69	71	100		
Functionality: % of improved water sources that are functional at time of spot check (rural). Ratio of the actual hours of water supply to the required hours (small towns)	Rural	82	83	84	82	84	90		
	Urban	Missing	84	87	86	87	95		

Source: Adapted from MWE (2013)

lowest (UNICEF and WHO 2012). Uganda is a good example of countries in sub-Saharan Africa that have undertaken reforms and devoted resources to their water supply sectors with the aim of scaling up effective service delivery. However, while these reforms are reported to have positively impacted on progress in the sector, the evidence shows that this progress has not adequately matched the level of investment (Barungi et al. 2003; Mwebaza 2010; O'Meally 2011). In particular, the rate of progress registered by the sector in the late 1990s to the mid-2000s, as indicated in the previous section, has remained difficult to replicate. Despite a remarkable recovery from very poor service delivery in the 1980s and early 1990s, Uganda's rural safe water access figures show that there is still a big challenge for the country in meeting the millennium targets and an even bigger challenge in meeting its own target of 77 per cent safe water access in rural areas by 2015.

Uganda's Ministry of Water and the Environment has actually set aside the indicators for rural safe water service delivery, which include, among others, the percentage of people within 1.5 kilometres of an improved water source, and the percentage of improved water sources that are functional. As indicated in Table 5.1, since 2009 access to safe water in rural areas in Uganda has remained static, at an average of 65 per cent (GoU 2011) and even declined to 64 per cent in 2013 (MWE 2013). It is worth noting that average access figures hide spatial and socio-economic access variations within the country or region. For example, some of the north-eastern parts of the country (the Karamoja region) have as little as 19 per cent coverage, while other urban and peri-urban areas and the south-western highlands have as much as 95 per cent coverage (GoU 2011).

Women and children have also long been more affected by water supply and distribution problems (Rudaheranwa et al. 2003; Water Aid 2012). They continue to bear the brunt of inadequate physical access to improved water sources, given that they are the major water collectors in rural households (Asaba et al. 2013).

Social-spatial disparities in a rural parish of Lwengo district

Problems of access to safe water in Uganda are not only shaped by the wider governance dynamics surrounding sustainability of safe water supply infrastructure, as Mugumya and Asingwire elaborate (see Chapter 6), but are further exacerbated by individual, household and community socio-economic dynamics. The remainder of this chapter discusses survey findings of household indicators in respect of access to safe water in a case study of a rural region in south central Uganda (Macri et al. 2013). The baseline survey assessed the livelihoods, health, gender and water governance issues in a rural parish in Lwengo district. This district was part of Masaka district prior to sub-national district boundary changes undertaken by government in 2010/11.

A quantitative approach was used in this research as it allowed us to measure specific socio-economic household characteristics for the purpose of analysing their impact on access, use and management of improved water facilities. A structured questionnaire was designed in order to collect information on the selected themes. Field work began in September 2011 and was completed in November 2011.

The fifteen villages in our study area have a combined area of 33 square kilometres, and contain approximately 1,730 households. In total, 606 households were selected proportionately across the fifteen villages to participate in the survey. This equated to approximately 35 per cent of the households in the survey area.

Socio-demographic profile of households

A brief look at the socio-demographic profile of the households participating in the survey indicates that the majority of respondents were females (63 per cent). With regard to age distribution, 25 per cent were aged between thirty-five and forty-four, followed closely by those in the age bracket of over fifty-five years, at 24 per cent (see Figure 5.1).

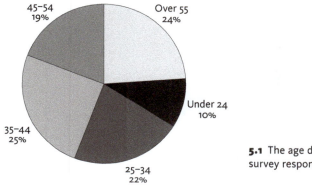

5.1 The age distribution of survey respondents

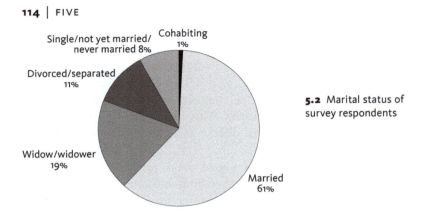

5.2 Marital status of survey respondents

A substantial percentage of respondents (69 per cent) were educated to primary level, while 20 per cent reported having no education. Most respondents were married (61 per cent), but a significant percentage was widowed (19 per cent) with a further 11 per cent divorced (see Figure 5.2).

Household composition and leadership

A total of 44 per cent of all households fit into the category of large-sized (i.e. between six and ten members), with 27 per cent medium-sized (i.e. four to five members). The percentage of respondents in small-sized households (i.e. two to three members) was around 20 per cent. Only slightly over 4 per cent of respondents belonged to very large households (i.e. over ten members) and a further 5 per cent came from single-person households (see Figure 5.3).

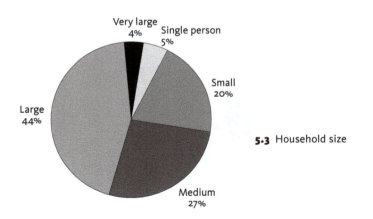

5.3 Household size

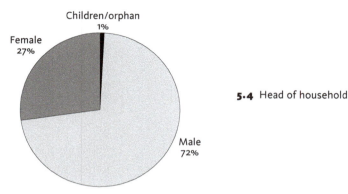

5.4 Head of household

The single-person households were more likely to be made up of elderly people (41 per cent of single-person households) and males (74 per cent of single-person households). It should be noted, however, that the total number of those households in the survey is small (twenty-seven cases), so no generalizations can be made from these particular findings.

The majority of the households were led by males (72 per cent), but 27 per cent were led by females. The survey also recorded that 1 per cent of households were led by children/orphans (see Figure 5.4).

Household poverty

The survey examined indicators of poverty among household members, including main source of income, money earned and dwelling type. In the case of the majority of respondents, the main source of income was agriculture, with 62 per cent earning their main income from crop farming and 20 per cent from mixed farming. Just under 7 per cent of respondents gave business as their main source of income (see Figure 5.5).

When analysing the level of the estimated monthly household income, the data shows that the vast majority of households (85 per cent) earned less than 50,000 UGX (Ugandan shillings); while fewer than 4 per cent of the households earned more than 200,000 UGX (see Figure 5.6).

Furthermore, the findings reveal that households with a high level of income (over 200,000 UGX) tended to be very large-sized households, suggesting that the relative income per household member may still be low (see Table 5.2).

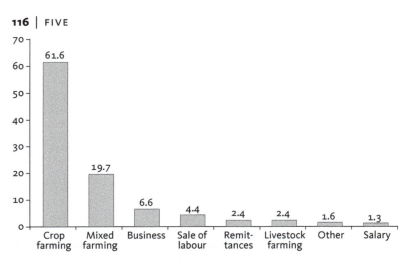

5.5 Household's major source of income (%)

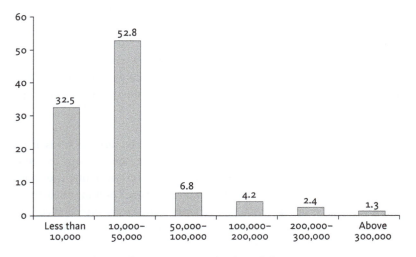

Note: $1USD was equal to 2,600 UGX at the time of the survey.

5.6 Estimated monthly household income (UGX)

With regard to dwellings, many households live in either a per-manent (38 per cent) or semi-permanent structure (35 per cent), but there are also a considerable number of respondents (18 per cent) living in households built with permanent materials, but with no cemented floors. While there does not seem to be a pattern of statistical correlation between the level of monthly household

TABLE 5.2 Estimated monthly household income and size of household (UGX/%)

Household	Less than 10,000	10,000– 50,000	50,000– 100,0000	100,000– 200,000	200,000– 300,000	Above 300,000
Single-person	7.30	4.50	0	4.30	0	0
Small-sized	25.80	17.60	16.20	8.70	15.40	0
Medium-sized	32.00	26.60	16.20	17.40	30.80	0
Large-sized	33.70	47.10	59.50	56.50	46.20	71.40
Very large	1.10	4.20	8.10	13.00	7.70	28.60
Total number of respondents	178 (100%)	289 (100%)	37 (100%)	23 (100%)	13 (100%)	7 (100%)

income and the type of dwelling, it is the case that 86 per cent of respondents with household incomes of over 300,000 UGX live in permanent dwellings.

When comparing earning patterns within the 'head of the household' variable, it emerges that all households with incomes over 300,000 UGX and a very high percentage (85 per cent) of those with an income of between 200,000 and 300,000 UGX are led by men. Hence, it appears that, overall, households led by women have lower levels of incomes than those led by men.

Household access to water

The survey sought information on water access in the area, including information on the type of water sources used, access to working improved sources in the vicinity, transportation, and cost of water.

Figure 5.7 shows the distribution of survey participants in relation to their nearest 'working' improved water source, including those within a 1-kilometre radius. As can be seen from the map, a large proportion of household participants (47 per cent), notably in the west and east of the survey area, are outside of these 1-kilometre catchment areas. In addition, approximately half of the working water pumps in the area are within 1 kilometre of the main roads in the region. Interestingly, almost all participants are within a 1-kilometre radius of 'an' improved water source but, owing to poor functioning and lack of maintenance, many of these are not working and are therefore of no use to the community.

Asked about the main source of water used, 40 per cent of all

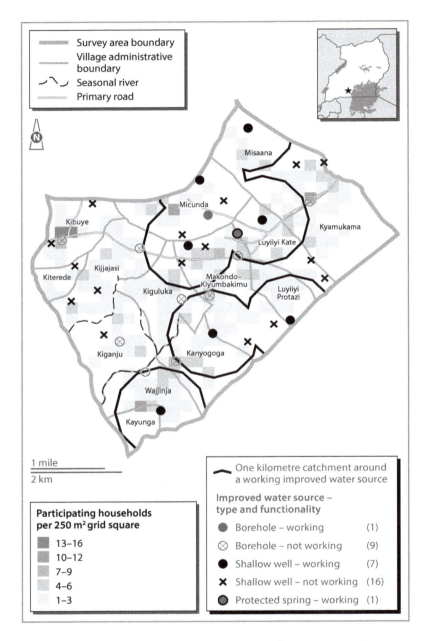

5.7 Map of those households within and outside of a 1-kilometre catchment area of working improved water sources

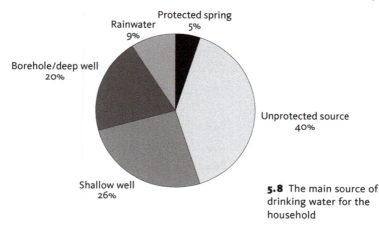

5.8 The main source of drinking water for the household

survey participants replied that they use an unprotected source for their main supply of water. A further 26 per cent use mainly a shallow well, while 20 per cent use a borehole/deep well. A small number of respondents also use rainwater (9 per cent) and protected springs (5 per cent) as their main water source (see Figure 5.8).

The top three reasons given for choosing a particular water source are linked to: water quality (54 per cent of respondents), its proximity to the household (38 per cent of respondents) and the ability to obtain the necessary quantity of water from that particular source in order to cover all of the household's needs (33 per cent of respondents). Respondents whose main source of water is an unprotected source use these sources mainly because they are permanent and reliable and can provide for all the water needs of the home. All other respondents choose their main water sources on the basis of the perceived quality of the water (see Table 5.3).

Figure 5.9 shows a map of the distribution of households using an unimproved/unprotected source as their main source of water. As expected, the vast majority of such households fall outside the 1-kilometre catchment area of improved water sources, and are located mainly in the west and east of the survey area. They make up 39 per cent of the entire sample. Remarkably, fifty-two households, almost 24 per cent of those accessing unimproved water sources, live within a 1-kilometre catchment of an improved water source and yet choose to use an unimproved source for their main water supply.

Forty-one per cent of respondents reported encountering

TABLE 5.3 Main source of water used and reason for using it as the main source of water (%)

	Borehole/ deep well	Shallow well	Protected spring	Rain-water	Unprotected source
Close to household	42.6	37.1	31.0	68.0	30.0
Permanent and reliable source of water	21.3	19.6	41.4	8.0	46.1
Has good-quality water	83.3	88.1	75.9	64.0	12.4
Meets all the water needs at home	20.4	34.3	17.2	12.0	46.1
No treatment required before drinking	38.9	23.1	41.4	20.0	2.8
No need to pay money in order to use it	3.7	4.2	3.4	24.0	31.8
It is the only source	0	0	0	2.0	2.8
Total number of respondents	108 (100%)	143 (100%)	29 (100%)	50 (100%)	217 (100%)

Note: Percentages are calculated from column totals

significant problems in collecting water from the main water source, owing mainly to their distance from it. Other problems of concern were the contamination of the main water source (30 per cent), congestion of users at the source (28 per cent) and the poor quality of the road to the source (27 per cent) (see Figure 5.10).

For those respondents using either an unprotected spring or borehole/deep well a major problem in collecting and using water is the distance from the household (48 and 40 per cent respectively). Congestion of users at the source is seen as the main problem by those whose primary water sources are protected springs (62 per cent), shallow wells (50 per cent) and boreholes/deep wells (48 per cent). Most of those who get their water mainly from rain collection (53 per cent) did not report any major problems associated with collecting and using water. In the case of those respondents

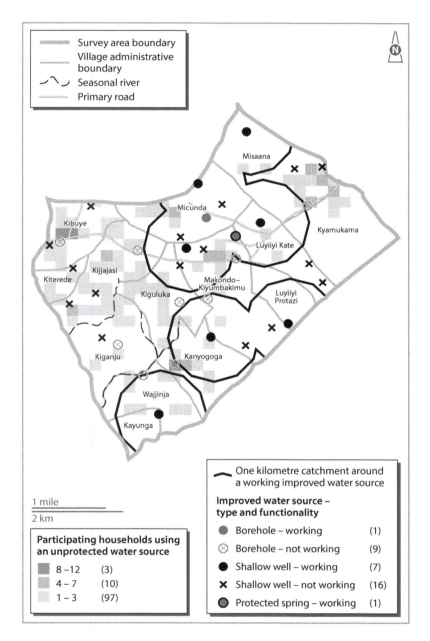

5.9 Map of household participants using an unprotected water source as their main water source

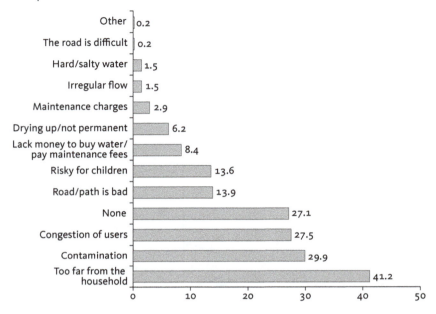

Note: Given the fact that this question allowed for multiple answers, the sum of percentages for each option exceeds 100

5.10 Major problems in collecting water from the main water source (%)

using an unprotected source, most problems reported relate to contamination of the source (63 per cent) (see Table 5.4).

In the case of the households using an alternative water source, the main reason for doing so cited by 37 per cent of respondents is the ability of the alternative source to cater for all the water needs of the household, followed by its perceived superior water quality in comparison with the main source (33 per cent). Other key reasons given relate to the reliability of the source and its proximity to the home (see Figure 5.11).

When asked about the means of transporting water to their homes, hand/head lifting is by far the most common method (91 per cent), followed by bicycle at 36 per cent. Table 5.5 shows that while adult females, children and youths of both genders are most likely to use hand/head lifting when collecting water, adult males and domestic workers/household helpers are more likely to use bicycles.

With regard to the length of time needed for water collection,

TABLE 5.4 Main source of water used and major problems in using/collecting water (%)

	Borehole/ deep well	Shallow well	Protected spring	Rain-water	Unprotected source
None	19.4	11.9	10.3	53.1	4.1
Too far from the household	48.1	39.9	58.6	22.4	40.6
Road/path is bad	13.9	25.2	41.4	16.3	35.5
Risky for children	7.4	7.7	10.3	8.2	22.1
Congestion of users	48.1	50.3	62.1	8.2	1.8
Irregular flow	1.9	3.5	3.4	0	0
Drying up/not permanent	1.9	1.4	0	2.0	13.4
Contamination	5.6	7.7	3.4	18.4	62.7
Maintenance charges	6.5	4.9	0	4.1	0
Lack of money to buy water/pay maintenance fees	13.0	14.7	6.9	6.1	2.8
Hard/salty water	0.9	0	0	2.0	2.8
The road is difficult	0	0	0	0	0.5
Other	0	0	0	0	0.5
Total number of respondents	108 (100%)	143 (100%)	29 (100%)	49 (100%)	217 (100%)

Note: Percentages are calculated from column totals

it emerges that adult females need more time than adult males to fetch water from the nearest water source (see Table 5.6). While more than half (55 per cent) of males in the households surveyed require less than thirty minutes to fetch water, only 38 per cent of women travel for less than thirty minutes to collect water. The majority of women (42 per cent) travel for thirty to sixty minutes and some (18 per cent) take one to two hours. This result does not necessarily mean that women take longer to fulfil the same task than men. More likely, it suggests that, in households which are located farther away from water sources, women are the ones bearing the task of water collection.

Both adult males and male youth carry larger quantities of water

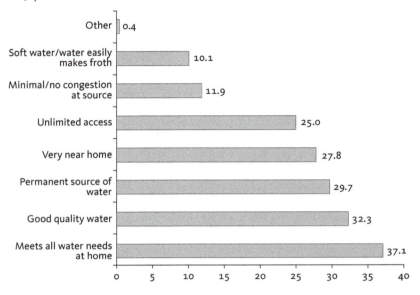

Note: Given the fact that this question allowed for multiple answers, the sum of percentages for each option exceeds 100

5.11 The reason for using alternative sources (%)

than do adult females and female youth respectively. Thus while over 47 per cent of adult males carry more than 20 litres of water per visit, only 4 per cent of adult women do so. Similarly, while over 28 per cent of male youth carry in excess of 20 litres of water on each visit, less than 6 per cent of female youth carry the same amount (see Table 5.7). Most respondents (45 per cent) use one to three jerricans of water per day on average, while a further 44 per cent use between four and six jerricans per day in their households. Fewer than a third of respondents buy water from water vendors, with the majority of these doing so only in the dry season.

When asked about water-related expenditure, 60 per cent of respondents indicated that most expenses are generated by the purchase of water storage equipment. Expenses related to repairing of the pumps ranked second with 39 per cent reporting having to pay these costs. There was also a significant number (19 per cent) of those surveyed who stated that they incurred no water-related expense (see Figure 5.12).

TABLE 5.5 Type of transport mainly used by the following categories of people in the household to collect water (%)

	Adult females	Adult males	Female children	Male children	Female youths	Male youths	Domestic workers/ household helpers
Bicycle	1.6	60.7	3.6	9.4	11.7	46.5	84
Hand/ head lifting	98.4	36.8	95.3	89.6	88.3	52.1	12
Wheel-barrow	0	0	0.7	0.7	0	0	0
Motor vehicle	0	0	0.4	0	0	1.4	0
Motor-cycle/boda boda	0	2.5	0	0.3	0	0	0
Other	0	0	0	0	0	0	4
Total	318 (100%)	163 (100%)	278 (100%)	298 (100%)	137 (100%)	142 (100%)	25 (100%)

TABLE 5.6 Length of time needed for the following categories of people in the household to fetch water from the nearest water source (%)

	Adult females	Adult males	Female children	Male children	Female youth	Male youth	Household helps/ domestic workers
Less than 10 minutes	4.5	8.0	1.9	1.6	4.3	4.3	15
10–30 minutes	33.0	46.6	15.4	13.8	13.6	23.9	10
30 minutes –1 hour	42.0	28.2	37.5	38.6	47.1	35.9	30
1–2 hours	17.9	13.5	31.1	32.5	26.4	30.8	25
2–3 hours	2.7	3.7	13.1	12.9	7.9	0	15
Above 3 hours	0	0	1.1	0.6	0.7	5.1	5
Total	336 (100%)	163 (100%)	267 (100%)	311 (100%)	140 (100%)	117 (100%)	20 (100%)

TABLE 5.7 Litres of water collected per visit by the following categories of people in the household (%)

	Adult females	Adult males	Female children	Male children	Female youth	Male youth	Household helps/ domestic workers
Never/ none	1.9	6.7	0	0	0.7	0.7	4.2
1–5	1.6	3.0	20.5	16.1	1.5	0.7	0
5–10	5.6	5.5	47.3	47.5	11.9	6.5	0
10–15	3.1	1.8	13.6	12.4	3.7	0.7	0
15–20	83.8	35.4	16.1	18.1	76.3	63.0	33.3
More	4.0	47.6	2.6	6.0	5.9	28.3	62.5
Total (count)	321 (100%)	164 (100%)	273 (100%)	299 (100%)	135 (100%)	138 (100%)	24 (100%)

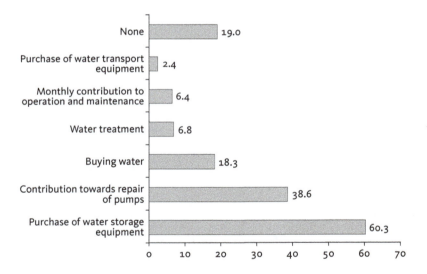

Note: Given the fact that this question allowed for multiple answers, the sum of percentages for each option exceeds 100

5.12 Forms of water-related expenses (%)

When asked about the qualities they would like to see in a water source, 70 per cent of respondents referred to the clean and safe quality of the water, while 56 per cent would like to have access to an improved water source and 53 per cent would like the source to be closer to home.

Health

The survey contained a number of questions relating to health. These included questions on strategies employed by respondents to ensure that water is safe, types of water-related disease suffered, cost to the household of these diseases, and steps taken to mitigate water-related diseases. Eighty-eight per cent of respondents cited their main strategy for ensuring that the water they use in the household is safe is boiling it. A considerable number also indicated that they ensure that water is kept in well-cleaned containers (57 per cent) and that they clean these containers regularly (46 per cent).

No clear pattern of distribution in responses emerged from cross-tabulating the main source of drinking water and the strategies employed by respondents in order to ensure that water is safe. This suggests that the household choices of such strategies are not significantly influenced by the actual water source used.

Referring to the types of disease suffered, findings indicate that, of the total number of households included in the survey, a large majority, 76 per cent, have experienced malaria, while 42 per cent have had at least one family member who has suffered from stomach aches. There was also quite a high incidence of diarrhoea at 37 per cent (see Figure 5.13).

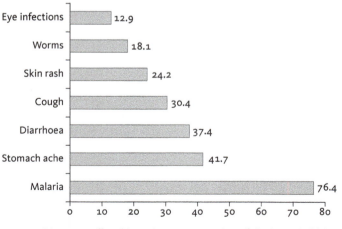

5.13 Diseases suffered by at least one member of the household (%)

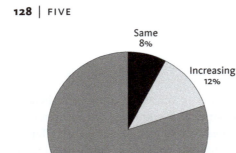

Same
8%

Increasing
12%

Decreasing
80%

5.14 Trend in prevalence of diseases in the household

Apart from their direct impact on the individual who is ill, water-related diseases seem to have a significant impact on the household overall, with 67 per cent of respondents indicating that these diseases have increased their usual household expenditure. They also have an impact on school attendance for 43 per cent of the households and on income for 38 per cent (owing to diminished family labour).

In order to cope with the burden of the expenses incurred from a water-related disease, the majority of households affected had to cut back on expenditure on other essentials. Forty-one per cent reported forgoing food with 17 per cent forfeiting clothing and 15 per cent education. Twenty-seven per cent reported being unable to remember what specific expenditure they had cut back on.

Encouragingly, a large majority of survey respondents, 80 per cent, reported that they believed the trend in the prevalence of diseases in the household is decreasing. Only 12 per cent considered it to be increasing (see Figure 5.14).

Referring to the benefits of using clean and safe water in the household, most respondents (90 per cent) felt that improved health of the household members and a reduction in the number of diseases are of paramount importance. Thirty per cent of interviewees also supported the view that cleaner and safer water would boost the usage and consumption level of water in the home.

Water usage in the home

Levels of satisfaction with water use at household level were considered a reflection of the challenges faced by households in accessing water. Several questions in the survey were focused on the

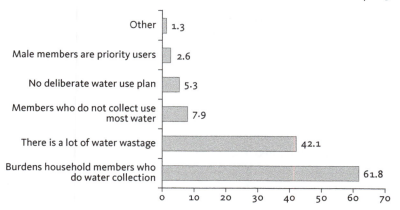

Other | 1.3
Male members are priority users | 2.6
No deliberate water use plan | 5.3
Members who do not collect use most water | 7.9
There is a lot of water wastage | 42.1
Burdens household members who do water collection | 61.8

Note: Percentages are calculated from the total of respondents who mentioned that they are not entirely satisfied with the way the water is used in the household. Given the fact that this question allowed for multiple answers, the sum of percentages for each option exceeds 100

5.15 Reason for not being satisfied with the way water is used in the household (%)

decision-making process around water use in the household. Results showed that 87 per cent of respondents were always satisfied with the way water was used in their household, with a further 7 per cent somewhat satisfied and just 6 per cent who were dissatisfied. These findings imply that communities cope well when faced with scarce resources such as potable water.

Among those respondents who were not entirely satisfied with the way the water is used in the household, 62 per cent felt that the usage of water in the home burdens those fetching the water. A further 42 per cent said that there was a lot of water wastage in the home (see Figure 5.15).

With regard to the question related to conflicts or disagreements over the use of water in the household, 89 per cent of respondents reported that they have never experienced conflict over water usage in the home while 11 per cent reported experiencing it sometimes.

Finally, in relation to usage, the survey data indicates that in 77 per cent of situations, adult females in the household are the ones who make the decisions as to how water is allocated and used. Only in 11 per cent of households is this decision made democratically, involving all household members.

Knowledge and perceptions about safe water service delivery

The survey assessed household perceptions around safe water provision in their locality and the respondents' involvement in securing these services. Results showed that the majority of respondents (96 per cent) rate the need for provision of clean and safe water as a top priority in their respective villages. More than half of them rated the delivery of safe water services in their community as either fairly good (38 per cent) or good (14 per cent), while almost 54 per cent of them rated the delivery of safe water programmes in their community as fairly good or good.

In Figure 5.16, the number of houses per 250 square metres who answered that safe water provision in their community was 'bad' or 'very bad' has been mapped. From this, it is clear that a substantial number of households falling within the 1-kilometre catchment area of a working improved water source still feel that safe water is not being provided in their community.

People who rated their water services as 'bad' or 'very bad' justified their opinion mainly by referring to the lengthy response time in case of a breakdown. Those who rated the services as 'good' or 'very good' cited the reduction in water-borne diseases as the most important reason for their rating.

Table 5.8 indicates that no significant differences can be noted between the males' and females' opinions on the level of involvement in deciding what water service to provide and where they are to be provided. Those who are happy with the water delivery programmes in their community mentioned that they appreciate the fact that they are involved throughout the planning services and in the decision-making process.

TABLE 5.8 Rating of the way safe water service delivery programmes involve locals in deciding what service to provide and where they are to be provided (%)

	Male	Female
Good	15.1	12.2
Fairly good	37.7	43.4
Bad	24.6	20.7
Very bad	10.1	5.8
Can't tell	12.6	17.8
Total	100	100

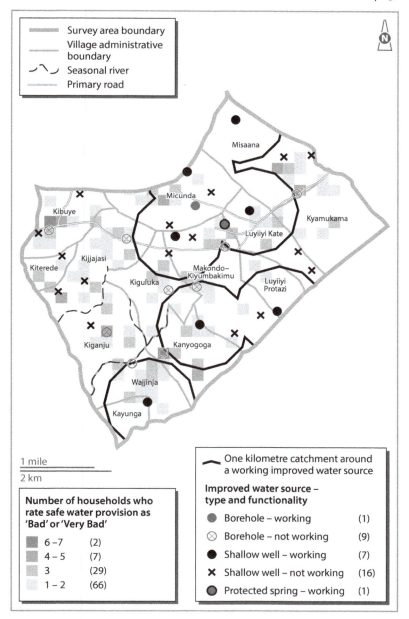

5.16 Map of those who rated the provision of safe water in their community as 'bad' or 'very bad'

When asked about the financial contribution made by their household towards the operation, maintenance and repair of their water source, 20 per cent of respondents had never made such a contribution; 22 per cent have made a financial contribution in the last few months, while a further 22 per cent have made a contribution within the past year.

Conclusion

This chapter seeks to set the scene for the detailed 'on the ground' chapters that follow based on the various interlocking research projects on water issues in a rural parish of the province of Lwengo in Uganda. We have found that this area of study is probably representative of rural sub-Saharan Africa in the broadest sense, being neither a clear success story nor a disaster. This national setting was followed by a social and spatial survey designed to establish the basic demographics of the area and household characteristics, again to set the context for the following much more detailed studies.

The survey reveals household characteristics that are pertinent in understanding water-related stresses. Geographical access to an improved water source that is functional is more important than access to the water infrastructure. Almost all survey respondents were located within a 1-kilometre radius of an improved water source but, owing to the poor functionality and lack of maintenance of some of these, several improved water sources remain idle and useless to the community. In rural point-water supply using hand pumps, communities are expected to own and manage the water facilities. Part of the expectation by policy-makers is that they ought to make monthly financial contributions towards operation and maintenance of the facilities. However, our survey findings indicate not only that households have limited income, but that they are also not happy with the quality of services provided, and so are unwilling to contribute. About 40 per cent of all participants in the survey reported using unprotected/unimproved water sources as their main source of water. In addition, the survey points to a number of factors that constrain choice of a water source, many of which reflect bad governance. For example, perceived water quality, its proximity to the household and the ability to obtain the necessary quantity of water from that particular source appear to be the top three reasons for choosing a particular water source.

In terms of internal household dynamics a total of 87 per cent of respondents mention that they are always satisfied with the way water is used in their household, with a further 7 per cent highlighting that they are somewhat satisfied. In 77 per cent of the situations, adult females in the household are making the decisions in relation to how the water is allocated. Only in 11 per cent of households is this decision made democratically, involving all household members.

The results of the survey contribute to a much-needed understanding of the key aspects of access to water in Uganda, while at the same time they raise a number of important questions which need to be answered through further research. For example, at the policy level, leveraging community capacity to participate in safe water service delivery programmes is not only essential for improving the sustainability of safe water services but also directly impacts on household well-being (e.g. perceived reduction in water-borne diseases), and may also serve as an incentive for community willingness to contribute to the operation and maintenance of safe water supply facilities. Furthermore, while communities may potentially be able to support policies and programmes that demand their direct involvement in or contribution to sustainable safe water service delivery, this potential may remain untapped for reasons that may prevent service providers from identifying/recognizing and developing/exploiting such community-based potential. Communities may be willing and able to make their contributions to operation and maintenance of their water supply infrastructure but may lack the necessary incentives or motivation to do so.

Notes

1 A country or region is said to experience water stress when annual water supplies drop below 1,700 cubic metres per person per year. When annual water supplies drop below 1,000 cubic metres per person, the population faces water scarcity, and below 500 cubic metres 'absolute scarcity'.

2 Events that led Uganda to become a British protectorate (1896–1962) began when two British explorers – Speke and Stanley – visited in 1862 and 1875 respectively.

3 The kingdoms were largely based on dominant tribal groupings, especially among the Bantu tribal groups in central, west and southern Uganda.

4 See Asingwire (2008); Lockwood and Smits (2011); MWE (2011); Mwebaza (2010); Quin et al. (2011).

References

Agarwal, A., M. S. delos Angeles, R.Bhatia, I. Chéret, S. Davila-Poblete, M. Falkenmark, F. G. Villarreal, T. Jonch-Clausen, M. Ait Kadi, J. Kindler, J. Rees, P. Roberts, P. Rogers, M. Solanes and A. Wright (2000)

'Integrated Water Resources Management', TAC Background Papers no. 4, Stockholm: Global Water Partnership.

Asaba, R. B., H. Fagan, C. Kabonesa and F. Mugumya (2013) 'Beyond distance and time: gender and the burden of water collection in rural Uganda', *The Journal of Gender and Water*, 2(1): 31–8.

Asiimwe, D. and N. B. Musisi (eds) (2007) *Decentralisation and the Transformation of Governance in Uganda*, Kampala: Fountain Publishers.

Asingwire, N. (2008) 'Shifting paradigms in social policy reform: a case of demand versus supply-driven approaches to rural safe water supply in Uganda', PhD thesis, Department of Social Work and Social Administration, Makerere University, Kampala.

Barungi, A., J. Kasaija, P. Obote and A. Negussie (2003) 'Contracts and commerce in water services: the impact of private sector participation on the rural poor in Uganda', Working paper series: 'New rules, new roles: does PSP benefit the poor'.

GoU (Government of Uganda) (2011) *Water and Environment Sector Performance Report 2011*, Kampala: Ministry of Water and Environment.

Lockwood, H. and S. Smits (2011) *Supporting Rural Water Supply: Moving towards a service delivery approach*, Warwickshire: Practical Action Publishing Ltd.

Macri, G., A. Rickard, B. Asaba, F. Mugumya, G. H. Fagan, R. Munck, N. Asingwire, C. Kabonesa and S. Linnane (2013) *A Socio-Spatial Survey of Water Issues in Makondo Parish, Uganda*, Dublin: Water Is Life, Amazzi Bulamu Project.

Muhangi, D. (1996) 'Towards an enabling government? Experiences from the water sector in Uganda', MA thesis, Netherlands Institute of Social Studies, The Hague.

MWE (2011) *Assessment of the Effectiveness of Community-Based Maintenance System for Rural Water Supply Facilities*, Kampala: Directorate of Water Development, Ministry of Water and the Environment.

— (2013) *Water and Environment Sector Performance Report*, Kampala: Ministry of Water and the Environment.

Mwebaza, R. (2010) *Sustaining Good Governance in Water and Sanitation in Uganda*, Pretoria: Institute of Security Studies.

O'Meally, S. (2011) *Uganda and Rural Water Supply: Major Strides in Sector Coordination and Performance*, London: Overseas Development Institute.

Quin, A., B. Balfors and M. Kjellén (2011) 'How to "walk the talk": the perspectives of sector staff on implementation of the rural water supply programme in Uganda', *Natural Resources Forum*, 35(4): 269–82.

Rudaheranwa, N., L. Bategeka and M. Banga (2003) *Beneficiaries of Water Service Delivery in Uganda*, Kampala: Economic Policy Research Centre, Makerere University.

UN (2000) *United Nations Millennium Declaration*, New York: United Nations.

— (2009) *Millennium Development Goals Report*, New York: United Nations.

UNDP (2006) *Human Development Report 2006: Beyond Scarcity: Power, Poverty and the Global Water Crisis*, New York: Palgrave Macmillan.

UNICEF and WHO (2012) *Progress on Drinking Water and Sanitation*, New York: United Nations.

Water Aid (2012) *Empowering Women and Girls: How Water, Sanitation and Hygiene Deliver Gender Equality*, online, www.wateraid.org/uganda/news/10407.asp, accessed 22 March 2012.

6 | GOVERNANCE AND SAFE WATER PROVISIONING IN UGANDA: THEORY AND PRACTICE

Firminus Mugumya and Narathius Asingwire

Knowing the right way forward is one thing, but achieving the rate of progress needed is quite another (Lockwood, 2004: 1)

Introduction

More than three decades of the neoliberal influence on public policies should have meant that governments of the developing world, and their development partners, were sufficiently aware of the social equity implications of state withdrawal from direct service delivery. This awareness should have resulted in the institution of governance measures, to address bottlenecks to development that would ascribe 'new' roles for 'new' actors, including networks of providers and targeted users of basic public services. The community-based management system (CBMS) is perhaps one of the now 'indispensable' governance approaches to ensuring functional sustainability of 'improved water supply'[1] infrastructure in rural sub-Saharan Africa. It was established on the basis of its potential to stimulate collective ownership, equitable access and use of rural point-water supply infrastructure and services (McCommon et al. 1988). It is well embedded in Uganda's rural domestic water supply policy and institutional framework and all new projects, whether instituted by government or the private not-for-profit sector, have to follow CBMS guidelines. Consequently, a range of actors, including public, private and voluntary, at different levels, are expected to work together to support community efforts towards *functional sustainability* of the water sources, i.e. the ability of a water source to continuously yield adequate clean and safe water for the users at any particular time (Carter and Danert 2003; Lockwood and Smits 2011).

Based on a study conducted in Uganda in 2011, this chapter examines the institutional framework for the rural safe water supply sub-sector in order to illuminate governance-related bottlenecks. It further examines policy-prescribed roles and responsibilities of the key sector actors, emerging relationships, and the extent to which these relationships impact directly or indirectly on the effectiveness of CBMS for rural safe water supply and sustainability. The study was conducted among key water sector policy actors and a rural community in central south Uganda, using both primary and secondary data collection methods.

Access to safe water and the governance challenge

Latest evidence shows that global efforts towards meeting the Millennium Development Goals (MDGs) target 7c[2] are reducing the number of people without access to safe drinking water, but these figures do not reflect the socio-economic and spatial disparities in regions and countries and also within countries. In 2012, only about 61 per cent of the people in sub-Saharan Africa had access to improved water supply sources compared to 90 per cent or more in Latin America and the Caribbean, northern Africa and large parts of Asia (UNICEF and WHO 2012). In addition, owing to cost and other logistical difficulties in most countries, a proxy indicator, i.e. the proportion of people using improved water sources, is being used, rather than the actual testing of microbial and chemical quality of water. About 187 million people (3 per cent of the global population) still use surface water for drinking and cooking, the majority of those, 94 per cent, being rural inhabitants (ibid.). Thus, despite 'global improvements', many rural dwellers continue to miss out on the benefits, with the burden of poor access to safe water still falling more on them, and most heavily on girls and women (ibid.; UN-Water 2006). As the UN has consistently observed, the problems of access to adequate domestic water are widely considered to have their root causes in governance:

The water crisis that humankind is facing today is largely of our own making. It has resulted chiefly not from the natural limitations of the water supply or the lack of financing and appropriate technologies (though these are serious constraints), but rather from profound failures in water governance, i.e., the ways in which individuals and societies have assigned value to, made decisions about, and managed the water resources available to them ... The scarcity at the heart of the global water crisis is rooted in power, poverty and inequality, not in physical availability. (UNDP 2006: 2)

Effective water governance, improved water management, enhanced capacity at the macro, meso and micro levels, and greater empowerment of the poor are, thus, key strategic means of accelerating progress towards meeting the Millennium targets (UNDP 2004, 2006; Rogers 2006; Bleser and Nelson 2011). While it is acknowledged that greater financing for the water sector is crucial in order to meet the 2015 targets, this is not to be seen in terms of greater aid flows to the developing world, but more in terms of ensuring effective cost recovery from the investments made. In stressing the need for further investment, the 2006 UNDP *Human Development Report* indicated that if funding gaps were met through cost recovery alone it 'would put water and sanitation services beyond the reach of precisely the people who need to be served to meet the 2015 targets' (UNDP 2006: 67). Hence, a combination of financing and targeted attention to the wider governance and public management issues is needed to meet the water development and service delivery goals at both local community level, and national and global levels.

Stoker (1998: 17) defines governance as 'the development of governing styles in which boundaries between actors in service provision have become blurred'. This view presupposes that actors work closely with one another and underscores the importance of collaboration in planning, implementation and monitoring activities for efficient and optimum results. Akiv Ozer and Yayman (2011) further define governance as: (i) a set of institutions that are drawn from, but are also beyond, government; (ii) breeding power dependence in collective action; and (iii) having the capacity to get things done without dependence on the power of government to command or use its authority.

Defining water governance

While there is a growing literature on 'water governance', there is a lack of clarity around the meaning of the term. It is partly used as an extension of the orthodox meaning of governance, but more specifically it encompasses the good governance framework that emphasizes networks made up of actors from the private, voluntary (including community) and public sectors. Most literature on water governance cites the definition developed by Rogers (2006: 16) in his work with the Global Water Partnership (GWP), which defines water governance as 'the range of political, social, economic and administrative systems that are in place to develop and manage water resources and the delivery of water services at different levels of society'. The definition builds on the view of governance as comprising a range of systems, including those of government and the public services provided by other sections of society (Franks and Cleaver 2007). Further, it recognizes that these systems relate, and link, to each other through political processes pertinent to managing natural resources such as water (Franks 2004; Franks and Cleaver 2007), and 'suggests a range of outcomes which go far beyond the management functions of individual organisations or groups'. Its reference to different levels of society implies recognition that outcomes may be different at different levels and that, for example, the poor may need special consideration while working out governance systems (Franks and Cleaver 2007: 292). Rogers' definition is useful in the analysis of relationships between different rural safe supply water actors at the meso, micro and macro levels of water policy implementation, and how these impact on community management.

One of the core issues in the water sector performance debate has been that governance weaknesses contribute to the current global, national or local water problems (Grigg 2011; Jiménez and Pérez-Foguet 2010; Jones 2011). Consequently, most countries, including Uganda, have embraced policy and institutional frameworks for water resource development and management that emphasize multi-stakeholder participation and more decentralized planning and management. The dominant assumption has been that these 'new' approaches bring about opportunities for sustainable supply and utilization of scarce water resources (Montgomery et al. 2009; Carter and Rwamwanja 2006). However, analysis of approaches in specific areas, such as Uganda in this case, may present an alternative paradigm.

An assessment of the extent to which government and its institutions are able to play an effective role that fits the contemporary understanding of governance is essential. Our study is based on the assumption that the multiplicity of public, private and voluntary actors in the rural safe water supply sub-sector depends on how central and local governments play their steering role. The steering role relates to policy management; the level of government commitment to guiding the rural safe water actors to adhere to the goals of CBMS and the effectiveness of local authorities in ensuring that community by-laws, which are crucial for compliance in operation and maintenance of water facilities, are put to work.

The new governance discourse also embeds public–private partnerships (PPPs), which in the New Public Management (NPM) paradigm relates to governments 'serving rather than steering' (Denhardt and Denhardt 2000: 549), 'governance without government' (Peters and Pierre 1998: 223) or a move within public service delivery from 'competition to collaboration' (Entwistle and Martin 2005: 234). While a flexible government, willing to collaborate and network with other actors rather than steering a predetermined course, is advocated in NPM, the complex relationships that result inevitably need a strong organization; a 'strong' public sector that does not control but rather 'influences' the activities of others (Peters 2011: 223). In the rural water sector in Uganda, PPPs have mainly operated in a manner which involves contracting out to the private for-profit sector and strategic partnering with the NGO/voluntary sector. Broadly speaking, contracting out, or tendering, involves separating the appointed service provider from the service purchaser while maintaining a relationship on contract management/monitoring (Savas 1981; Skelcher 2005). Central, or local, governments contract private firms or individuals to carry out stipulated tasks or series of tasks, such as routine maintenance, repairs of water systems, provision of training courses, etc. The public authority remains the sole owner of the utility but pays the contractor for the service under conditions stipulated in a service agreement. But there is a question as to whether these relationships are sufficiently well managed to ensure that high efficiency levels are maintained.

Actors, roles and responsibilities in Uganda's institutional framework for rural water supply

The rural water supply sub-sector in Uganda operates within the decentralized service delivery framework instituted in the early 1990s. This framework takes the traditional intergovernmental decentralization of authority (Conyers 1983) and devolves to the market in the form of private sector participation (Hambleton et al. 1989). A number of actors at macro and meso levels take on specific roles and responsibilities that together are expected to augment those of the community at the micro level, with a view to providing sustainable water service delivery. Using evidence gathered through the combination of policy document analysis and interviews with relevant informants and actors, this chapter will now go on to interrogate the governance challenges in the institutional framework, and to consider how these impact on the effectiveness of CBMS.

Macro-level actors, their roles and relationships The Central Government (CE), through the Ministry of Water and the Environment (MWE), is mandated to ensure appropriate legislation and regulatory controls are in place to support and govern the actions of all actors engaged in safe water service delivery. It is also charged with setting standards and guidelines for guaranteeing that domestic water supply demands are given priority over other water demands, such as those of industry, agriculture and hydropower production. As indicated in Figure 6.1 below, Central Government and its institutions are specifically mandated to provide financial and technical support to districts for the operation and maintenance (O&M) of water sources, ensure availability of spare parts in the country, undertake policy regulation, monitor water quality and conduct studies to inform sector and service improvements.

Our study indicated that, while the MWE provides leadership in coordinating the roles, functions and responsibilities of relevant government departments with regard to water, it is unable to dictate to them as to how they should engage. These departments have individual autonomy and generally pursue individual mandates, requiring continuous follow-up and lobbying. Central Government-level departments and ministries also work in close collaboration with donors and non-governmental organizations to execute macro-level functions. These collaborations and linkages, especially with sister ministries such as Local Government, encounter challenges in terms of networking or multilevel governance, which subsequently impact on CBMS.

Within the decentralized service delivery architecture, the Ministry of Local Government (MoLG) is responsible for ensuring that sound decentralized government systems are in place. It has been hampered in the discharge of this responsibility by delays in the provision of funds to local governments that are charged with overseeing implementation of rural safe water service delivery activities. An analysis of national budget allocations for the water and environment sector reveals a steady reduction in the budget share for the water sector, particularly for rural water supply, delays in disbursement of funds, hurried implementation and poor budget performance (MWE 2011b). Furthermore, the disbursement of funds to the districts for rural water supply tends to favour *hardware activities*, e.g. installation of new water sources or repair and rehabilitation of existing ones, as opposed to providing funding for *software activities*, such as awareness-raising, community mobilization, post-construction follow-up and community support, all of which are central to CBMS. Our study revealed that over 70 per cent of the rural water budget in Uganda is allocated to hardware activities as compared to an allocation of 11 per cent for software activities, with the remaining 19 per cent used to cover administrative costs and sanitation activities. The analysis also revealed that, while Central Government may set ceilings or guidelines for expenditure on certain activities, local government has discretion to adjust budgets as it sees fit.

In terms of local government and human resources management, the MoLG works closely with the Ministry of Public Service (MPS) to streamline planning in relation to staffing structures and job descriptions and salaries, among other functions which impact on safe water service delivery mechanisms. Similarly, the Ministry of Gender, Labour and Social Development (MoGLSD) partners with the MoLG and MWE in executing water sector programmes, specifically in relation to community mobilization and sensitization. The MoGLSD is also responsible for supporting sub-national governments in building system capacity for gender-responsive decision-making, while the Ministry of Health (MoH) and the Ministry of Education and Sports (MES) are, together, responsible for hygiene education in communities and in institutions such as schools. Our study examined how these institutions, at national district and sub-county local government level, coordinate their work to promote CBMS and the functional sustainability of water facilities. The results of our analysis indicated a lack of commitment on the part of Central Government actors to building an effective and consistent collaborative framework in support of CBMS. This

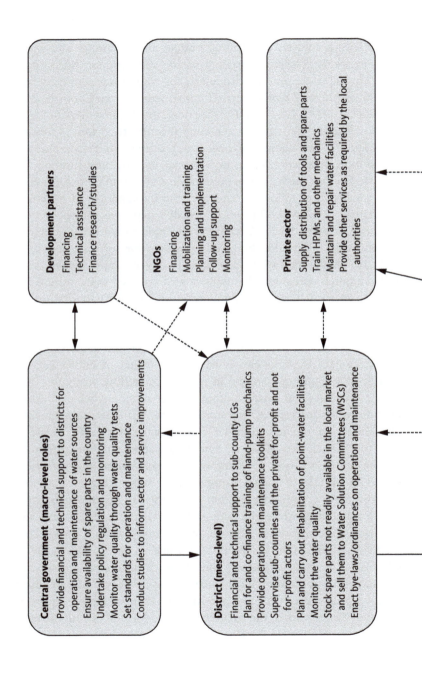

Water user community

Participate in planning and decision-making

Elect WSCs

Participate in site selection and cleaning water-source surroundings, etc.

Contribute to capital cost of water source construction and to operation and maintenance of water source

Source caretaker

Organize the community for orderly use of water source

Clean surroundings of water facilities

Undertake minor servicing of water source (oiling)

Protect the water catchment area

Maintain the fence around the source

Collect the O&M funds

Sub-country (meso-level)

Select and pay for the training technicians (HPMs)

Train WSCs and provide follow-up support

Supervise and monitor the HPMs

Provide custody of operation and maintenance tool kits

Plan and allocate resources to operation and maintenance

Monitor the functionality of water sources

Enact by-laws on operation and maintenance

WSCs (micro-level)

Plan for and oversee O&M; report problems

Together with users select caretakers

Engage HPM/plumber and pay for spares and repairs

Set water-user charges

Hire and pay caretakers

Promote sanitation in the community

Make rules and regulations on use of the source

6.1 Water sector actors and their relationships vis-à-vis CBMS of rural safe water facilities (source: adapted with minor modifications from MWE 2011a: 12)

was evident across a range of areas, including local participation, contribution to repair, O&M of water facilities and collaboration on the general issues of hygiene and sanitation in households.

Furthermore, in 2002 the MWE had established eight Technical Support Units (TSUs) to provide technical support to a cluster of districts and to report directly to the ministry on key rural water supply issues. They were composed of specialists in civil engineering, public health and community mobilization and training, and it was intended that their work in the districts would enhance the effectiveness of CBMS. However, our study revealed that their impact is yet to be felt at the district and community level and, indeed, that some of the district local government staff had a negative view of the TSUs and saw them as watchdogs rather than as contributors to the improvement of local government water sector performance.

The Ministry of Finance, Planning and Economic Development (MoFPED) plays a key role in rural water supply governance, in that it is responsible for the allocation of funds as well as for coordinating donor inputs. Following efforts initiated in 2002 to enhance aid effectiveness in recipient countries, a sector-wide approach (SWAP) to planning, financing and monitoring water and sanitation programmes was adopted. It means that within a decentralized delivery system the allocation of all significant public sector funding follows a common approach, is within a framework of a single sector expenditure plan and relies on government procedures for disbursement, accounting, monitoring and reporting on progress. The SWAP meant that aid to the water sector should significantly shift from the conventional project-based funding to national budget support in the form of a 'basket fund', through which all donors to the sector channelled their support. In the same vein, government institutionalized the Water Policy Committee (WPC) and the Water and Sanitation Sector Working Group (WSSWG), with responsibility for overall policy and technical guidance to the sector respectively. This institutional and funding mechanism was intended as an enabling strategy for the development of efficiency and effectiveness. However, the extent to which these funding mechanisms are effective in supporting decentralized public programmes, including water and sanitation, is in question, particularly with regard to timely allocation of funds and control of financial leakages.

Partly as a consequence of this uncertainty, the MWE established the Good Governance Working Group (GGWG) in 2007, which is tasked with identifying and recommending measures to promote and monitor transparency, accountability and good governance in the water sector. One of the initial initiatives of the GGWG was to undertake research to inform the first joint action plan to address corruption and public resource mismanagement in the sector. The extent to which these efforts have impacted on CBMS and the functional sustainability of rural point-water supply facilities is, as yet, unknown.

In sum, the Central Government institutional architecture for rural safe water supply is well intentioned but the delivery mechanisms are ineffective. We argue, therefore, that a deliberate and conscious effort is required to make these work, which calls for a shift in thinking among Central Government actors on intergovernmental decentralization and its role in enhancing principles of subsidiarity.

Local government meso-level actors, roles and functions The key meso-level actors in the rural safe water service delivery system are the district and sub-county local governments (LGs). Local Government Councils (LGCs), made up of elected politicians, constitute the planning authority of LGs and are supported by Technical Planning Committees (TPCs), which are made up of local government technical staff, employed and supervised by the district and sub-county LGCs. Hence, the nature of relationships between TPCs and LGCs, and the dynamics that shape these relationships, are critical in determining the effectiveness of service delivery programmes and strategies. The LGCs also monitor and coordinate the activities of NGOs operating within their jurisdiction, initiating self-help projects and mobilizing people, material and technical assistance for such projects. The governance and service delivery roles and functions of LGCs run over five levels, from the village, through the parish, to the sub-county, county and district council.

With support from the District Health Office (DHO) and the Community Development Office (CDO), District Water Officers (DWOs) are responsible for the provision and sustainability of water supply services in districts and sub-counties. Our study revealed challenges and problems in coordination, prioritization, implementation and follow-up of activities that offer greater leverage for CBMS systems. At regional and district level, water sector stakeholder coordination meetings were supposed to be convened at least once a year, bringing together political leaders, technical officers, NGOs and private sector representatives to discuss and share district- or region-specific water and sanitation experiences and challenges. This did not happen; meetings were reported to be irregular, owing to lack of funding. These meetings were intended to serve as forums for sharing experiences among meso-level actors and as an opportunity for TSU staff to create an understanding of water sector policy issues.

The MWE guidelines stipulate that community mobilization for rural point-water supplies should be undertaken by Community Development Officers (CDOs), Community Development Assistants (CDAs) and health assistants (HAs) or health inspectors (HIs) in the districts and sub-county LGs. HAs and CDAs not only form part of the sub-county LG extension services workforce, but are also members of the sub-county LG TPC. As members of the TPC, they are responsible for identifying community needs using participatory planning methods. In essence, while they are regarded as support staff, HAs and CDOs are part of the technical team which is directly responsible for rural safe water and sanitation. However, the DWOs frequently bypass the community development department which is responsible for software, and allocate resources directly for hardware purposes. This is a significant governance issue that undermines CBMS. This tendency not to involve the technical staff responsible for software activities not only reflects the lack of capacity of DWOs, but also directly impacts negatively on functional sustainability for improved rural point-water facilities.

Private sector actors Private companies, individual technicians/ mechanics and spare-parts dealers constitute the main actors in the private sector that support rural safe water supply at all levels – macro, meso and micro. The services they provide for CBMS and for rural water supply generally range from undertaking research to providing training and to construction and repair of water supply facilities, as well as supply of spare parts. Hand pump mechanics (HPMs) and spare parts dealers were the primary actors from the private sector who featured in our study, which examined the extent to which their roles and responsibilities supported CBMS, and the extent to which external factors impacted on their capacity to influence and contribute to CBMS effectiveness. The study found that HPMs have a great deal of power and discretion in determining prices and selecting customers to whom they supply hand-pump spare parts. Privatization, in the context of CBMS, does not automatically lead to free market behaviour (Pérard 2008); rather, it brings with it a new responsibility to ensure that communities are not exploited. It is particularly imperative for local authorities and other not-for-profit rural water supply service providers to recognize this responsibility. Recent efforts to regulate the activities of HPMs, through the formation of the Hand-pump Mechanic Associations (HPMAs), are yet to yield success. The fact that they are geographically scattered, owing to the nature of their work, and many of them semi-literate, makes the formation of credible representative regulating organizations difficult.

NGOs and donors/development partners Most NGOs involved in water and sanitation activities in Uganda are coordinated by Uganda Water and Sanitation NGO Network (UWASNET), a national umbrella organization for civil society organizations (CSOs) in the water sector in Uganda. UWASNET works closely with government-sector institutions at the macro level on policy and collaborates with other non-governmental agencies. Within the new governance framework, there is a strongly articulated advocacy for the creation of networks, collaborations and partnerships with a view to leveraging service delivery (Skelcher 2005). However, networking at the meso and micro levels does not always reflect the ambitions of its advocates. Our study examined the working relationships of the NGOs and other actors at the macro and meso levels in their efforts to support CBMS for rural safe water supply. It found that initiatives such as the formation of the UWASNET in 2001 did provide opportunities for more effective NGO and government collaboration and engagement on issues of policy and sector governance. However, it identified difficulties in collaboration and networking at lower levels of service delivery. Collaborations and networks such as the GGWG exist between Central Government actors, national NGOs and development partners and address issues such as policy budgeting, finance and sector performance. However, the effectiveness of these networks tends to be weak at the meso and micro levels. There were tendencies for the different actors at the meso level to place blame on one another as being responsible for failures in CBMS. In addition, some NGOs positioned themselves in opposition to local government and as being more 'for the people'. This, understandably, led to considerable levels of discomfort on the part of the technical staff of the local authorities. Also, distrust and bureaucratic behaviour at a local government district level tended to drive NGOs to implement their activities with minimal, and sometimes no, district involvement. Consequently, the NGOs were accused of 'hurrying water projects' without consultation with districts, undertaking water quality tests or training and sensitizing communities effectively about their roles. In theory, LGs are responsible for monitoring the activities of NGOs and community-based organizations (CBOs) in their jurisdictions, but it is clear that, in practice, this function is challenged and undermined by attitudes, misunderstandings and poor communication.

The micro-level actors: the water user community In a demand-responsive approach (DRA) to development, promoted under the decentralized service delivery and governance framework, the water user communities are key actors in the initiation of the water project, but also in the O&M of the water source. Water user communities are charged with taking major governance decisions with regard to the sustainable management of their water sources. In general, as was the case in this study, water user communities need to be supported in order to be effective in this regard, underpinning the importance of effective collaboration and governance. In this case, the village executive council leaders and the Water Sanitation Committee (WSC) members are the primary actors on whom CBMS of point-water facilities depend. While both committees have a role, the WSC is the critical one. The CBMS model operates on the premise that when WSCs are functioning effectively (e.g. meeting regularly, collecting funds for O&M, ensuring proper sanitation and hygiene at water sources, signing and initiating and maintaining contracts with HPMs, reporting hand-pump breakdowns and formulating and enforcing by-laws), high levels of functional sustainability of water sources are realized (Lockwood and Smits 2011; MWE 2011a, 2011b; Schouten and Moriarty 2003). However, studies have consistently shown dismal performances by the WSC (below 50 per cent) on most of their policy-designated roles (MWE 2011a). They have also found that WSCs tend to be active immediately after inauguration of newly constructed water sources, but lose interest later, owing partly to losing contact with the service providers that initially mobilized them. In addition, willingness to contribute to O&M of water sources depends on the level of trust the community hold in their leaders and in other actors, including government and NGOs.

Conclusion

Uganda's institutional framework for rural safe water supply provides a potentially enabling structure for effective governance of rural water service delivery, and eventual sustainability. Theoretically, the well-developed CBMS provides the tools for effective governance of rural water supplies but, in practice, there have been many challenges and barriers to creating an effective CBMS. The enabling potential, as revealed in this study, is reflected in the fact that Uganda's water sector has more ambitious targets than those set in the MDG target 7c. The MDG target is aimed at halving the proportion of the global population without sustainable access to safe drinking water and sanitation by 2015, whereas Uganda is aiming towards a target of between 77 per cent and 100 per cent.

The 'right way' for sustainable community-based management models for rural safe water supply is certainly known in Uganda's policy and planning framework, but 'achieving progress' remains problematic. As Lockwood (2004: 1), puts it, 'knowing the right way forward is one thing, but achieving the rate of progress needed is quite another'. From our study, we conclude that, while CBMS is well recognized in Uganda as a desirable approach to achieving sustainability of rural point-water supply, the authorities, particularly government authorities, are not taking the necessary steps to ensure its effectiveness. This failure is at the very heart of the weaknesses within the post-welfare policy agenda, with its commitment to decentralization, marketization, participatory and demand-responsive approaches, as well as networks and partnerships in the provision of public services. We do not completely reject the notion of government withdrawal from public service delivery but we argue for public authorities to take account of context-specific circumstances and conditions that can disable good policy and programme proposals such as those embedded within the CBMS model. We advocate for a more effective central and local government authority that will consciously and creatively fulfil its 'new roles' as conceived under New Public Management (NPM) and good governance models, which position government as 'enabler'.

Notes

1 Water sources which, by the nature of their construction, are protected from outside contamination, particularly fecal matter. They include, for example, boreholes, protected springs and shallow wells.

2 To halve, by 2015, the proportion of the population without sustainable access to safe drinking water and basic sanitation.

References

Akiv Ozer, M. and H. Yayman (2011) 'Deviation from classical management thought: governance, transformation and the Third World view', *International Journal of Business, Humanities and Technology*, 1(1): 84–94.

Bleser, C. S. and K. C. Nelson (2011) 'Climate change and water governance: an International Joint Commission case study', *Water Policy*, 13(6): 877–94.

Carter, R. C. and K. Danert (2003) 'The private sector and water and sanitation services – policy and poverty issues', *Journal of International Development*, 15(8): 1067–72.

Carter, R. and R. Rwamwanja (2006) *Functional Sustainability in Community Water and Sanitation: A Case Study from South West Uganda*, Diocese of Kigezi/Cranfield University/Tearfund.

Conyers, D. (1983) 'Decentralization: the latest fashion in development administration?', *Public Administration & Development*, 3(2): 97–109.

Denhardt, R. B. and J. V. Denhardt (2000) 'The new public service: serving rather than steering', *Public Administration Review*, 60(6): 549–59.

Entwistle, T. and S. Martin (2005) 'From competition to collaboration in public service delivery: a new agenda for research', *Public Administration*, 83(1): 233–42.

Franks, T. (2004) 'Water governance – what is the consensus?', ESRC-funded seminar on 'The water consensus – identifying the gaps', Bradford Centre for International Development, Bradford University.

Franks, T. and F. Cleaver (2007) 'Water governance and poverty: a framework for analysis', *Progress in Development Studies*, 7(4): 291–306.

Grigg, N. S. (2011) 'Water governance: from ideals to effective strategies', *Water International*, 36(7): 799–811.

Hambleton, R., B. Hoggett and F. Tolan (1989) 'The decentralisation of public services: a research agenda', *Local Government Studies*, 15: 39–56.

Jiménez, A. and A. Pérez-Foguet (2010) 'Challenges for water governance in rural water supply: lessons learned from Tanzania', *International Journal of Water Resources Development*, 26(2): 235–48.

Jones, S. (2011) 'Participation as citizenship or payment? A case study of rural drinking water governance in Mali', *Water Alternatives*, 4(1): 54–71.

Lockwood, H. (2004) *Scaling Up Community Management of Rural Water Supply: Thematic Overview Paper*, Delft: IRC International Water and Sanitation Centre.

Lockwood, H. and S. Smits (2011) *Supporting Rural Water Supply: Moving Towards a Service Delivery Approach*, Warwickshire: Practical Action Publishing.

McCommon, C., D. B. Warner and D. I. Yohalem (1988) 'Community management of rural water supply and sanitation services', *Wash Technical Report*, 67(4).

Montgomery, M. A., J. Bartram and M. Elimelech (2009) 'Increasing functional sustainability of water and sanitation supplies in rural sub-Saharan Africa', *Environmental Engineering Science*, 26(5): 1017–23.

MWE (2011a) *Assessment of the Effectiveness of Community-based Maintenance System for Rural Water Supply Facilities*, Kampala: Directorate of Water Development, Ministry of Water and the Environment.

— (2011b) *Water and Environment Sector Performance Report*, Kampala: Ministry of Water and the Environment.

Pérard, E. (2008) *Private Sector Participation and Regulatory Reform in Water Supply: The southern Mediterranean experience*, OECD.

Peters, B. G. (2011) 'Steering, rowing, drifting, or sinking? Changing patterns of governance', *Urban Research & Practice*, 4(1): 5–12.

Peters, B. G. and J. Pierre (1998) 'Governance without government? Rethinking public administration', *Journal of Public Administration Research and Theory*, 8(2): 223–43.

Rogers, P. (2006) 'Water governance, water scarcity and water sustainability', in P. Rogers, M. R. Llamas and L. Martínez-Cortina (eds), *Water Crisis: Myth or Reality?*, Leiden: Taylor & Francis/Balkema, pp. 1–35.

Savas, E. S. (1981) 'Alternative institutional models for the delivery of public services', *Public Budgeting & Finance*, 1(4).

Schouten, T. and P. Moriarty (2003) *Community Water, Community Management – from System to Service in Rural Areas*, London: ITDG Publishing.

Skelcher, C. (2005) 'Public–private partnerships and hybridity', in E. Ferlie, L. E. Lynn, Jr, and C. Pollitt (eds), *The Oxford Handbook of Public Management*, New York: Oxford University Press, pp. 347–70.

Stoker, G. (1998) 'Governance as theory: five propositions', *International Social Science Journal*, 50(155): 17–28.

UNDP (2004) *Water Governance for Poverty Reduction: Key Issues and the UNDP Response to Millennium Development Goals*, New York: United Nations.

— (2006) *Human Development Report 2006: Beyond Scarcity: Power, poverty and the global water crisis*, New York: Palgrave Macmillan.

UNICEF and WHO (2012) *Progress on Drinking Water and Sanitation*, New York: United Nations.

UN-Water (2006) *Gender, Water and Sanitation: A Policy Brief*, New York: UN-Water.

7 | WOMAN WATER KEEPER? WOMEN'S TROUBLED PARTICIPATION IN WATER RESOURCE MANAGEMENT

Richard Bagonza Asaba and G. Honor Fagan

Introduction

Despite women's recognized responsibility as domestic water keepers, albeit a traditional, culturally and politically constructed role, the fact remains that they have been under-represented and constrained in their participation in the governance of water resources. However, their traditional responsibility as water keepers, given their daily work in accessing water for domestic use, has increasingly been seen by policy-makers as a rationale for their inclusion in community management water schemes. This has led to legislation being enacted to ensure their proportional participation in new public management and governance frameworks for community-based management systems (CBMS) in rural water supply.

This chapter looks at the dynamics at play in the expanded role of women, from domestic water keeper to community water keeper, in one particular Ugandan rural locale where the legislation advocates equal participation in community water management. The subtleties and highs and lows of the fluctuating process of their inclusion are traced in the words and stories of men and women from fifteen villages in a Ugandan parish where this study took place. The outcomes of the study point to the fact that women's participation in management of water resources remains peripheral and is deeply marked by patriarchal domestic structures.

Women as community water keepers

There are gendered dynamics at play in expanding the role of women to include community responsibility for safe water provision. Traditionally in Uganda, women have borne the burden of being the domestic water keeper and now their role has been expanded from that to community water keeper. As in most developing countries, the governance framework of neoliberal New Public Management (NPM) advocates equal participation of men and women in CBMS for a safe and sustainable water supply. Thus, securing the success of CBMS, and indeed the community's cash contribution, wherein the community has to act as providers and beneficiaries of public water services, now involves the inclusion of women. So it is within this policy framework, of CBMS for safe water provision, that we examine the instance or progress of what could be considered 'women's empowerment' as community water keepers. The current dominant trend in development of 'instrumentalizing' women as key providers of development for their families, communities and countries (Porter and Wallace 2013) provides the context for our question – can women be the community water keepers?

First we look at the key water actors and assess women's involvement at this level, and then we consider their role in the construction of pumps and wells. Finally their involvement and participation in Water User Committees (WUCs) is examined closely from the point of view of the villagers themselves. The field work[1] for this study comprised a socio-economic survey of the case study area, it being fifteen villages in a rural parish in Lwengo district. This was followed by a series of in-depth interviews and focus groups in four of the villages. The key actors or 'water service provider groups' were identified in the case study area where CBMS was in place. These included water users, non-governmental actors and government actors.

The WUCs for each water source comprised men, women, boys and girls with varying sociocultural backgrounds. Water users, or what are sometimes described as 'beneficiary communities', in rural water policies are, *inter alia*, required to participate in 'all aspects' of community-based management (broadly classified as pre-construction and selection of an 'improved' water source; construction of the water source; and post-construction, or operation, repair and maintenance), with equal representation or involvement of women and men. The main civil society actors were non-governmental organizations (NGOs), particularly the Medical Missionaries of Mary (MMM) (a Catholic order of nuns, all non-Ugandans), who had funded the construction of most of the shallow wells, and World Vision and UNICEF, who had constructed the only protected spring in the parish.

The main government or local government actors included: Water User Committees (WUCs) and village chairpersons at village level; the hand pump mechanic (HPM) and health assistant at sub-county level; and the District Water Officer (DWO) at district level.[2] The sub-county HPM played a very important role, in that his relationship with the local water users and village chairpersons, among others, determined the functionality of pumps and the ability of women and children to obtain safe water for their households. Through these relationships, he also had the potential to influence the participation of men and women in the management of their water sources. The Water Statute and Uganda National Framework for Operation and Maintenance of Rural Water Supplies (UNFOMRWS) states that responsibility for many aspects of water management – for example, supporting and training WUCs and water users – lies with both the sub-county health assistant and the Community Development Officer (CDO). But in this sub-county all these roles were assigned to the sub-county health assistant (SHA), who himself acknowledged that he was supposed to work with the DWO, the CDO and NGOs in the execution of his duties but did not have adequate resources to do so. The sub-county and district local government had established water sources in the area, many of which were boreholes.

While there is multilevel involvement in the organization of the water resources in the case study area, the major actors in water delivery are men, or are led by men, the exception being one key non-governmental organization, the Medical Missionaries of Mary. For example, the DWO and SHA were men; all the village chairpersons and HPMs were men; and the WUCs were led and dominated by men, contrary to rural water policy provisions. Despite the fact that the identification of HPMs, including those trained during pre-construction and construction phases of water points, should be gender sensitive, the position was locally maintained and stereotyped as a 'man's job'. One local leader, commenting on the absence of female HPMs in the parish, sub-county and district, said:

> Culturally, HPMs are known to be men. If a woman becomes a pump mechanic, people will say she is *kikulasaja* [she is a 'man-like' woman]. Others say 'how do they see a woman repairing a pump? It looks awkward.' (Male district key informant)

In this locale the government actors, such as the SHA and the DWO, took gender issues in the governance of water resources as more of an addition than as an integrated component. Despite their mandate as stipulated in the UNFOMRWS, a degree of insensitivity to the gender issues was expressed by them in interview situations, and they did little to emphasize the active involvement of women in water management or even support and train water users and WUCs. It was explained to us that the District Water Office 'lacked staff with social and gender skills' necessary to adequately implement 'software' activities.

The failure by government actors to perform such important 'software' activities has been reported previously in some rural parts of Uganda (e.g. Kanyesigye et al. 2004; Asingwire 2011). The explanations for such failure included inadequate finances and inadequate gender-focused training. In Uganda generally, both female and male community members are trained to make minor pump repairs in rural and peri-urban communities, but the numbers of trained females are fewer by far (see Kanyesigye et al. 2004: 16). There are also few female HPMs: for example, in 2011 women constituted only 16 per cent of HPM trainees in Kiboga District (GoU 2011). Another study revealed that, across sixteen districts in the country, 97 per cent of 'improved' water source technicians (such as HPMs) were male (Asingwire 2011: 26). Earlier research has cited constraints faced by serving female HPMs, such as restriction of their movement by their husbands or partners to avoid their being 'in the company of men and in isolated areas', and lack of the 'enormous energy' necessary to carry heavy toolkits or perform repair or maintenance tasks (GoU 2011: 18).

And so, despite the rhetoric of inclusion, and indeed legislative provision to promote inclusion, significant impediments remain to women being recognized as key actors or community- or government-level water keepers.

Gender and construction of water technologies

Following current theorization of water planning (Panda 2007; Lockwood 2004; Rydhagen 2002), greater involvement of women in the establishment of water technologies is one of the potentially transformative, participatory ways to achieve sustainable water governance. Local water policies (e.g. GoU 1999, 2011) also state that both women and men should be involved in the construction of 'improved' water points.

Asked to assess the way safe water service delivery programmes involved them in decision-making at the level and location of water service, the majority of survey respondents (65 per cent of the females and 35 per cent of the males) rated them as only 'fairly good'. Most of these cited their participation in planning and pre-construction meetings (59 per cent of the females and 40 per cent of the males), whereas those who rated the programmes as bad alleged that the programmes involved 'just a few community members' (61 per cent females and 40 per cent males); or never involved them at all (57 per cent females and 43 per cent males). These statistics show that more female than male survey respondents were dissatisfied with their inadequate involvement in pre-construction programmes.

Men tended to dominate the activities involving the actual construction or 'sinking' of the water points. Traditionally, culturally men were presumed to be more 'energetic' than women, and this guaranteed that they would have a greater representation in setting up the water sources. Focus group discussion (FGD) participants noted that communal activities that required a lot of 'physical force', such as the construction of 'improved' water sources and the carrying of materials (such as bricks), were the preserve of men.

> It was mainly men who attended and participated in the construction of our shallow well. This was because men have more physical energy than women. The construction work itself was strenuous ... it involved carrying bricks, stones, gravel and lifting pipes and other metallic parts of the well, tasks which are best performed by men. (FGD with WUC members)

> During the construction of our shallow well, men worked more than women. They [manually] dug the hole where the shallow well was sunk and carried gravel and stones for the concrete that was used. Women did lighter tasks, although a few also carried gravel. Women brought food for the male builders and also cooked it. (FGD with women, Misaana Village)

The above indicates that some women attended the construction of improved water sources and participated in what was perceived as less strenuous work, such as cooking food for the labourers, or what Coles and Wallace (2005) described as 'ancillary labour'. Indeed, during the field work we observed that the local patriarchal ideologies were observed, evident in men's higher involvement in the repair of a borehole (an activity that required similar tasks as those undertaken during construction) in one village. At the request of the chairperson of the village for volunteers to undertake the repair, up to eleven male water users turned up, including a number of youths. They helped the HPM to carry the toolbox to the site, open up the borehole and also lift the pipes. The HPM said: 'It is very difficult to repair a borehole without the presence and help of male community members. Men are more energetic than women and can help you to lift the toolbox and the tools.'

Representation in Water User Committees

Under Uganda's CBMS, Water User Committees are the established and recognized bodies responsible for the management, operation, maintenance and sustainable use of improved water sources (see GoU 1999, 2011). According to Agarwal (1997), Cornwall (2003, 2008) and Cleaver (2004), women (or the disadvantaged) are represented in decision-making in development, collective action institutions or natural resource management through being members of relevant groups or committees. Institutions such as formal water user groups and water management committees are key decision-making arenas in which the inclusion of men and women in water governance can be assessed (Plummer and Slaymaker 2007; Singh 2008; Cleaver and Hamada 2010), and in which women can assert control over their own lives (Cleaver 2004). Women's membership of water committees may, however, be shaped by what Foucault (1982) calls acquiescence, as well as patriarchy, or 'cultural messages' that prompt women to view themselves as shy, self-doubting and lacking entitlement (O'Grady 2005).

In the case study area all the improved water sources had WUCs, but many of them were inactive. The primary outcomes of this inactivity were their failure to act promptly whenever the water sources broke down, and their failure to convene regular meetings for water users to get to know the committee members. A higher number of female survey respondents (43 per cent, compared to 36 per cent of the males) were unaware of the existence of WUCs for water sources in their villages. Also, more male than female community members occupied positions on WUCs (including key positions). Of the 602 survey respondents, only ten indicated that they were members of WUCs for particular improved water sources in their villages. Seven of the ten were women (three *de jure* female household heads and four *de facto*). Most of the survey respondents, who knew that their improved water sources had WUCs, indicated that they believed the committees had more male than female members

Seventy-seven per cent of the survey respondents did not know the required gender make-up of WUCs. Of those that had some knowledge, only 32 per cent of females and 25 per cent of males knew that a WUC ought to have an equal number of women and men.[3] Perhaps the main reason why most of the survey respondents did not know their WUCs or the make-up of their membership was that the committees rarely held meetings with the water users. In the case of inactive committees, meetings never took place, and nor did they take steps to repair the pumps whenever they broke down. It is important to note that, whereas a number of the survey respondents did not know the WUCs or their members, many knew the village chairperson or village committees. This again indicates the recognition that local administrative persons and institutions had, hence their higher power and influence in improving access to water.

In our study, the situation in four villages was examined in more detail to better define the patterns. One of these villages had females in some key positions while the other three had males in all of the key positions. All four WUCs had male chairpersons but the one which had three females in key positions (treasurer, vice-chairperson and secretary) was reportedly functioning best. A number of parish key informants (and a few survey respondents) expressed the view that this particular WUC was one of the most active in the case study area, arguing that it collected repair fees promptly and acted swiftly whenever the pump broke down. The women on the WUC were considered to have good mobilization skills, and this was confirmed in the community meeting by a number of water users. Focus groups in the four selected villages also confirmed that female water users were more willing to pay the repair fees than men but a particular difficulty was that most women were reliant on men to pay the repair fees. The leadership qualities of women on WUCs were also generally perceived to be central to improving the performance of the local water organizations:

Women on WUCs perform better than men. They possess a spirit
of ownership of the water facility that is unlike that of men. Men
have little time for water-related community work. (Male parish
key informant)

Communities that have many women on their committees seem to
have their water sources functioning well for most parts of the year.
I have examples of K ... and T ... villages that I know very well in
K ... Sub-County [another sub-county in Lwengo District] (Male
district key informant)

It was clear that where female leadership was employed it worked
well, and there was a view from those most involved in ensuring
that water sources functioned that women in leadership roles on
committees were effective. However, the cases remained infrequent.

Further dialogue in focus groups and interviews on how to
include women in leadership roles revealed some non-inclusive
processes and patriarchal ideologies that privileged men, hence
men's domination of WUC positions. Female members in one focus
group (who used a particular protected spring) complained about
the election of its WUC:

Our current WUC members were elected when a few people had
gone to clean the protected spring [many were men as local norms
assigned them this role]. While they were there, elections were
organized. So the committee members we have were elected in the
presence of only a few people who had gone to clean and desilt the
spring. (Women's FGD)

This means that the process and timing of the election of the
WUC members of the protected spring was 'functional' or 'instru-
mental' (White 1996). By virtue of the location and timing of the
meeting, it was attended only by men, who were seen as being
responsible for the cleaning of the spring. Thus, because the meeting
to elect the committee took place when a particular type of work,
defined as male, was being carried out, women were excluded from
the possibility of membership.

Also playing a key role were the culturally embedded ideologies that asserted men's superiority over women with regard to
representation on WUCs for deep boreholes and shallow wells. For
example, female, and some male, survey respondents reasoned that

men had more physical energy or were more 'energetic', a quality
that made it easier for them to perform tasks required of members
of WUCs, such as lifting the heavy parts of the hand pumps (e.g.
whenever the HPM was doing repairs) or doing minor repairs on
the pumps as required for one to be a caretaker. Many female
respondents also perceived that some of the tasks of the WUC
members required unwavering or 'strong personalities'. They gave
examples such as caretakers, who have to deal with, and sometimes
discipline, children who misuse the pumps, or chairpersons, and
other committee members, who are required to make household
visits to collect repair and maintenance fees and also to deal with
water fetchers from defaulting households where sometimes it is
necessary to 'forcefully' collect fees from them.

However, it is also additionally acknowledged by the women that
the processes of exclusion go beyond simple 'consensual' cultural
gender-role arrangements, and into the terrain of female subjugation
and harassment. The unequal nature of the gender order is internal-
ized, enforced and reinforced, as women in a focus group put it:

> The chairperson of our shallow well has to be a man because he
> commands more respect. People tend to undermine us [women]
> if we take up such a position. Men undermine us most. They say
> 'how can a woman ask me to go for a meeting?' Even the caretaker
> needs to be a man because when a man talks, he can be listened to
> and will not be disrespected. If a woman becomes a caretaker, the
> people who come to collect water will abuse her – even young boys
> can abuse you. (Women's FGD)

As has already been discussed, there are some men who are
cognizant of the requirements for inclusion and of the success of
women in leadership roles and who are trying to involve women.
But they still explain the lack of women on WUCs in cultural rather
than political terms:

> We try to emphasize the fair representation of women on the WUCs,
> including the four key positions of chairperson, vice chairperson,
> treasurer and secretary. But in most of the communities, women are
> shy ... In some communities, we even fail to get women who can vol-
> unteer to be on the committees and yet we cannot force them. Basing
> on my experience, I usually get only two women who are willing to be
> on the committee. (Male NGO key informant)

When we are electing WUCs, we want women to at least hold some key positions. For example, women are very good at keeping money and making accountability, and so a lady can be chosen as a treasurer. We also need somebody from the political wing, who is at least someone from the village local council, and a youth. A local council person on the same committee can help women to enforce the by-laws, while a youth can guide his fellow youth. The only challenge we face is that women fear to take up these positions … When some people in the meetings nominate them for various positions, they say no, not me. (Male district key informant)

Another key informant concluded:

Women can take up these positions [on WUCs] but after being sensitized. Among the Baganda [the dominant ethnic group], there are many beliefs that make women inferior to men, and these prevent women from taking positions on water committees. (Male parish key informant)

In other words, the inferiority of women to men and boys is built into the terrain of the cultural practices of the majority, and this has to be tackled or overcome through training or 'sensitization' of men and women to ensure that women are allowed into a position of authority.

From the above analysis, it is clear that non-inclusive and un-democratic election processes, cultural beliefs and practices that hold women as inferior, women's fear of being regarded as inferior, and the reality of them being regarded as inferior limits their ability to serve on WUCs. Although there is both regulation and policy to support the inclusion of women, without training, and both men and women 'being sensitized', under-representation will continue within the patriarchal organizing structure of the case study area.

Conducting meetings

When women step up and involve themselves there is further struggle involved. As theorized by White (1996), transformative or 'empowering' participation offers the practical experience of being involved in considering options, making decisions and taking collective action against unfairness. Agarwal (1997) and Cornwall (2008) add that this involves an individual's ability to attend or be 'physically present' in an activity. In the case of water governance, it involves the physical presence of men and women in local governance spaces (Franks and Cleaver 2007; Singh 2008; Cleaver and Hamada 2010). In the case study area gender sensitivity in community participation, and involvement in 'all levels of decision-making' (including post-construction and maintenance), were prerequisites (GoU 1999, 2011). However, and unfortunately, WUC meetings for the operation and management of improved water sources were rarely convened, and thus there was little or no formal engagement between the WUCs and the water users in the area. This meant that the spaces and places where women and men would conduct dialogue on issues around water were limited. This was affirmed in most of the FGDs, and by some key informants:

> We always encourage the WUCs to meet regularly and make reports to their respective communities of water users, but they often fail to do so. Instead, they tend to meet when there is a breakdown [that is, when a pump has broken down]. In fact, it is not good for them to wait for a breakdown in order to meet or raise contributions from the community. (Male NGO key informant)

Village chairpersons (sometimes with a few members of the village council or WUC) convened the few water meetings that took place, and also had the responsibility of inviting water users. Unless the village chairperson was also the WUC chairperson, or worked closely with him, it was very difficult for a WUC to convene meetings. By virtue of their authority, village chairpersons had more power in this regard than either the WUC members or chairpersons.

While water meetings occurred infrequently in the case study area, it is noteworthy that where they did occur, more women than men were reported to have been in attendance. Most of the FGD participants and key informants confirmed that water meetings were mainly attended by women. This fact was also reflected in the community meetings conducted in the case study villages, where women outnumbered men. Also, women were more likely to remain until the end of a meeting, whereas men drifted away slowly and quietly through the course of the meeting. Thus by the time a meeting concluded, the attendance consisted of significantly more women. For example, one village meeting had about thirty men and thirty-three women present at the beginning, but only fifteen men stayed until it ended.

According to women:

> Most of the meetings we have been having since our borehole was constructed are attended by women ... It is us who are responsible for all water-related issues in the household ... We are more concerned about water because we fetch it [with children]. Do men collect water? ... They just sit down and wait for us to give them water for drinking and bathing ... You are the one who fetches water, washes utensils, bathes the children, cooks and everything else you wash requires water. So it is our concern and responsibility for water in the households that encourages us to attend water meetings. (Women's FGD)

> We attend water meetings more than men because we care more about water. Men do not care about water and so prefer to do their own things when meetings are called. Men do not care about where and how you get water ... all they want is water in the household. When the shallow well breaks down, it is us who walk a distance of over one kilometre to M ... [a neighbouring village] to fetch clean water from another [functioning] shallow well. (Women's FGD)

According to men active in keeping water resources flowing:

> It is women who attend water meetings because they usually stay at home. Women are more responsible for water issues compared to men. (Male village key informant)

> Women attend water meetings more than men. Women use water most and suffer the consequences if water is not available. In fact, when water is not available, you can expect domestic violence to occur in a household [i.e. men becoming violent against women]. (Male village key informant)

Both male and female FGD participants attributed men's low attendance at water meetings to a combination of laziness, men's lower level of mobility, limited interest or indifference and the lack of monetary or other material reward.

Setting the agenda

As theorized by Lukes (1974), power is exercised not only through securing desired outcomes in decision-making processes, but also through procedures of preference-shaping and 'institutional practices' of bias mobilization and control over political agenda. For example, Stewart and Taylor (1995) argue that determining which issues a community are allowed to be involved in, and controlling the agenda for discussion, is a covert dimension of power central to an understanding of participation and empowerment.

We have seen that men determined who attended water meetings while women were more physically present in the meetings. Men, as the primary conveners of water meetings, were also the ones who set the agendas and dictated the tempo of meetings by virtue of chairing them. Despite their generally being in the majority at meetings, female water users had little input into the agendas. The issues of repairs and raising of repair fees dominated WUC meetings, while cleanliness, hygiene and safeguarding of the water sources were the dominant items on the agendas of the first post-construction meetings (or when the water sources had just been handed over to the communities by either NGOs or the sub-county local government). Other issues discussed in water meetings included the safeguarding of water points (perhaps related to maintenance), running of WUCs and child fights at the water sources, many of which were raised by women:

> ... the foremost issue that we often discussed in the meetings was the broken-down pump [a shallow well] and how to repair it. And of course the payment of the fees was the most important thing. We discussed the amount to ask from every individual and once it was agreed, the WUC [chairperson or another committee member] communicated it to the various households in our village. And whenever you had your own money, you would pay it to the committee there and then without having to go home and asking your husband to give it to you. (Women's FGD)

As theorized by White (1996), Cornwall (2003, 2008) and Gaynor (2010), the ability of marginalized groups to have a voice offers the potential to transform societal and gender relations and the direction of development. This resonates with Agarwal's (1997) notion of women 'being heard' in meetings. In formal water resource management institutions, this ability to exercise voice and choice also offers the potential to transform gender relations (Plummer and Slaymaker 2007; Cleaver and Hamada 2010). Women's power, or voices in water institutions, or their ability to resist male-dominated water spaces, can be affected by patriarchy, whereby they may see themselves as powerless, anxious, shy or even lacking entitlement (O'Grady 2005). This is also akin to Foucault's notion of a 'normalizing gaze' in which individuals, in this case women, may behave in certain ways because men will classify and judge them. Men's power during water meetings was summed up in the following FGD:

> In our culture, men are more powerful and women have to follow what they say. A man's decision cannot be overturned. Some women, especially young ones [such as those who have been 'sensitized' or have attended various trainings on water and other aspects of community development], do not know what they need to do to achieve what they want. They think they should also give rules and do everything that men do. (Male FGD participant, WUC)

It is apparent that, regardless of training, patriarchal men cannot accommodate women as rule-makers nor even as equals, but rather must keep them within patriarchal norms of obedience to men.[4] Women's participation in water governance, particularly in meetings, was challenged by patriarchal beliefs, and men felt uncomfortable with women's articulation of their views and interests. A key informant explained how training and attendance at relevant sensitization workshops was necessary to encourage better participation:

> The few women who can state their views in meetings are those who attend various trainings and sensitizations or development-related workshops in our parish, and those who are actively involved in women's associations. The women who do not attend these workshops and those who are not members of associations, such as housewives [the majority], are usually very quiet in the water meetings and cannot air out their views freely. (Male village key informant)

Certainly, observations in the community meetings held in the four case study villages revealed that fewer women contributed to the discussions. A number of women were silent during the meetings and some, who perhaps had important issues that should have been considered, were seen murmuring among themselves. It was also observed that most of the women who tried to express themselves held more socially recognizable positions in the villages. They included 'elders' (fifty years and above); those involved in businesses such as shop attendants or owners; a nurse; and members of women's village, or community-based, associations. The domestic patriarchal arrangement can be seen to directly undermine the involvement of women here, in that the women who attended with husbands were seen to be much less willing to contribute:

> Some women attend water meetings with their husbands and when the husband talks, she keeps quiet. You [referring to women] may say something in a meeting which a man [husband or partner] may not be happy about. (Women's FGD)

It is noteworthy that the majority of the FGD participants (both male and female), and WUC members, all observed the degree to which women's voices, needs and interests were subjugated in water meetings. It was noted that men had more opportunities to give their views during water meetings, and that women's needs and interests were rarely taken into account by the respective WUCs:

> In most cases here, men take the floor more than women, unless the chairman says 'let us also listen to women'. Depending on what idea you propose during the meeting, men can challenge you. Women's ideas may not be taken into account. If a woman comes up with a good idea, there is a small likelihood that it might be considered. Women are usually dull in the meetings because they are shy. You may propose an idea and they [men] quash it or do not take it as important, so you also decide to keep quiet and just let the meeting move on while you only listen. (Women's FGD)

In addition to not being heard because they might not be sufficiently forthcoming, or can be easily 'quashed', their concerns may be quite different to those of men, specifically arising from their domestic caring role as mothers.

> ... a woman's views may not be taken seriously. For example, we raise issues concerning our children who collect water from the shallow well, such as fights between themselves, and the caretaker denying them access to the well even after we have paid repair fees ... The mistreatment of our children because of 'not paying repair fees' is often not adequately discussed and is not taken seriously by the chairperson of the meeting and his committee. (Women's FGD)

The above responses indicate that women were not entirely free to express their opinions in water meetings and that their specific concerns were not given much priority in the meetings.

A few FGD participants and key informants expressed the view that things were changing and that women were now participating more fully in WUC meetings and being heard some of the time.

> In the past [1960s and 1970s], women were reticent in all village meetings. But these days, women can raise their views in water meetings and are even capable of discussing issues better than men. (Male FGD participant, WUC)

> ... these days, women can talk in meetings because our communities have been sensitized about gender by various organizations and NGOs such as World Vision and the MMM. Some women even encourage their fellow women to be more active in meetings [and other social gatherings]. (FGD with WUC)

> During the last meeting we had on cleaning [and desilting] our protected spring, both men and the few women who attended were given an opportunity to talk. For example, I was able to speak, and I proposed a name for one of the committee members [when electing the committee] and it was seconded. (Women's FGD, the study area village)

> I think that women's views are considered during water meetings [in K ...]. During one of the meetings for our shallow well, Miss Carol [not her real name] proposed that we should refence the well. Her wish was granted later on, as the committee refenced the well after a fortnight. (Male village key informant)

Another example was given of a case where women had an impact on decisions and indeed personnel.

> Some women make good contributions during water meetings for our shallow well. At one time, women who attended our meeting argued that the treasurer on our committee was 'misusing his powers' by giving his children preferential treatment whenever they went to the well to collect water. He, for example, wanted his children to jump the queue. Because the women insisted, it was decided that the treasurer should be replaced by a woman and this was done. (Male village key informant)

While the above examples indicate that some women did speak out in water meetings about issues that concerned them, and in some cases influenced outcomes, the evidence is, as the majority of the FGD participants and key informants assert, that men generally had more power and privileges during water meetings.

This in essence resonates with Andrea Cornwall's (2003) idea that representation does not guarantee voice. What we see here is Foucault's (1982) disciplinary or 'normalizing' power of traditional patriarchy: where 'empowerment' is 'given' through policy designed to ensure female representation and voice in WUCs, it is challenged in cultural practices. Women's silence in water meetings can further subjugate them and privilege men or reproduce men's domination (Kerfoot and Knights 1994; Connell 2005). And apart from a few occasions when women tried to resist the patriarchal norms, such as the election of WUC members, replacing an underperforming WUC member and fencing of a water source, there is limited evidence of women's water choices being respected and implemented in the male-dominated water spaces.

Conclusion

How do the words and experiences of the poor women and men in this rural locale help our understanding of current development processes for securing safe water? Returning to the analysis of the strategy to create women as community water keepers given their traditional domestic role as domestic water keepers, what lessons can we learn?

Traditionally women, as carers, have borne the burden of being domestic water keeper, and now their role has been expanded to that of community water keeper in a neoliberal New Public Management arrangement. This arrangement, in line with some development theory, advocates equal participation of men and women in CBMS for the maintenance of a safe and sustainable water supply in Uganda. Securing the success of CBMS, and indeed the community's financial contribution to those schemes, is now intended to involve women in their governance; this despite the fact that, as carers in poor communities, they have the least likelihood of having access to finance to meet water maintenance fees.

We would contend that this case study indicates that, though the policy is presented as incorporating women in governance as if they are empowered actors, it takes no account of the fundamental constraints on female participation in the economy and polity arising from the persistent gender inequalities which shape their lives. A façade of opportunity is presented in these policy arrangements wherein women's empowerment is conceptualized as an outcome. Conceptualizing equality as an outcome, without challenging the dominant sexist norms and the gendered constraints on women, may in fact create an additional burden on them. At best it presents an impression of opportunity that the women have little or no way of seizing.

Legislation promoting the increased participation of women in New Public Management and governance frameworks for CBMS has failed in that regard. It has instead furthered the myth of women being unencumbered by gender relations (Cornwall 2012). In this chapter we have endeavoured to unpick the encumbrances at play in the dynamics of instrumentalizing women as community water keepers. Women's participation in choice, maintenance and management of water resources remains peripheral despite, and probably because of, the prevalent agenda in neoliberal development policy which seeks to override, as opposed to reverse, the reality of poor women's lives. Gender-transformative, and sustainable, water governance can occur only when women effectively participate in all the political processes of decision-making and when they have a voice (White 1996; Panda 2007; Cornwall 2003, 2008).

Notes

1 The field work was undertaken with technical and financial support from the Water Is Life: *Amazzi Bulamu* Project (WIL), which was funded through the Irish Aid/HEA Programme of Strategic Co-Operation.

2 Also generally or specifically stipulated in the Water Statute and NFOMRWS (GoU 1995, 2011).

3 Fifty per cent, as outlined in the revised UNFOMRWS; earlier versions and policy documents hinted at 33 per cent for female Water User Committee members, and some respondents and key informants mistakenly took this as the recommended composition.

4 This view was expressed in the context of a male-on-male interview; hence we see the subject position of a male investigating gender as particularly useful in uncovering the patriarchal order.

References

Agarwal, B. (1997) '"Bargaining" and gender relations: within and beyond the household', *Feminist Economics*, 3: 1–51.

Asingwire, N. (2011) *Assessment of the Effectiveness of the Community-based Maintenance System for Rural Water Supply Facilities*, Kampala: MWE and DWD.

Cleaver, F. (2004) 'The limits of participation in development', in A. M. Lykke, M. Kirkebjerg Due, M. Kristensen and I. Nielsen, *Current Politics in West Africa; the Use of Local Knowledge in Applied Research; Participation in Project Planning and Capacity Building*, Proceedings of the 16th Danish Sahel Workshop, 5/6 January, Aarhus: Sahel-Sudan Environmental Research Initiative (SEREIN).

Cleaver, F. and K. Hamada (2010) '"Good" water governance and gender equity: a troubled relationship', *Gender & Development*, 18: 27–41.

Coles, A. and T. Wallace (2005) *Gender, Water and Development*, Oxford: Berg.

Connell, R. W. (2005) *Masculinities*, 2nd edn, Cambridge: Polity Press.

Cornwall, A. (2003) 'Whose voices? Whose choices? Reflections on gender and participatory development', *World Development*, 31: 1325.

— (2008) 'Unpacking participation: models, meanings and practices', *Community Development Journal*, 43: 269–89.

— (2012) 'Framing women in international development', Presentation at the Development Studies Association, London, November 2011.

Foucault, M. (1982) 'The subject and the power', in H. L. Dreyfus and P. Rabinow (eds), *Beyond Structuralism and Hermeneutics*, Chicago, IL: University of Chicago Press, pp. 208–26.

Franks, T. and F. Cleaver (2007) 'Water governance and poverty: a framework for analysis', *Progress in Development Studies*, 7: 291–306.

Gaynor, N. (2010) *Transforming Participation? The Politics of Development in Malawi and Ireland*, London: Palgrave Macmillan.

GoU (1999) *The National Water Policy*, Kampala: Ministry of Water and the Environment.

— (2011) *Water and Environment Sector Performance Report, 2011*, Kampala: Ministry of Water and the Environment.

Kanyesigye, J., J. Anguria, E. Niwagaba and T. Williamson (2004) *Are National Water and Sanitation Objectives Achieved on the Ground? A Review of Service Delivery, Planning Monitoring and Evaluation in Tororo and Wakiso Districts*, Kampala: WaterAid.

Kerfoot, D. and D. Knights (1994) 'Into the realm of the fearful: power, identity and the gender problematic', in L. Radtke and H. J. Stam (eds), *Power/Gender: Social Relations in Theory and Practice*, London: Sage.

Lockwood, H. (2004) *Scaling Up Community Management of Rural Water Supply: Thematic Overview Paper*, The Hague: IRC International Water and Sanitation Centre.

Lukes, S. (1974) *Power: A Radical View*, London: British Sociological Association.

Macri, G., A. Rickard, B. Asaba, F. Mugumya, G. H. Fagan, R. Munck, N. Asingwire, C. Kabonesa and S. Linnane (2013) *A Socio-Spatial Survey of Water Issues in Makondo Parish, Uganda*, Dublin: Water Is Life: *Amazzi Bulamu* Project.

O'Grady, H. (2005) *Woman's Relationship with Herself: Gender, Foucault and Therapy*, Oxford: Routledge.

Panda, S. M. (2007) *Women's Collective Action and Sustainable Water Management: Case of Sewa's Water Campaign in Gujarat, India*, International Research Workshop on 'Gender and Collective Action', 17–21 October 2005, Chiang Mai, Thailand: Institute of Rural Management (IRMA).

Plummer, J. and T. Slaymaker (2007) 'Rethinking governance in water services', Working Paper 284, London: Overseas Development Institute.

Porter, F. and T. Wallace (2013) 'Introduction', in T. Wallace, F. Porter and M. Ralph-Bowman (eds), *Aid, NGOs and the Realities of Women's Lives: A Perfect Storm*, Rugby: Practical Action Publishing.

Rydhagen, B. (2002) *Feminist Sanitary Engineering as a Participatory Alternative in South Africa and Sweden*, Karlskrona: Blekinge Institute of Technology.

Singh, N. (2008) 'Equitable gender participation in local water governance: an insight into institutional paradoxes', *Water Resources Management*, 22: 925–42.

Stewart, M. and M. Taylor (1995) *Empowerment and Estate Regeneration*, Bristol: Policy Press.

White, S. C. (1996) 'Depoliticising development: the uses and abuses of participation', *Development in Practice*, 6: 6–15.

*Joyce Mpalanyi Magala, Consolata Kabonesa
and Anthony Staines*

Introduction

This chapter presents an ethnographic understanding of the world of women and water, gained over fourteen months in one rural semi-arid village in south-western Uganda. Life in the village studied is characterized by long droughts, resulting in limited water availability, with the women having to adapt and manage the water resource sparingly. An exploration of the role of women in water management at household level was undertaken; and the daily experiences of women with regard to water management were characterized. The chapter further examines discourses surrounding women as gatekeepers of water in the home.

The gendered perspectives with regard to patriarchy, masculinity, power and submissiveness provided a theoretical framework for understanding the issues around women, water management and health. Field work included participant observation at household level, at community meetings and at village water sources. Formal and informal interviews were conducted, involving both men and women in the village. Data was recorded in field notes and analysed, based on critical incidents that illuminated the in-depth search from the 'how to the why' of events. In sum, the women's daily experience of limited access to a water supply was explored as a microcosm of the broader issues around gender and water politics in a development context.

Despite the numerous water and health interventions, women still struggle with limited access to water, which has persisted in sub-Saharan Africa and Uganda in particular. They bear the impact of 'inadequate, deficient or inappropriate water and sanitation services' (GoU 2010: vii). Therefore water access is a key determinant in the lives and health status of women in Africa. Moreover, Gupta et al. (2010: 301) assert that 'access to water should be physically safe', especially for women and children who generally collect the water on a daily basis. The nature of the women's domestic work revolves around availability of water and water management. Water management involves the collection, use and storage of water at the household level. The principal elements are: personal hygiene as exhibited in the handling of water for drinking, food preparation, bathing, washing of utensils and clothes, and watering animals. These, and the other household activities in which women engage, have implications for their health and for their ability to fulfil their roles and realize their goals. The availability of water is key to women's role performance as well as to their hygiene and behavioural practices. This, in turn, has an effect on household health outcomes.

Women, water and health

The Millennium Development Goal MDG7 focuses on halving the proportion of the population without sustainable access to safe drinking water and basic sanitation by 2015 (WHO and UNICEF 2012). Access to adequate supplies of water is considered a right and an 'indicator of human well-being ... and [plays] a role in helping to resolve some of the manifold problems associated with poverty, exclusion and disease' (Potter 2010: 115). According to the United Nations (UN 2012), women and girls bear the primary responsibility for water collection. Therefore, achievement of the MDG target should benefit women, as the managers of domestic water needs. However, Ray (2007), among others, observed that there is still a proportion of women without access to water for domestic and general livelihood needs. Water scarcity, especially in rural areas, puts a heavy burden on women, who often spend considerable time planning and coordinating household water needs (Ennis-McMillan 2001). They also expend significant time and effort in collecting household water, which impacts on their health and their families as well as on their possible income generation and education activities (AbouZahr et al. 2009). WHO and UNICEF (2010) also recognized that, at household level, women carry the largest burden in terms of collecting and managing water.

The WHO (1978) defined health as a state of complete physical, mental and social well-being, and not merely the absence of disease or infirmity. This definition challenges the common belief, which links health to the absence of disease, without paying adequate attention to sociocultural perspectives on health. Some health disorders are non-medical, and it is important to explore the factors that lead to the occurrence of these disorders. Smith (1983) emphasized the need to understand these factors, to be able to describe 'one's health as healthy or unhealthy from a socio-cultural perspective' (ibid.: 30). Similarly, Jablensky (2005) emphasized the need to understand the sociocultural perspectives on disease which are rooted in people's lives over the generations. However, in Africa, many health interventions, such as water development, have consistently focused on the biomedical model of health, with limited attention to the sociocultural dimension. Such interventions have, therefore, not addressed those sociocultural issues which also have gender-specific aspects to them.

Gender perspectives

Masculinity symbolizes manhood, which is associated with status and power, given the influence of patriarchy in society, while femininity symbolizes womanhood and subordination. Society in Uganda accords different rights, privileges, duties and obligations to both men and women by virtue of their sex. Women are traditionally considered to be subordinate to men, owing to the higher power and authority attributed to men (Tibatemwa-Ekirikubinza 1999). Gender perspectives are embedded and demonstrated in the way of living and in interaction between males and females in society and, hence, greatly influence attitudes and behaviours. Nannyonga-Tamusuza (2009: 367) argues that the 'collective social and cultural forces that shape the gendering process are structured by relationships with each other'. Tamale (1999: 28), speaking specifically of Uganda, observed that 'the gender concept exerts a major effect on individual and social interactions'. Writing in 1991 (ibid.: 1), he stated: 'it is popularly believed that women are not supposed to speak or express their opinions in public, a view that is deeply embedded in African patriarchal values, which relegate women to the domestic arena of home and family'.

Gender and water – evidence from Uganda

This study, which was conducted in the south-western part of rural Uganda, revealed that water is one of the key elements that define masculinity and femininity within the household, largely as a result of the gender-prescribed roles with regard to water management. At household level, water management, which involves collection, usage and storage, is perceived as women's work with men not expected to have a role, other than stepping in in circumstances where the women and/or the children are not available or are unable to collect water.

This gender division of labour results from the socialization process whereby the girl-child is initiated by the mother into the key activity of water collection at an early stage. This process prepares the girl-child for a role as wife and mother, responsible for the family's domestic chores, including that of water provision, which is a key element of most household activities. The children begin, in these early stages of life, to develop lifelong attitudes to themselves and their role, becoming victims to a 'socially ascribed – and prejudicial – meaning to gender' (Kiyimba 2005: 253). From an ethnographic understanding of Ugandan society, the paternal aunt locally known as *Ssenga* plays a key role in this socialization process and in preparing the girl (her niece) to be submissive as a wife. Tamale (2006) observed that the notion of *Ssenga* is a respected and important role, which inculcates the gender role of the woman in the culture. *Ssenga* also plays a large role in institutionalizing masculine ideologies and the patriarchal power, and in the social construction of water management in relation to woman and womanhood.

The men, as the head of the household, are more economically empowered than women. They are the breadwinners and, within this role, they are expected to provide resources for collection and management of water. For example, generally water has to be fetched from long distances, in some cases up to one or two kilometres, and the provision of suitable water containers for this purpose lies with the men. While women are ostensibly responsible for the management of water, they have little influence over the resources necessary to do so. This gendered construct with regard to control and management of household resources gives the men power over the women, who are economically dependent, and charged with the 'burden of unpaid care work' (UNDP 2014: 74).

Patriarchal tendencies involved in the process of water management are characterized by domination, power and control. The gendered construction of water collection, with women's lack of power over resources and limited participation in decision-making, makes them vulnerable. Within the prescribed gendered roles, they learn to be submissive while, at the same time, demonstrating confidence in their ability to act as managers of water within the home. Owing to changes in the socio-economic environment, women have become increasingly more involved in activities beyond the household to provide for the family's welfare needs. However, despite their increased engagement in income-generating activities, the responsibility for water management remains in their domain. Concomitantly, the evidence indicates that men are becoming less engaged in domestic provisioning, spend significant periods of time away from the home and spend much of their meagre incomes on the attractions of the growing trading centres. This increases the pressure on the women exponentially. Ms Najjuma[1] said: 'The responsibility for water is too difficult for me on top of other household needs. The man leaves home in the dark and returns in the dark. There is no help I get from him with regards to water' (interview).

In a minority of cases the roles, including that of water management, are shared between the men and the women. This is mainly in situations where women have acquired a level of education and skills for income generation and/or have had engagement with women's groups. In these cases, it seems clear that education has contributed to the women's sense of self-worth and given them the confidence to better negotiate water management issues. Ms Nabiryo said: 'In my home, my husband appreciates the big role I play. He helps me with the purchases of water containers and also buying water when it is necessary' (interview). Women such as Ms Nabiryo demonstrate a sense of fulfilment and contentment about the gender division of labour around water in the household. It was also the case that some men, who had acquired a level of education and had some exposure to debates on the issues of concern to women, were more willing to support their wives, most particularly in the area of water management. Such exposure was critical to changing the attitudes, beliefs, practices and behaviours of the men and women around water management. Mrs Kityo, a woman's leader, remarked: 'The women who were active in the women's group have gained a lot of skills in managing their homes and generating some income' (interview). But the majority of the women, who did not have the benefit of such engagement, remained as powerless as before and dependent on their husbands. These women continued to expend vast amounts of time managing water and negotiating around it, and thus had limited time for self-improvement and confidence-building by way of education or social engagement.

The scenarios outlined above indicate a level of gender equality in the households where husbands were supportive, with inequality more prominent in households where the men paid less, or no, attention to water issues. Hence, 'in households, rights become embedded in the wider intra-household relations and negotiations' (Ahlers and Zwarteveen 2009: 418).

Water and health – a sociocultural perspective

The health of an individual can be viewed from different perspectives, including that of the ability to achieve role performance. Role performance, as a model of health, focuses on 'one's ability to achieve maximum expected performance of social roles' (Smith 1983: 48). Similarly, Saylor argued that 'healthy individuals demonstrate accomplishment and execution, and they carry out their roles and tasks successfully in ways that are valued culturally' (2004: 108). In the discussion on women's health and water, AbouZahr et al. (2009: 10) have illustrated that women's health may also 'be at risk as a result of their traditional family responsibilities'. The requirement to adapt to one's environment and/or circumstances was observed to be central to the health of women. Analysis of the findings of this research supported this and revealed that limited availability of water had consequences for the women's role performance. The women were constantly negotiating, making decisions, taking action and specifically prioritizing water use, reuse and, indeed, rationing depending on the levels of water available.

The notion of health as an ability to perform one's role and the ability to adapt to the environment is further reflected in the women's specific approaches to the collection and use of water. When collecting water, the location of the water source was a major determinant; the women prioritized convenience of access to the water source over water quality. While they desired to have clean water for their households, the distance to a source of clean water (1–2 kilometres) was an off-putting factor. Ms Nakazzi said: 'it is not unusual for women to collect water from open wells and ponds which are nearer to their homes even though it is not safe for home use' (interview). Moreover, though the women had acquired some knowledge from health workers of the importance of good hygiene in avoiding disease, they had a limited amount of water at their disposal, which was a major obstacle to maintaining even basic levels of hygiene. More often than not, the women compromised on their own hygiene in order to conform to the expected norms of community behaviour, such as sending children to school with clean uniforms. For example, practices such as washing the feet only and ignoring the rest of the body were common. This approach can be described as concentrating on being 'good wives and mothers to care for their households' (Shadle 2007: 334). For the women, the consequence of inadequate water translates into limited role performance and possible compromise of their own, and family, health in favour of societal approval.

Conclusion

> Despite the numerous water and health interventions, women still struggle with the limited access to water and the poor health which has persisted in sub-Saharan Africa and Uganda in particular. Women bear the impact of 'inadequate, deficient or inappropriate water and sanitation services'. (GoU 2010: vii)

This study reveals that water management is a social role ascribed to women, with water being a symbol of womanhood and with restricted masculine participation and engagement. The cultural complexity with regard to water management faced by women is set by society with the gendered roles, prescribed through the socialization process, contributing to the patriarchal control of resources, which, in turn, limits the decision-making power of women. Women are ascribed the role of principal 'gatekeepers' of water at a household level, but have limited power in carrying out this role. Further, limited availability of water constrains the women's domestic role performance, hinders fulfilment of their full potential and limits their capacity for self-actualization. It also influences their approach to health in terms of issues around hygiene and disease. It is critical for the women themselves to develop an understanding of their key role in water management and how they might seek to empower themselves within it. In this regard, it is important to think beyond the supply-driven approach of providing water sources and engage with issues affecting women in water management.

In seeking for a meaning of health beyond that of the mere absence of disease, this study explored role performance, adaptation and self-actualization models of health. It rejects the dominant disease paradigm of health, and advances an alternative view based on a critical understanding of the sociocultural dimension of health and the conflictual politics of gender. The process of water management should not be viewed only from the disease point of view, but more importantly from the perspective of role performance and adaptive models of health. Development programmes should go beyond the predetermined approaches that focus on the biomedical model, and engage with the broader sociocultural and gender issues around the water management process, issues which demand the women's constant attention and which require key decision-making on a daily basis. This supports Leite's finding that 'water and sanitation projects which go further than supporting women's domestic role, and actually support women to take leadership roles within community water management programmes, are among the most successful both in addressing health and sanitation goals, and in challenging gender inequality: empowered women can make water projects work better' (2010: 70).

Note

All names have been changed for reasons of confidentiality.

References

AbouZahr, C., I. de Zoysa and C. Moreno (2009) *Women and Health: Today's evidence, tomorrow's agenda*, Geneva: WHO.

Ahlers, R. and M. Zwarteveen (2009) 'The water question in feminism: water control and gender inequities in a neo-liberal era', *Gender, Place & Culture, a Journal of Feminist Geography*, 16(4): 409–26.

Ennis-McMillan, M. C. (2001) 'Suffering from water: social origins of bodily distress in a Mexican community', *Medical Anthropology Quarterly*, 15(3): 368–90.

GoU (Government of Uganda) (2010) *Water and Sanitation Sub-sector Gen-der Strategy (2010–2015)*, Kampala: Ministry of Water and the Environment.

Gupta, J., R. Ahlers and L. Ahmed (2010) 'The human right to water: moving towards consensus in a fragmented world', *Review of European Community & International Environmental Law*, 19(3): 294–305.

Jablensky, A. (2005) 'Disease and health in the cultural context', in S. W. A. Gunn, P. B. Mansourian, A. M. Davies, A. Piel and B. M. Sayers (eds), *Understanding the Global Dimensions of Health*, New York: Springer, pp. 231–9.

Kiyimba, A. (2005) 'Gendering social destiny in the proverbs of the Baganda: reflections on boys and girls becoming men and women', *Journal of African Cultural Studies*, 17(2): 253–70.

Leite, M. (2010) 'After the summit: women's access to water and policy making in Brazil', *Gender and Development*, 18(1): 69–79, www.tandfonline.com/loi/cgde20.

Nannyonga-Tamusuza, S. (2009) 'Female-men, male-women and others: constructing and negotiating gender among the Baganda of Uganda', *Journal of Eastern African Studies*, 3(2): 367–80.

Potter, R. (2010) 'Contemporary social variations in household water use, management strategies and awareness under conditions of "water stress": the case of Greater Amman, Jordan', *Habitat International*, 22: 115–24.

Ray, I. (2007) 'Women, water and development', *Annual Review of Environment and Resources*, 32: 421–49.

Saylor, C. (2004) 'The circle of health, a health definition model', *Journal of Holistic Nursing*, 22(2): 97–115.

Shadle, B. L. (2007) 'What shaped the lives of working women in Uganda? Women, work and domestic virtue in Uganda (1900–2003)', *Journal of African History*, 48(2): 333–4.

Smith, J. A. (1983) *The Idea of Health: Implications for the nursing professional*, New York: Teachers College Press.

Tamale, S. (1999) *When Hens Begin to Crow: Gender and parliamentary politics in Uganda*, Kampala: Westview Press.

— (2006) 'Eroticism, sensuality and "women's secrets" among the Baganda: a critical analysis', *Feminist Africa*, 37(5): 89–97.

Tibatemwa-Ekirikubinza, L. (1999) *Women's Violent Crime in Uganda: More sinned against than sinning*, Kampala: Fountain.

UN (2012) *Millennium Development Goals Report*, New York: United Nations.

UNDP (2014) *Human Development Report 2014: Sustaining Human Progress: Reducing Vulnerabilities and Building Resilience*, New York: UNDP, hdr.undp.org.

WHO (1978) *Alma-Ata Declaration, 1978*, Declaration of the Alma-Ata international conference on primary healthcare, Alma-Ata, USSR, 6–12 September.

WHO and UNICEF (2010) *Progress on Sanitation and Drinking-water*, 2010 update, Geneva: WHO Press.

— (2012) *Progress on Drinking Water and Sanitation*, 2012 update, New York: WHO Press.

9 | UNDERSTANDING ADAPTIVE CAPACITY ON THE GROUND: A CASE OF AGRO-PASTORALISTS IN A RURAL PARISH, UGANDA

Mavuto D. Tembo

Introduction

Uganda is arguably the African country most at risk from climate change impacts on precipitation and freshwater resources (IPCC 2014), with agriculture accounting for more than 24.2 per cent of gross domestic product (HDR 2014) and up to 66 per cent of exports and employment (GoU 2010). In terms of pastoralism, climate change is likely to lead to increased conflicts over pasture and water for livestock and food crop production (Deininger and Castagnini 2006; IPCC 2007). For pastoral communities in Uganda, Ruettinger et al. (2011) argue that, first, droughts and high temperatures threaten cattle life, feed and water; secondly, climate variability is raising the degree of vulnerability inequality between pastoralists and crop cultivators and exacerbating poverty. Some pastoralists may shift from livestock to crop cultivation, from nomadism to sedentary livestock keeping, from pastoralism to agro-pastoralism (Sserunkuuma and Olson 2001; Wurzinger et al. 2008). In addition, extreme climatic events have historically been shown to be costly to pastoralists, reducing consumption or forcing the sale or destruction of assets, thereby reinforcing poverty (Nyariki et al. 2009; IPCC 2014).

Agro-pastoralism is a major livelihood for forty-five households in the study area, where the majority are crop cultivators (Tembo 2013). Access to water and pastureland is vital to enhancing the adaptive capacity of agro-pastoralists and sustaining animal-keeping livelihood in the study area. In 2011 I noticed that agro-pastoralists were not attending community meetings and focus group discussions that I had organized as part of data collection for this research. They are considered a minority group in the study area and are frequently and purposefully excluded from community meetings and other events. This exclusion is compounded by the fact that they spend all day with their cattle and, therefore, have difficulty attending village meetings, which are generally held in the daytime (ibid.).

While nomadic or semi-nomadic agro-pastoralists are found all across Uganda, there has been a broad process of sedentarization in the twentieth century, with growing numbers of agro-pastoralists opting to practise mixed crop/livestock farming. Government policy has encouraged sedentarization (Wurzinger et al. 2008). The state claims it is easier to provide services to settled communities, including veterinary services to cattle, which helps control diseases such as bovine tuberculosis (Inangolet et al. 2008). Recent policy programmes such as the Programme for the Modernization of Agriculture (PMA) are also heavily oriented towards settled cattle farmers rather than (semi-)nomadic agro-pastoralists (Butler and Gates 2012). Indeed, as noted by Behnke (1985), government policies such as PMA describe nomadic agro-pastoralists as 'backward' and practising a way of life that needs to be modernized. Rather than supporting (semi-)nomadic agro-pastoralism, then, the government increasingly favours a form of supposedly modern cattle ranching in controlled herds, supported by veterinary services and intended to supply distant urban commercial markets instead of local subsistence (Butler and Gates 2012).

The research approach

In the study area, the case of agro-pastoralists reflects these broader changes in Ugandan society. Agro-pastoralists – who tend to belong to the Munyalwanda, Munyankole, Mukiga and Munyolo tribes, in contrast to the Baganda people in the area, who constitute the majority – are often referred to as backward, or out of touch with modern life. They are viewed with suspicion and, with literacy rates improving among many households in the parish, the mostly illiterate agro-pastoralists are effectively excluded from village life.

In the literature on adaptive capacity in sub-Saharan Africa, however, forms of inequality or exclusion that might exist at a local level have not been given much explicit attention. As a consequence of this oversight in the literature, there is no guide to dealing with minority groups when trying to assess adaptive capacity (Tembo 2013). Hence, developing an understanding of adaptive capacity to climate change in rural areas such as the study area requires attention to micro-scale practices within groups and between groups at community level. The 2013 study revealed that, first, agro-pastoralists display context-based adaptive strategies such as application of local knowledge about water point construction. Their knowledge and water management practices were designed to suit a mobile liveli- hood, which the agro-pastoralists (then pastoralists) still believe to be ideal practice. Agro-pastoralists were able to cope with dry season pasture constraints and regulation of access through customary systems, dependent on negotiation and reciprocity. Secondly, agro- pastoralists exchange milk-based goods for cash or other products while, at the same time, circulating a wide range of information about life in the area. Finally, this study concluded that the adap- tive capacity of agro-pastoralists can only sustain them to a certain extent, in that it can help them cope with normal drought and the dry season but drought related to climate change variability is disastrous for them. Their overall adaptive capacity is constrained by an agricultural modernization policy that is promoting micro-scale practices, most particularly 'enclosure', which limits how future adaptive capacity will develop. This is further complicated by local economic development, which takes water and pastureland from agro-pastoralists.

Understanding adaptive capacity at the micro level should be of interest not just to academics, but to development practitioners and policy-makers too. A better understanding of the dynamics of small rural communities and their local politics is essential both to Ugandan policy-makers and to NGOs which come with agendas for modernizing livestock farming and poverty alleviation.

Limitations and constraints The agro-pastoralists are a minority group in the study area who are viewed by the wider community as primitive and nomadic, which posed difficulties for this research. I was faced in the first instance with the challenge of attempting to engage with a community that had anxieties about my very presence. I was an outsider and was viewed with distrust and with scepticism about my agenda. But in order to conduct my research it was essential that I develop a relationship of trust with potential respondents. I began this process by talking with village leaders, one of whom told me that the community thought I was a govern- ment agent sent to spy on their land with a view to either buying it myself or bringing in other potential buyers. This conversation happened in Kiganju village, whose people were loyal to an opposition party and distrustful of the ruling party. A major factor which contributed to this view of my purpose was the fact that I carried a global positioning system (GPS) and camera, leading people to believe that I was measuring their land. There were others among the community who questioned why I had travelled from Malawi to ask them about water governance and climate change. I was often asked, 'Is there no water in Malawi?'

The constraints brought about by this atmosphere of suspicion meant that I was forced to continually negotiate my relationships. Some of the negotiation strategies I pursued were similar to those of Sultana (2007), and included attending local events such as wedding and funeral ceremonies, and church and mosque functions. During these functions I often endeavoured to engage in conversations in the local dialect, Luganda. Gradually my rapport with the community improved and I developed a relationship of trust, specifically with three agro-pastoralists, who later helped me to connect with the wider community of agro-pastoralists in the study area. I am aware that I was only able to partially access the lives of the researched community members because of other unresolved anxieties people held about my research.

A further constraining factor was the tarnished reputation of the local NGO, brought about by the behaviour of the local coordinator, who owned a guest house in the community, which he also operated as a brothel. I lodged at this guest house for seven months, and this led to me being seen as associated with the coordinator and the brothel. I was unaware of the situation for some time until a team of co-investigators told me about it. Although I attempted to reassure the researched community that I had nothing to do with the brothel and, indeed, was not connected to the NGO, I was not believed, particularly as the other doctoral students who were there identified themselves with the NGO.

Research methodology This study used a 'dynamic assessment' approach, which involved a combination of Participatory Geographical Information System (PGIS) and ethnography (for details, see Tembo 2013). This approach helped to reveal elements of the agro-pastoralists' adaptive capacity to climate change. The research was conducted in three main stages, the first of which took place in February and March 2011. During this stage, data about agro-pastoralists' movement was captured to identify times and spaces when they met up with the wider community – that is, to identify how they managed to negotiate their interactions with others in the study area.

In a second stage, during the wet season of April/May 2011, hand-held GPS units were used to gather detailed information about where agro-pastoralists go to get water and access pasture. The data collected at this stage helped to trace the movements of agro-pastoralists and identify 'flashpoints' – that is, moments when their movements entailed dilemmas and negotiations, which later formed the basis of interview questions. The data also enabled me to add their movements to the overall GIS database which I had compiled of the study area parish.

Five agro-pastoralists took hand-held GPS units to record their travel distances, times and average speeds, first during the April/May 2011 wet season and then secondly during the June/August 2011 dry season. The GPS recordings revealed how they moved and where they went, and this data allowed me to ask the respondents about what was happening during their time with the herd. In this regard, the data from the GPS units required ground observations. During the dry period observation of agro-pastoralists' adaptive strategies enabled me to uncover some of the dynamics of adaptive capacity pertaining to cattle, the herders and their interactions with resources. Alongside this work, I also recorded ten semi-structured interviews with some of the agro-pastoralists.

In the third and final stage, July/August 2011, thirty-five agro-pastoralists completed a short survey with a view to increasing understanding of the anticipated future for cattle keeping. This questionnaire focused on their perceptions of water and pasture scarcity and climate change, their coping mechanisms, their connections within and without the community, and what they anticipated would be the future of cattle keeping.

Agro-pastoralists' adaptive capacities and their importance in the wider community

To identify the agro-pastoralists' adaptive capacity it is necessary to consider a range of practices engaged in to cope with dry periods. There are five practices which signal a degree of adaptive capacity: knowledge, mobility, cooperation and sharing, culling the herd, and diversification.

Knowledge Agro-pastoralists' knowledge of water point construction significantly pre-dates the involvement of the state and other actors in the study area. Traditionally water management practices by agro-pastoralists were (and still are) tailored to a mobile livelihood system, which itself is a method of coping with seasonal variations and climate variability. Agro-pastoralists use water management as a means of managing the wider wetland rangelands, given that access to, and availability of, water affects who and how many have access to surrounding pasture in the wetlands (Tembo 2013). In the 1950s the agro-pastoralists drew upon their local knowledge about water in the wetlands to appropriately locate water points. As one respondent noted:

> We have explored the wetland and we know where water springs can be found. And we dug our wells there ... We know where there is ... fresh water around the villages ... (personal interview, 27 April 2011)

During my experience of accompanying herders on the grazing trail (May and June), we counted thirty-three open wells that contained water. Observation of the wells indicated that water retention in the wells differed: almost one third of the wells dug in the 1950s were observed to maintain water till the next rainy season, while those wells dug between 2000 and 2009 had run dry by the end of July. Herders explained that the more recent open wells can run dry from mid-July depending on the characteristics of the rainy season; for example, if rains are erratic and low or if a drought occurred. However, in a good rainy season water can remain in the open wells until the next season. The assessment of recent wells in the grazing field concluded that cattle walked into the open wells to drink water, which contributes to sedimentation and rapid drying.

Mobility Mobility itself is a sophisticated response to the unique characteristics of pastoral systems, and is central to ensuring that pastures can recover seasonally, allowing the agro-pastoral livelihood to remain sustainable in an environment where other sedentary land uses have failed (Nyariki et al. 2009).

Historically, agro-pastoralists would have moved far and wide throughout the wetlands during the dry season (Tembo 2013). There is still a significant level of mobility as they try to cope with water and pasture scarcity: 55 per cent of the survey respondents indicated that they moved to other parts of the parish when local water and pasture were exhausted. In doing so, they drew upon family connections, such as brothers and uncles, and also 'good' friends outside the study area, even in exceptional circumstances moving as far away as Masaka (54 kilometres from the study area).

Within the study area there is what we might refer to as 'micro-scale' mobility. The results of the GPS observation revealed the micro mobility of herders on the grazing field during May to July. It recorded the movements of a herd from their kraal to regular grazing fields in the wetland (Kibuye-Michunda wetland). These movements demonstrate a degree of flexibility on the part of the herders across space and time that helps them cope with water and pasture variations.

Mobility can also vary between and within seasons: for example, GPS observations from one herder showed that in 2011 he moved 4.8 kilometres in May; 9.3 kilometres in June; 14.6 kilometres in mid-July; and 19.3 kilometres at the end of July. I observed that adjustments in movements depended on local knowledge and experience regarding pasture and water availability in the wetland. One day when I participated in grazing cattle, I counted fifteen herds grazing together for nine hours (from 6.30 a.m. to 3.30 p.m.). A brief discussion with herders on the ground corroborated GPS observations about micro-scale movements and increasing trends of walked distance as the dry season intensifies and pasture becomes problematic. One respondent explained:

> Now it is wet season [March–May], I graze near my house. There is pasture and water. My cows can feed and drink. During June all grass will dry and there will be dust here. We share this little pasture with colleagues from neighbouring villages. Our village doesn't have enough grazing land, so, from June until next rainy season [September–December], we will all graze in Kibuye and Michunda wetland …

He further clarified the situation with regard to difficulty of movement which had been previously signposted:

Where we graze during the dry season, there is part of the wetland that is still open to everyone. My job is to ensure I find the best way to get there without trespassing on people's assets and work with my friends on the ground … (personal interview, 25 July 2011)

But such movements were not possible for all. For one thing, only Ankole cattle are capable of walking such long distances to access water, but most Baganda agro-pastoralists stocked cross-breed (crosses between Ankole and Friesian) that are not as adaptable to long distances as pure Ankole cattle (Kugonza et al. 2012). In addition, 17 per cent of the respondents (specifically of the Muganda tribe) said that they shared pasture locally but never migrated to other places outside the study area because they are not nomadic. They commonly disassociated themselves from agro-pastoralists who were formally nomadic pastoralists by saying 'we are not wanderers' (i.e. nomadic). I observed that they kept fewer cattle than the agro-pastoralists and often fed their cattle with banana peel in the evening to supplement grazing. Some would also tether their herd in the wetland, a common practice mainly among agro-pastoralists with fewer than ten cattle.

The Baganda confined their cattle in small 'communal' grazing pockets and watered their animals late in the afternoon after grazing. In addition, their cattle shared open wells with people. For example, in Micunda, Moses[1] had four cattle which he always tethered. Each day he went out to the village and to nearby restaurants to fetch banana peel to feed his herd. He also used the nearby open well called Kidabada to water his cattle in the evening.

Cooperation and sharing Cooperation and sharing resources are used as mechanisms to aid cattle survival and human well-being. Adger (2003) calls this 'social capital'. In particular, the agro-pastoralists turn to relatives to share information and knowledge regarding diseases and to exchange bulls for breeding and restocking. Respondents belonging to the Munyalwanda, Munyankole, Mukiga and Munyolo tribes, who were originally nomadic pastoralists, particularly emphasized the importance of these alliances.

There is also evidence of other forms of cooperation, for example between the rich and the poor. During key informant interviews, I found that two brothers from the Munyalwanda tribe depend on cooperation with a landlord in the study area. Since 1995 they have been keeping cattle for this landlord in order to benefit from the use of his portion of wetland and upland. The landlord has an area of wetland with one perennial open well that was dug in the 1950s and which is used to water animals. At the time of interview they were keeping twelve cattle in their herd belonging to this landlord. They said, 'we have a place to graze cattle but the land belongs to one rich landlord. My brother negotiated a deal to take care of his cattle in 1995. We entirely depend on this cooperation' (personal interview, 17 June 2011). During my follow-up visit in February 2014, I found that this cooperation had broken down and the land had been sold and is now physically fenced. The agro-pastoralist's herd has been reduced from eighty cattle to thirty, and he indicated that this would soon be reduced further to ten animals because of grazing-land challenges (this is discussed in detail in the next subsection).

Also, survey results showed that 5.71 per cent of other agro-pastoralists have connections with private landowners, but these respondents indicated that they pay the landlord either in kind or in cash to access water when the dry season intensifies or drought occurs. Another form of cooperation engaged in was herders taking it in turns to be in charge of grazing. For example, they would graze in turns of three or seven days and then, during their free days, engage in other activities such as cultivating crops or vending milk.

The agro-pastoralists also cooperated with local leaders in their villages in order to resolve disputes, especially around issues such as cattle trespassing on other people's fields or use of someone else's water source. Some agro-pastoralists (7.2 per cent) also had relations with livestock management services from the local government, as well as with some private service providers. Most services focused on disease diagnosis and treatment and less on water access. The service providers themselves favoured working with agro-pastoralists who stocked cross-breed cattle, as promoted by government livestock projects. Agro-pastoralists in Kiyumbakimu and Kibuye villages who were involved with such services were advised to have an underground water reservoir, which they stocked by harvesting 1,000 litres of rainwater; enough to provide for their cattle for two months. However, respondents noted that this underground water was also used for domestic chores, such as washing dishes and laundry.

Culling the herd Agro-pastoralists also try to cope with dry spells by culling their herd. In the survey 86 per cent agreed that the potential for live cattle sales tends to increase during the dry season. The respondents associated the dry season with greater deterioration of pasture and water, increased incidences of certain diseases and occurrences of sudden death of animals. All interviewees observed that periods of drought are extremely difficult and frequently catastrophic. Of those surveyed, 60 per cent mentioned increased sales of live animals during the drought years compared with normal dry seasons; 71 per cent pointed to increased mortality of animals. For example, most respondents claimed to have lost their herd during the 1999/2000 drought and had to restock. One interview respondent said:

> When drought strikes hard, it is not me to decide on which
> animals to keep. All of them may die. You accept what remains. I
> don't have a clear answer on this because a disaster is disaster ...
> I have control during normal dry season when I cull usually four to
> six animals per year ... (personal interview, 24 June 2011)

However, agro-pastoralists mentioned that sale of cows is the last option. From their explanations, it seems that 'sequencing' was key before a live animal was sold. For instance, they first sought sales of milk to the wider community in order to earn money to buy cheaper forms of calories such as maize grain. Secondly, they would consider selling sick animals when lactating cows ran dry and only then would they move on to sell heifers and old members of the herd, bulls, and lastly cows with production limitations.

Diversification In the study area parish, there are a number of minority tribes, the Munyalwanda, Munyankole, Mukiga and Munyolo. This study revealed that in the case of the Munyalwanda tribe, women are mostly responsible for household food security. I specifically observed the Munyalwanda women because they were found in my two study villages of Kiganju and Micunda. They tended newborn calves around the homestead. The married women spent much of their time indoors making butter, ghee and yogurt that was then sold alongside fresh milk. They kept some milk, yogurt and ghee for their own domestic consumption but sold the butter and most of the milk. In addition, I observed that milk, butter, yogurt and increased meat availability during the dry season provided a source of adaptive capacity to the community in terms of nutritional security. Sales of milk and animals increased integration of these minority tribes into the wider community. The income enabled women in agro-pastoralist households to invest in containers for storing water and transporting milk. It was also used to buy food supplies, mainly bananas and cereals such as maize and millet, to supplement household food requirements among other needs. Women also made and sold mats to increase and diversify household income.

Since milk yields varied across, and within, seasons, most respondents said that they depended on crops during the dry season when milk production was lowest and the requirement for labour energy to tend herds at its peak. Male respondents said that lower milk production was compensated for by higher sales of live animals during the dry season. Some agro-pastoralists, in particular those of the Muganda tribe, were not engaged in the local milk trade and butter-making, while in the case of the Baganda agro-pastoralists their cattle generated income via the sale of live animals and domestic milk supply.

Interaction between adaptive capacity and the process of land enclosure

It is anticipated that the adaptive capacity of agro-pastoralists will be increasingly expected to interact with a multiplicity of stressors which will further compromise their capacity, most notably large-scale land conversions and conflicts (IPCC 2014). Climate variability will exacerbate the risk of land enclosure and, in turn, intensify land-use conflict in the wetland which mainly supports agro-pastoral livelihoods. Socially disadvantaged people, exposed to persistent inequalities and discrimination, based on factors such as ethnicity, are particularly negatively affected by climate and climate-related hazards (IPCC 2007). It is widely acknowledged that context-specific conditions of marginalization shape multidimensional vulnerability and differential impacts (IPCC 2014).

Current policy responses in Uganda to climate change adaptation result in mixed, and in some cases detrimental, outcomes for agro-pastoralist and marginalized people, despite numerous potential socio-economical synergies between climate change policies and poverty reduction in Uganda (GoU 2010). For example, PMA policy is encouraging commercialization, as in production for export and local consumption. But it is well known that such a process can create new levels of social inequality and exclusion regarding resource utilization, particularly around access to water in agro-pastoral systems (Adano et al. 2012). Because they require access to a wide range of land, enclosure has a particularly problematic effect on agro-pastoralists (Bassett and Turner 2007). If land parcels are privatized then agro-pastoralists will encounter enormous difficulties in moving cattle to, and through, the wetland areas where water is available (Tembo 2013). In the study area parish, as a whole, agro-pastoralists reported grave concerns about the removal of communal pastureland, with 71 per cent of survey respondents stating that local leaders at village level are involved in land transactions with wealthy buyers, many of whom are not from the study area. The outcome is that only 41.5 per cent of the 629 hectares of pastureland in the study area is now freely accessible to agro-pastoralists.

Agro-pastoralists understand that their adaptive capacity can be drawn upon only to a limited extent, particularly when it comes to mobility, because of growing enclosure dynamics on the ground, as experienced by herders in the study area. People are buying land for ranching and new landowners are building 'fences' (often simple barriers or signposts indicating that the land is privately held) and fines are being imposed on herders if an animal trespasses on those private parcels. The introduction of these barriers fundamentally complicates the herders' adaptive capacity, and raises questions as to whether their adaptive capacity can withstand the future challenges.

Moreover, because they now have access to only a little over 40 per cent of the pastureland in the parish, herders are increasingly confined to small 'communal' grazing pockets where the cattle graze on a daily basis during the dry season. The herders make the point that grazing is becoming more tiring in those drier months because the cattle graze faster and herders have to move faster too, making them get thirsty and hungry more quickly. During participant observation with herders, I also found the work to be immensely challenging during the drier months. At every stop and turn the herders had to shout and prevent the animals from crossing boundaries. Thus, as one herder said to me, 'It is a zigzag and an unplanned movement. If you sit down and fall asleep you might find that cattle are deep in private pastureland.'

The IPCC (2014) notes that exhaustion from exposure to heat and increased workload undermine agro-pastoralists' ability to carry out physical work that supports diversification. As one herder said to me, 'I'm up very early to milk my cows. After that I come to graze cattle. I keep walking. I am thin and weak. I can't do other jobs tomorrow ...' (personal interview, 17 June 2011).

The GPS data visualized and charted the movements of the herders, illustrating how enclosure increases agro-pastoralists' work-load in the dry season. The policy of commercialization, though it embraces climate adaptation strategies at a micro scale, acts as a threat multiplier, often with negative outcomes for agro-pastoral livelihoods. A detailed analysis of movements, over four-hour periods, indicated that mobility is overlapping. For example, in one case, a herder came to the same spot every four hours and carried out the same action at the same position at different times without himself realizing. Such spots were usually adjacent to good pasture in private land.

A second pattern which was observed was the frequency of actions by herders to stop their cattle from trespassing. During participant observation with herders in July, I noted that cattle were grazing much faster than they had been in May. They were generating much more dust because the animals were grazing in the same places day after day. In other words, as July progressed, the herders were reaching the limits of the land's carrying capacity, resulting in erosion in some areas from overgrazing and overstocking. But this outcome only made the cattle graze faster because there was no grass on the ground, which made it harder again for herders to keep their cattle from the longer, more luscious grass on private land parcels within the wetland areas.

Conflicts with other resource users

Evidence from literature shows high confidence that marginalized people such as agro-pastoralists will suffer disproportionately from climate variability because of competing needs for water and land (IPCC 2007, 2014). Indeed, in the Makondo area, brick-making and increased cultivation of eucalyptus trees have put demands on the wetland where agro-pastoralists feed their cattle.

Demand for bricks has increased in the study area as a growing number of households look to convert grass houses into more permanent dwellings. To meet that demand many entrepreneurs have established small-scale brick-making enterprises. Making bricks requires clay, water and space in which to dry the bricks. The dry season is the obvious high point of the brick-making season, hence numerous brick-making sites have been established close to water sources for when the rains cease. Brick makers have erected fences around their drying bricks, stacked on top of one another almost like a pyramid, but they have also fenced off some reliable water sources for their exclusive use. This has posed a problem for herders because it reduces the availability of water but also takes away from them small, but much needed, parcels of land on which their cattle can graze. Furthermore, brick makers, intent on keeping cattle away from the bricks, have sought to have fines imposed on herders whose cattle stray too close to their plots.

Cultivating eucalyptus trees to supply the growing market for poles used in the construction of houses is also taking away rangeland. This land use has also entailed fencing off portions of the wetland and thus adding an extra burden to herders. In June and July, I observed the tree growers weeding their plots to protect them from bush fires and also building thorn fences to prevent trespassing cattle from damaging the young trees. I also noted the significant amount of time spent by herders moving around the grazing herd with the aim of keeping cattle from trespassing on brick-making sites, eucalyptus trees, other portions of cultivated land and private pasture land.

A final source of tension was between agro-pastoralists and the wider community that wanted to use water for domestic purposes. In interviews with village leaders and well caretaker committees numerous complaints were made against agro-pastoralists. Village leaders blamed the herders for watering cattle in open wells where water was designated for drinking and cooking. This was a particular issue during the dry season. Consequently, the reaction from many users of the wells was highly negative towards the herders (Tembo 2013).

The consensus view from survey respondents in the villages was that herders were 'irresponsible' people. This perception of agro-pastoralists contributed to decisions by community and village leaders that undermined the ability of agro-pastoralists to cope with the dry season. For instance, some village leaders suggested fencing water sources to keep cattle away, as had been done in other villages.

For example, a delivery pipe had been constructed at the study area spring, supported by a concrete slab, which meant that cattle could no longer access the water. Such measures severely constrain the adaptive capacity of agro-pastoralists on the grazing field. About 20 per cent of those I surveyed felt that their entitlements to water and pasture had been violated as a result of decision-making processes that always favour the wider community.

Conclusion

Climate change is likely to have far-reaching effects on the livelihoods of agro-pastoralists, leading to increased conflicts over pasture and water for livestock. For agro-pastoral communities in the study area, dry seasons and high temperatures already threaten cattle life, feed and water. While some pastoralists may shift from livestock to crop cultivation, others will struggle to retain their existing lifestyles and livelihoods. In the study area, agro-pastoralists draw upon their local knowledge about water to know where they might dig new wells if existing wells run dry. In addition, mobility enables them to cope with seasonal fluctuations, although such mobility is differentiated, with those who own herds of more than ten animals and who are without access to banana peel tending to be more mobile than others. Mobility relies upon a level of cooperation and resource sharing in terms of information and knowledge, as well as in terms of breeding and restocking. Agro-pastoralists have developed particular methods of coping with dry spells which can involve herd culling, and they have developed new income streams by diversifying into areas such as the sale of milk products. This, in turn, increases their integration into the wider community. These minority tribes are important actors in understanding the adaptive capacity of the overall community in the study area, and they make a significant contribution to the life of the community.

Agro-pastoralists are increasingly aware that their adaptive capacity can only sustain them to a certain extent, in that it can help them cope with normal drought and the dry season but drought related to climate change variability brings a whole new set of challenges. Furthermore, the effect of macro policies at a local level can be detrimental to the overall adaptive capacity of agro-pastoralists, through the promotion of micro-scale practices which can lead to 'enclosure', which, in turn, limits the effectiveness of the traditional grazing system, i.e. nomadism. This is further complicated by local economic development initiatives such as those outlined above (brick-making and tree cultivation) that further reduce the availability of pastureland and water in the wetland. All of these non-climatic factors interact to impact on the ability of agro-pastoralists to cope with seasonal fluctuations within their environment.

On the basis of these findings, I conclude that it is becoming increasingly more difficult for agro-pastoralists to cope with dry seasons, which in turn means that their capacity to adapt to climate change is heavily constrained. The types of actions they might pursue in the event of longer dry spells have limitations imposed on them by the prevailing socio-political arrangements, as exemplified here. Looking at these micro-scale practices – trying to understand adaptive capacity using a dynamic approach – illustrates just how difficult it is becoming to remain an agro-pastoralist. Given this, it is not surprising to hear agro-pastoralists speak negatively about their future prospects. To quote one herder:

> ... even if we have *balaalo* [herders] grouping it can't guarantee our survival. Our weakness is that we are landless and, therefore, powerless. How shall we get pasture in future if we can't afford land today? (Personal interview, 15 June 2011)

Note

1 All names have been changed for reasons of confidentiality.

References

Adano, W. R., T. Dietz, K. Witsenburg and F. Zaal (2012) 'Climate change, violent conflict and local institutions in Kenya's drylands', *Journal of Peace Research*, 49: 65–80.

Adger, W. N. (2003) 'Social capital, collective action, and adaptation to climate change', *Economic Geography*, 79: 387–404.

Bassett, T. J. and M. D. Turner (2007) 'Sudden shift or migratory drift? FulBe herd movements to the Sudano-Guinean region of West Africa', *Human Ecology*, 35: 33–49.

Behnke, R. H. (1985) 'Measuring the benefits of subsistence versus commercial livestock production in Africa', *Agricultural Systems*, 16(2): 109–35.

Butler, C. K. and S. Gates (2012) 'African range wars: climate, conflict, and property rights', *Journal of Peace Research*, 49(1): 23–34.

Deininger, K. and R. Castagnini (2006) 'Incidence and impact of land conflict in Uganda', *Journal of Economic Behavior & Organization*, 60: 321–45.

GoU (2010) *Agriculture for Food and Income Security: Agriculture Sector Development Strategy and Investment Plan: 2010/11–2014/15*, Kampala: Ministry of Agriculture, Animal Industries and Fisheries.

HDR (2014) 'Sustaining human progress: reducing vulnerabilities and building resilience', *Human Development Report 2014*, New York: UNDP.

Inangolet F., B. Demelash, J. Oloya, J. Opuda-Asibo and E. Skjerve (2008) 'A cross-sectional study of bovine tuberculosis in the transhumant and agro-pastoral cattle herds in the border areas of Katakwi and Moroto districts, Uganda', *Tropical Animal Health and Production*, 40: 501–8.

IPCC (2007) *Climate Change 2007: Impacts, Adaptation and Vulnerability. Contribution of Working Group II to the Fourth Assessment Report of the Intergovernmental Panel on Climate Change*, Cambridge: Cambridge University Press.

— (2014) *Climate Change 2014: Impacts, Adaptation, and Vulnerability. Part A: Global and Sectoral Aspects. Contribution of Working Group II to the Fifth Assessment Report of the Intergovernmental Panel on Climate Change*, ed. C. B. Field, V. R. Barros, D. J. Dokken, K. J. Mach, M. D. Mastrandrea, T. E. Bilir, M. Chatterjee, K. L. Ebi, Y. O. Estrada, R. C. Genova, B. Girma, E. S. Kissel, A. N. Levy, S. MacCracken, P. R. Mastrandrea and L. L. White, Cambridge and New York: Cambridge University Press.

Kugonza, D. R., M. Nabasirye, O. Hanotte, D. Mpairwe and A. M. Okeyo (2012) 'Pastoralists' indigenous selection criteria and other breeding practices of the long-horned Ankole cattle in Uganda', *Tropical Animal Health and Production*, 44: 557–65.

Nyariki, D. M., A. W. Mwang'ombe and D. M. Thompson (2009) 'Land-use change and livestock production challenges in an integrated system: the Masai-Mara ecosystem, Kenya', *Journal of Human Ecology*, 26: 163–73.

Ruettinger, L., D. Taenzler, P. Musana and B. Narcisio (2011) *Water, Crisis and Climate Change in Uganda: A Policy Brief*, Kampala: Adelphi.

Sserunkuuma, D. and K. Olson (2001) 'Private property rights and overgrazing: an empirical assessment of pastoralists in Nyabushozi County, western Uganda', *Economic Development and Cultural Change*, 49: 769–92.

Sultana, F. (2007) 'Reflexivity, positionality and participatory ethics: negotiating fieldwork dilemmas in international research', *ACME: An International E-Journal for Critical Geographies*, 6: 386–94.

Tembo, M. D. (2013) 'A dynamic assessment of adaptive capacity to climate change: a case study of water management in the study area, Uganda', PhD thesis, National University of Ireland, Maynooth.

Wurzinger, M., D. Ndumu, A. M. Okeyo and J. Solkner (2008) 'Lifestyle and herding practices of Bahima pastoralists in Uganda', *African Journal of Agricultural Research*, 3: 542–8.

10 | FUNCTIONAL SUSTAINABILITY OF HAND PUMPS FOR RURAL WATER SUPPLY

Michael Lubwama, Brian Corcoran and Kimmitt Sayers

Introduction

Background Populations' access to safe water supply is fundamental to daily existence and well-being. One of the key elements of a rural water infrastructure is a hand-pump system, which is expected to convey groundwater to the surface in a safe and reliable manner. Quantitative maps of groundwater resources in Africa have indicated that groundwater is the largest and most widely distributed store of fresh water in Africa (MacDonald et al. 2012). The hand pump is a robust technology that provides a cost-effective means of access to groundwater, and therefore has an important role to play in delivering safe and sustainable water supplies to communities in developing countries (Reynolds 1992; MacDonald et al. 2012). However, observations in sub-Saharan Africa have shown that many hand pumps have fallen into disuse shortly after installation once the development partners hand over to the local community, resulting in a large number of non-functioning hand pumps (Harvey 2004).

The non-functionality of hand pumps has been attributed to a complex issue of sustainability (Esposto 2009; Harvey 2002, 2004; Murphy et al. 2009). This implies that the hand pump as a technology has to be examined in the context of: policy issues (local, national and international); institutional arrangements; financial and economic issues; community and social aspects; natural environment; spare-parts supply; maintenance systems; and monitoring (Harvey 2004). However, a retrospective view on the International Drinking Water Supply and Sanitation Decade of 1981–90 (IDWSSD), when hand-pump technology was promoted as a technology of choice for rural water supply in developing countries, noted that by the end of the decade 'software' was beginning to eclipse hand-pump 'hardware', despite the fact that pertinent design issues regarding hand pumps were yet to be optimized (Black 1998). Innovation on the hand pump was stifled for financial reasons alone as a result of the need to provide rural populations with water at the lowest cost possible (Arlosoroff et al. 1987), and this resulted in very few design changes to it over the years. Therefore, the hand pump, which is a now a very old technology, is still being used in the twenty-first century, and yet society as a whole has changed significantly in terms of population growth and societal needs, and hydrogeological conditions. Success stories of hand-pump technology in India and other Asian countries have resulted in technology transfer of hand pumps to sub-Saharan Africa, only for them to fail soon after installation. However, the success in India, for example, was due to a dense population and a well-developed bicycle industry, which enhanced the development of a standardized supply chain and maintenance management system. These conditions were, and still are, lacking in sub-Saharan Africa (Reynolds 1992). It has also been noted that technology transfer of the world's most widely used hand pump, the India Mark II, to Sudan failed because of the differences in the hydrogeological conditions (Esposto 2009). These factors explain, in part, the frequent tendency towards inadequate performance and/or breakdown shortly after installation. Therefore, the large number of non-functioning hand pumps in Africa requires a novel and holistic approach to tackling this problem.

Functional sustainability concept Different definitions of sustainability abound in the literature. However, the common theme in all of the definitions is the principle that the water supply system continues to work over time without external support (Carter et al. 2010; Esposto 2009; Harvey 2004; Murphy et al. 2009). The underlying premise in the definitions provided on sustainability of hand pumps is the ability of the hand-pump users to maintain the hand pumps o that they provide reliable services and are available at any given time (Murphy et al. 2009). The other aspects of a sustainable rural water supply system, i.e. policies, institutions, financing, community, technology, spare-parts supply and monitoring, are really 'enablers' for effective and efficient maintenance so that the water supply system can continue to work over time.

Different maintenance strategies have been proposed and implemented for hand pumps. These basically fit into two types of system: a centralized system and a village/community-led operation and maintenance (VLOM) system. Implementation of the centralized system has been impractical in sub-Saharan Africa as a result of an underdeveloped supply-chain system and lack of financing for implementation. Significant effort was put into developing a VLOM system leading to hand-pump designs that would satisfy the ability of local users with simple tools to carry out maintenance activities. This has not solved the issue of non-functioning hand pumps. As an 'old' technology it has persistent design issues which remained unresolved after the IDWSSD. Few attempts are being made to understand failure modes in order to systematically refine hand-pump designs and improve their performance and reliability (Reynolds 1992).

Reliability is an important consideration in hand-pump technology. A reliable hand pump is one that supplies 30 litres per head per day for 95 per cent of the year. Hand-pump reliability is determined on the basis of the probability that the hand pump is in operating condition on any one day, calculated as the sum of operating time before failure divided by the total time. This definition is similar to that of mechanical availability, and has been adopted to account for the period of time during which many hand pumps stand idle while waiting to be repaired (Arlosoroff et al. 1987; Reynolds 1992). This implies that hand-pump modifications that lead to a reduction in maintenance interventions would increase the availability and, hence, the reliability of the hand pump.

The literature has shown that below-ground components have been responsible for 75 per cent of all hand-pump repairs. Wear of the nitrile rubber piston seals was singly responsible for most hand-pump maintenance interventions at 25 per cent (Reynolds 1992). Therefore, wear of the nitrile rubber piston seals contributes significantly to low availability and unreliability. The nitrile rubber piston seals are low-cost materials but dysfunctional supply chains inhibit routine replacements. Piston seals are responsible for maintaining pressure levels during upstroke and downstroke operation of the piston assembly in the hand pump. This directly affects water output at the spout. Therefore, a worn piston seal results in significant problems for hand-pump users. Leakage rates increase, resulting in lower water flow rates. This may lead to a perception of hand-pump unreliability by the hand-pump users (Gleitsmann et al.

2007). The long time it takes to acquire replacements and personnel to instal these replacements means that people in rural communities are faced with the realization that their only source of safe water, groundwater, is unreachable. One of the aims of the projects during the IDWSSD was to increase hand-pump availabiliy through longer operation time of the piston seals with reduced frequency of piston seal replacements (Arlosoroff et al. 1987; Aspegren et al. 1987). Seal-less pistons (e.g. the Volanta pump) were considered, but were not widely adopted, owing to inherently high leakage rates and the high pressures required for operation (Reynolds 1992). There is a Dutch-designed hand pump, the blue pump, which uses seal-less piston design, but maintenance of this pump is very difficult as the entire unit is closed (Van Beers 2011).

Functionality is not the same as sustainability, but functionality provides the best indication of sustainable water supply. Functionality of a water supply service should trigger detailed investigations on sustainability (Carter et al. 2010). However, a new perspective on the hand pump recognizes that other aspects of sustainability are meant essentially to enhance the availability and reliability of the hand pump. Therefore, functional sustainability of a hand-pump technology can be defined as 'the availability and reliable operation of a hand pump over a significant period of time with minimal maintenance interventions'. For such functional sustainability to be achieved, major effort and emphasis has to be given to understanding the behaviour and mechanisms of operation of components that fail most, including the piston seal. Such an approach would ensure that a robust hand pump is developed that meets the targets of high reliability and consistent performance.

Methodology

We now go on to present the results of the field visit to the study area parish, Lwengo District in Uganda. The visit involved the documentation and discussion of the problems identified by hand-pump users, during which wear modes and mechanisms for the nitrile rubber piston seal were determined. It provided the basis for the development of a new approach to increasing the functional sustainability of hand pumps by increasing the wear resistance of the nitrile rubber piston seal through a surface engineering approach.

In total fifteen villages were visited, namely: Luyiiyi Kate, Misaana,

Micunda, Makondo, Luyiiyi Protazi, Kiyumbakimu, Kijjajasi, Kigan-ju, Kibuye, Kitereede, Kiguluka, Kanyogoga, Kayunga, Kyamukama and Wajjinja. The objectives of the field visit were: (1) to determine availability of the hand pumps as measured by the number of functional and non-functional hand pumps; (2) to determine problems that hand-pump users face as they operate the hand pumps; (3) to identify the hand-pump component that is replaced most frequently; (4) to ascertain the extent of wear of piston seals. The total number of participants was 328. This included 46 men, 78 women, 154 primary schoolchildren and 50 secondary schoolchildren. There were at least two women representatives from each of the fifteen villages. Primary schoolchildren were aged between nine and fourteen, and secondary schoolchildren ranged in age from fifteen to eighteen. All the participants were randomly chosen, but there was a requirement that they be regular hand-pump users.

The study involved the use of both qualitative and quantitative research methods. Observation was used to physically locate the hand pumps, monitor users and determine hand-pump functionality. Semi-structured interviews were carried out with the men, women and primary schoolchildren. Participatory approaches were used, with the respondents being given A4-size photographs of different hand-pump types to identify hand pumps in their village and then asked about the problems they faced when using hand pumps. Secondary schoolchildren filled in structured questionnaires dealing with hand-pump identity in their villages and problems they faced when using hand pumps. Structured interviews were also used with the two hand-pump mechanics in the study area parish. These interviews sought to determine which hand-pump component failed most; the possible reasons for failure; and the maintenance interventions used.

At the first stage a level of surface examination was used to determine possible wear modes and mechanisms of the nitrile rubber piston seal. In this approach a hand pump was dismantled and worn piston seal surfaces cleaned for examination. Sensory judgement (using visual inspection, touch, smell, etc.) was used to make a first assessment of the environment in which the surfaces were operating. Observation of particular patterns using a 10X eyepiece magnifying glass was used. Surface physical characteristics and the processes that produce them based on the observation of pits, ploughed ridges and cracks on the surface were used to determine the wear mechanisms (Ludema 1996).

Results and discussion

Hand-pump types and functionality Only ten out of thirty-four hand pumps were functional in the study area parish during the research period, representing less than one-third functionality. Although this is a snapshot, it provides the best indication of inadequacies in sustainable hand-pump water provision in the area (Carter et al. 2010). The respondents identified three types of hand pumps in Makondo Parish – the India Mark II, the India Mark III and the U3M pump. These pumps have similar external components, but differ significantly in their internal components. The India Mark II was designed in the 1970s, pre-dating the VLOM concept, and it relied heavily on centralized maintenance. These hand pumps require a minimum of four semi-skilled workers with a mobile van and special tools to repair below-ground components. The India Mark III is a VLOM derivative of the India Mark II. This model uses an open-topped cylinder and a 2.5-inch galvanized pipe for the rising main to enable the piston seal to be withdrawn for maintenance without extracting the rising main. Repairs to India Mark III pumps take one third of the time needed to carry out similar repairs on below-ground components to India Mark II pumps. A mechanic carrying all of the necessary tools on a motorbike or bicycle could extract the nitrile rubber piston seal with the assistance of a pump caretaker or any other member of the user community. In the U3M hand pump a polyvinyl chloride (PVC) rising main replaces the typical galvanized steel rising mains used in the India Mark II and India Mark III hand pumps (Arlosoroff et al. 1987; Reynolds 1992). The modification of the U3M pump incorporated appropriate technology by making use of standard pipes manufactured by the plastics industry in Uganda to replace the heavier galvanized steel rising main, to ease maintenance when the below-ground components are removed. The correct identification of hand-pump types by users showed that the hand-pump users were knowledgeable on the types of hand pumps in their villages through their frequent interaction with them.

Problems identified when using hand pumps Problems users faced as they operated the hand pumps are highlighted in Table 10.1.

TABLE 10.1 Percentage representation of problems different categories of respondents face in operating hand pumps

	Primary children	Secondary children	Women	Men
Difficult to operate; short handles	42	80	33	43
Low output in terms of flow rate	57	96	72	39
Long queues at the pump	97	88	85	83
Long distance to the pumps	9	88	33	39
Water tastes salty (bad)	9	56	18	26
Water is reddish brown in colour in morning	25	76	36	30
Pumps are always breaking down	35	76	87	83
Pumps take a long time to repair	4	72	87	22
Pumps stall before delivering water	26	52	15	17
Water smells bad	8	16	0	0
High pump fees	6	20	56	61
Blockages	100	4	10	13

The results indicate that men, women, primary schoolchildren and secondary schoolchildren rate the problems differently based on the social dynamics of the community. It should be noted that in this community the main 'water bearers' are the primary schoolchildren who fetch water for home use in the mornings before school and in the evenings after school. Women tended to fetch water in the afternoons when the water that the children had fetched was gone. Secondary schoolchildren fetched water for personal use while men who fetched water did so as an economic activity.

The problems that the hand-pump users identified can all be related to hand-pump sustainability. Primary schoolchildren were most concerned about blockages and long queues at the pumps. Blockages usually result from insertion of foreign objects down the spout of the hand pump by the children. However, some blockages can arise from poor pump siting, resulting in blockages in the foot valve. Blockages cause more force to be applied when pumping water, which results in general operational difficulty. Long queues result from low output from the hand pump. This is due to leakages as a result of worn nitrile rubber piston seals. The primary schoolchildren were less concerned about distance to the hand pumps because these trips provided them with an opportunity to play with friends along the way. This also applies to their lack of concern about pumps taking a long time to be repaired. The salty taste of water and bad odour were not a problem for the primary schoolchildren because they were not the ones who used the water for chores in the home. Also, high pump fees did not bother the primary schoolchildren as they were not the ones who paid them. As can be seen, the secondary schoolchildren identified both different and more issues as being major ones. Over 50 per cent of them were affected by most of the problems. High pump fees were a problem for 20 per cent, which is probably due to the fact that they had to work to supplement the household income and thus would be more aware of the utilization of income. Among the women respondents, 87 per cent reported that hand pumps were always breaking down with long repair times. This is expected as the women tended to worry about the long duration their children spent queuing at the pumps. For the men who fetched water as an economic activity or to enhance economic production, e.g. brick-making, house construction, etc., over 80 per cent mentioned frequent hand-pump breakdowns and long queues at functioning hand pumps as their main problems. These results clearly show that different users have different perspectives on hand-pump problems, depending on their position and their experience. This variation is seldom mentioned in the literature. Hand-pump users are lumped into one category, and yet, as can be seen, the experiences and needs of the women, men, primary schoolchildren and secondary schoolchildren all vary. The water service that the hand pump delivers serves different purposes for the hand-pump users beyond providing safe drinking water.

The hand-pump mechanics verified hand-pump types as identified by the users. They identified the piston seal as the component that is most frequently replaced during breakdown maintenance interventions. The seals become worn and quite frequently need replacing within a year. Many of the problems identified in Table 10.1 are due to worn piston seals, such that the sealing function is inadequate. Long queues at the pump can be due to low output in terms of flow rate or frequent breakdowns of other pumps in nearby villages, resulting in people converging at a functional pump with consequent heavy use of that hand pump. The maintenance approach used by the mechanics was similar. Both would try to involve the community in the maintenance activities by first inviting community members to be present on the day the repairs were to be carried out; and by then allowing them to participate in the activities of greasing the chain and lifting pipes from the ground. The mechanics also reported that the fee paid by hand-pump users to the local water committee for the maintenance work was not enough for them to make a living and to maintain a stock of spare parts (which were located in Kampala and hence not easily accessible when required). This resulted in the hand-pump mechanics working in other sub-counties and districts, explaining in part why the hand pumps can remain unrepaired for some time.

Piston seal wear Figure 10.1 shows a typical examples of a worn-out nitrile rubber piston seal obtained after the first level of surface examination. From Figure 10.1 (a) distinct features can be observed on the seal which are identifiers of the type of wear taking place. The distinct crack is a sign of fatigue wear. The wave pattern parallel to the direction of seal movement indicates adhesive wear. The deep plough mark was most probably caused by an abrasive material, hence indicative of abrasive wear (Mofidi 2009; Moore 1980; Myshkin et al. 2005). Figure 10.1 (b) shows a seal with a distinct reduction in seal thickness. It is practically impossible for such a seal to perform its sealing function, leading to some of the problems identified in Table 10.1, including low output; long queues; frequent breakages; pumps stalling; and difficulty in operation. The brownish colour is due to rust formation caused by oxidation of the iron pipes. This confirms what some of the hand-pump users identified as problems, including reddish-brown water in the morning, bad odour and taste. The identification of these wear mechanisms indicates that wear of nitrile rubber piston seals is complex, involving the combination of adhesive, abrasive and fatigue processes. This implies that any solution that reduces even one of the mechanisms contributes significantly to the wear resistance of the seals. This increases hand-pump availability and reliability, thus enhancing functional sustainability.

A surface engineering approach to piston seal repair involves the application of a very thin layer of wear-resistant material to the nitrile rubber piston seal. Experiments have been carried out

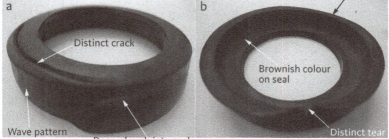

10.1 Worn-out piston seals showing identifiers of wear mechanisms (a) on the base of seal and (b) on the underside

with diamond-like carbon-based thin film applied to nitrile rubber for this purpose. The results show that the wear rate of the coated nitrile rubber is significantly reduced (Lubwama et al. 2012a, 2012b, 2013, 2014). The application of the thin film minimizes maintenance interventions by enhancing the capacity of the material to resist wear.

As most of the problems identified by the hand-pump users related to the wear of the seal, and it has already been reported that wear of the seal is singly responsible for most hand-pump interventions, the surface engineering approach provides a new and unique way of dealing with the problem. An increase in the wear resistance of the seals implies that the hand pump will be available for longer durations without any maintenance interventions, thus increasing its reliability and enhancing its functional sustainability. A major advantage of this approach is that it does not require change of the hand-pump systems and mechanisms already in place. Hand-pump manufacture, spare-parts supply and maintenance systems are not affected. However, after the seals are manufactured, a specialized surface engineering method is used to apply the thin film coating. This obviously adds an extra cost to the seal, but at the same time it has the possibility of increasing hand-pump usability over time. While further research on this new approach is required to make it a viable solution, it presents an alternative approach to the current thinking on non-functioning hand pumps. It addresses the hand pump as a technology that needs continuous design effort in order for it to be a viable solution for water service delivery in the twenty-first century.

Conclusion

The fact that large numbers of hand pumps in sub-Saharan Africa become non-functioning shortly after installation by development partners is, and has been, a major issue and one which requires a novel approach to a possible solution. The focus to date has been on 'software' issues with emphasis being put on hand-pump sustainability. Different aspects of sustainability have been defined in the literature, and yet all these aspects seek to enhance the ability of hand-pump users to maintain the hand pumps installed by the development partners. Technology transfer from one geographical region to another has also not been as successful as anticipated. In this chapter we have sought to adopt a new perspective on the hand pump by seeking a solution to the problem of non-functionality that begins with the most problematic components. This resulted in the identification of the wear of the piston seals as singly responsible for most hand-pump maintenance interventions. Problems identified by hand-pump users were related directly and indirectly to the piston seals.

The identification of this issue has led us to develop a new approach to sustainable hand-pump functionality as presented in this chapter. We have taken a surface engineering approach to increase the availability and reliability of hand pumps by increasing the wear resistance of the nitrile rubber piston seals, thus increasing the functionality of the hand pump. Whereas functionality and sustainability are not the same thing in the classical sense, functionality is usually the only means of identifying a sustainable water supply service. Hence, we use the definition of functional sustainability as 'the availability and reliable operation of a hand pump (water supply service) over a significant period of time with minimal maintenance interventions'.

References

Arlosoroff, S., G. Tschannerl, D. Grey, W. Journey, A. Karp, O. Langenegger and R. Roche (1987) *Community Water Supply: The Handpump Option*, Washington, DC: World Bank.

Aspegren, H., R. Hahn and P. Johansson (1987) *Piston Seals for Handpumps*, Lund: Department of Environmental Engineering, Lund Institute of Technology.

Black, M. (1998) *Learning What Works: A 20 year retrospective view on International Water and Sanitation Cooperation*, Washington, DC: World Bank.

Carter, R. C., E. Harvey and V. Casey (2010) *IRC Symposium 2010 Pumps, Pipes and Promises: User financing of rural handpump water services*, The Hague: IRC International Water and Sanitation Centre.

Esposto, S. (2009) 'The sustainability of applied technologies for water supply in developing countries', *Technology in Society*, 31: 257–62.

Gleitsmann, B. A. G., M. M. Kroma and T. Steenhuis (2007) 'Analysis of rural water supply projects in three communities in Mali: participation and sustainability', *Natural Resources Forum*, 31(2): 142–50.

Harvey, P. A. (2002) 'Sustaining handpumps in Africa: lessons from Zambia and Ghana', *DfID Water*, 15: 4.

— (2004) *Rural Water Supply in Africa: Building Blocks for Handpump Sustainability*, Loughborough: WEDC.

Lubwama, M., B. Corcoran, K. Sayers, J. B. Kirabira, A. Sebbit, K. A. McDonnell and D. Dowling (2012a) 'Adhesion and composite microhardness of DLC and Si-DLC films deposited on nitrile rubber', *Surface and Coatings Technology*, 206: 4881–6.

Lubwama, M., K. A. McDonnell, J. B. Kirabira, A. Sebbit, K. Sayers, D. Dowling and B. Corcoran (2012b) 'Characteristics and tribological performance of DLC and Si-DLC films deposited on nitrile rubber', *Surface and Coatings Technology*, 206: 4585–93.

Lubwama, M., B. Corcoran, K. V. Rajani, C. S. Wong, J. B. Kirabira, A. Sebbit, K. A. McDonnell, D. Dowling and K. Sayers (2013) 'Raman analysis of DLC and Si-DLC films deposited on nitrile rubber', *Surface and Coatings Technology*, 232: 521–7.

Lubwama, M., B. Corcoran, K. A. McDonnell, D. Dowling, J. B. Kirabira, A. Sebbit and K. Sayers (2014) 'Flexibility and frictional behaviour of DLC and Si-DLC films deposited on nitrile rubber', *Surface and Coatings Technology*, 239: 84–94.

Ludema, K. C. (1996) *Friction, Wear, Lubrication: A textbook in tribology*, Boca Raton, FL: CRC Press.

MacDonald, A. M., H. C. Bonsor, B. É. Ó. Dochartaigh and R. G. Taylor (2012) 'Quantitative maps of groundwater resources in Africa', *Environmental Research Letters*, 7(024009): 1–7.

Mofidi, M. (2009) *Tribology of Elastomeric Seal Materials*, Lulea University of Technology.

Moore, D. F. (1980) 'Friction and wear in rubbers and tyres', *Wear*, 61: 273–82.

Murphy, H. M., E. A. McBean and K. Farahbakhsh (2009) 'Appropriate technology: a comprehensive approach for water and sanitation in the developing world', *Technology in Society*, 31: 158–67.

Myshkin, N. K., M. I. Petrokovets and A. V. Kovalev (2005) 'Tribology of polymers: adhesion, friction, wear and mass transfer', *Tribology International*, 38: 910–21.

Reynolds, J. (1992) 'Handpumps: towards a sustainable technology', Report no. 11467, Washington, DC: UNDP-World Bank.

Van Beers, P. H. (2011) 'Reliable low-cost maintenance handpumps are the key for sustainable rural water supply', in R. Shaw (ed.), *The Future of Water, Sanitation and Hygiene: Innovation, adaptation and engagement in a changing world*, Proceedings of the 35th WEDC International Conference, 6–8 July, Loughborough University.

PART THREE

BALANCE SHEET

11 | BEYOND THE MDGS: CAN THE WATER CRISIS FOR THE POOR FINALLY BE RESOLVED?

David Hemson

Introduction

In 2012 the Joint Monitoring Programme (JMP) of the United Nations Children's Fund (UNICEF) and the World Health Organization (WHO), which monitors progress towards the Millennium Development Goals (MDGs) internationally, struck a note of optimism about worldwide progress in accessing water. The global MDG drinking water target, to halve the proportion of the population without sustainable access to safe drinking water between 1990 and 2015, was met in 2010. This was regarded as a 'tremendous achievement' which should be applauded (JMP 2012b: 4). Between 1990 and 2012, 2.3 billion people gained access to an improved drinking water source, raising global coverage from 76 to 88 per cent (JMP 2014). However, this welcome news was immediately followed by a number of riders and reservations. Universal coverage, the goal of the International Drinking Water Supply and Sanitation Decade (IDWSSD) of 1980–90, is some distance away *more than* twenty-five years after that target had been set. Could more have been achieved with more defined targets and the provision of funding from wealthy countries, as set out in the MDG declarations? Did the MDG strategy provide the best mobilization of resources? What was achieved? Where was it effective and ineffective? How also can this be set within the trend of global inequality and poverty? And then also what lessons have been learnt and what strategies are needed beyond 2015, or are the same methods to be used, simply allowing more time for progress?

To answer these questions we need to gain an understanding of the approach, method and perspective behind the MDGs, find out precisely what was achieved and not achieved; and decide whether this approach provided the necessary support and expertise to accelerate the rate of change in coverage in safe drinking water and improved sanitation. A 'bottom-up' perspective from rural areas provided by the Ugandan case studies in Part Two reinforces this statistical analysis.

The main issues

One of the themes running through discussion of development policy is that of a 'water crisis'. This crisis is not often precisely defined and the term is usually applied to the issue of water scarcity. But this is a misperception as essentially the crisis relates to millions of poor people not having access to sufficient water to satisfy human needs, rather than to physical limits of the water resource. There is also a second sense of crisis: that the readily available resource is finite while the demand generated by rising populations for better levels of service is exponential. The first form of crisis is immediate, acute and demands a resolution; the second appears on the horizon in Africa, following consistent economic growth. The focus on water governance in Part Two is in relation to the first sense of crisis: the lack of access to safe drinking water and improved sanitation for millions who are vulnerable to diarrhoea, cholera and other water-related diseases.

A quick scan of the data on delivery of the MDG targets reveals uneven rhythms in progress, perhaps not surprising, given the existence of uneven development at global, regional and country levels. The promise of the MDG approach was one of *combined developments* with the provision of additional funding assistance, technical expertise, and tested and proved technology to resolve the primary water crisis. Evidence for such concerted development can be found in the convergence of institutions, technologies and delivery systems which would, in theory, allow for a catch-up effect for more disadvantaged countries. Since such a concerted development process depends on the integration of a complex of agencies, funding, state capacity, information systems and leadership, its magnitude has to be inferred from the results achieved.

The objective of combined development was that the latecomers, the less developed countries, would be able to employ innovations in soft and hard technology. Francis and Bessant (2005) define soft technologies as human-mediated processes (and hard technologies as physical) to reach or surpass the rate of change in more advanced developing countries. This catch-up is undeniably linked to the availability and use of the 'right' technology by the often isolated countries which are undertaking this task.

Since the MDGs are intended to provide greatest benefit to the most disadvantaged, evidence of an 'evening up' of uneven development (between, for instance, regions, countries, wealth groups and rural and urban sectors) would provide evidence that the combination of support, funding and expertise was having the desired impact. In this chapter the results of the analysis of the MDG data will be further examined to identify these trends. The long duration of the MDGs has provided at least three universal data points (the baseline 1990, the MDG declaration in 2000 and the last available data point in 2012) in accessible databases from which these trends can be measured. The method used here is critical, analytical and empirical; to arrive at findings on the course of development in the water sector from the available data it will be possible to understand what has, and has not, been achieved before moving on to future perspectives and approaches. The extraordinary quality of data gathered through surveys, analysed and synthesized in readily available databases, provides the evidence to test the dynamics of change in coverage in water and sanitation over much of the MDG period and to draw conclusions.

The chapter sets out to explore the progress attained through all the factors making up the MDG approach in the water sector, such as international expertise and monitoring to implement improved water and sanitation facilities. It is divided into three sections, starting with a discussion of the MDG method and its application in the water and sanitation section, followed by an examination of the results of the MDG period by region and with particular reference to Africa. It concludes with a presentation of some ideas, policies and perspectives for the post-2015 period.

Strategy in water and sanitation delivery

The goal of MDG7 is to halve, by 2015, the proportion of the population without sustainable access to safe drinking water and basic sanitation. Not all MDG indicators were so seemingly modest. In the area of maternal and infant mortality, for instance, much more demanding goals and measures were set. For some reason, however, those planning for the water and sanitation sector adopted a more conservative character. Previously, the staff of the WHO and of international water bodies had anticipated that there would be a renewed commitment to the achievement of *universal coverage*. As the Review of the IDWSSD in 1992 concluded: 'The objective of the water supply and sanitation sector is to advance towards realistic goals established for the year 2000 on the road towards universal coverage. This was reaffirmed as the ultimate goal at various international fora' (WHO 1992: 1).

It is not clear, then, how more modest proposals were arrived at with the dawn of the millennium, when precisely the opposite could be expected. MDG7 was phrased to remove the goal of comprehensive coverage presumably to ease demands on the developed countries to provide the additional assistance necessary. The strategy of the MDG thus became to halve the problem of access rather than resolve the pressing challenges of sustainable water systems and achieve all-round development.

The Millennium Conference in Johannesburg, which set goals for the fifteen years to 2015, can be compared to previous international development strategies which set the target to achieve universal access, such as the International Decade for Water (Hemson et al. 2008). The target of the International Decade for Water which was to be met in 2000 was put off, in a sense, indefinitely. Curiously, when faced with the development challenge of the millennium, the sights were lowered rather than raised, additional capital spending was cautious, and debate tended to limit, rather than endorse, commitments. The goal of improved sanitation was, for instance, included in MDG7 only after intense debate in which South Africa (which had a key role in influencing the outcome owing to the recent ending of apartheid) took the lead.[1]

Unlike the International Decade for Water, which was cast in a period in which neoliberal policies were still to take hold (the early 1980s), the MDGs were introduced and considered in the early 2000s, a time of neoliberal ascendancy which also tended to undermine the authority of international organizations and stress private initiative. The capital budgets for assistance to developing countries were being cut back and the policies of austerity and structural adjustment were enforced. All this – economic austerity, limited international financial support and the placing of responsibility on developing states themselves – can be seen to have led to a strategy for scaling down of goals and their related targets.

It appears that the funding available was generally put together from existing budgets and commitments from donor countries and regions, such as the EU, and did not actually add up to a decisive change in support for the most challenged regions. The following features characterized the delivery system which emerged:

Devolution of MDGs to national states, integration into national plans and budgets In the water sector, as in others, the responsibility for meeting the MDGs was devolved to national states with assistance being promised to developing states for this purpose. The volume of international assistance is hard to estimate as it was not funnelled through an international agency but rather flowed in the form of bilateral assistance from individual developed countries and regional bodies such as the EU. However, it is clear that the total funding was nowhere near that required for the targets to be reached. Over the entire period international funding was entirely disproportionate to the size of the problem, particularly in relation to improved sanitation (Hutton and Bartram 2008).[2] The estimated total spending, excluding programme costs, required in developing countries to meet the water component of the MDG target was authoritatively estimated at US$42 billion, while for sanitation it was more than three times higher at US$142 billion.

Monitoring and evaluation accorded a high priority If a comparison could be made, the emphasis in the IDWSSD, in an earlier phase of sustainable water development, was on ensuring the availability of appropriate technology, particularly in the form of more robust hand pumps. During the MDG period it has been more on the improvement of delivery systems and aspects of sustainability. Closely associated with this trend has been an insistence on improved monitoring and reporting.

In previous planning epochs the data on progress was very difficult to establish at a national, regional and local level; in most cases it consisted of fuzzy estimates at the national level from water service providers and did not deal with the problem of failing water systems. The key question then was access to infrastructure, irrespective of whether it was functioning or not. Statistical review has improved substantially during the fifteen years of the MDGs. There has been much greater surveillance of progress, more rigorous definitions of improved service and increasing numbers of surveys of beneficiaries. These include the Census, General Household Surveys, Demographic and Health Surveys (DHS), Reproductive and Child Health Surveys, HIV/Aids Indicator Surveys, Household Budget Surveys, Living Standards Measurement Studies (LSMS), and Multiple Indicator Cluster Surveys. While sampling can vary and results do not always display identical patterns, these surveys, over time, present a coherent portrait of past and fairly recent access to improved drinking water sources and improved sanitation.

In addition the Joint Monitoring Programme (JMP) interacts with statistical agencies to standardize indicators and measures, authenticate trends and promote improved practices. This concentrated effort has considerably improved the quality, depth and potential disaggregation of the country data on water and sanitation services and created an unparalleled database, built on a wide range of data sources and with a depth of data points. This is available nationally and in aggregate, and can be checked against the data available in national and international datasets over decades. It has been assembled, checked and refined for the purposes of MDG monitoring and evaluation and is an invaluable source. The JMP is fairly open about its methods of establishing definitions and creating estimates from available data and compensating for gaps in data.[3] In many cases (e.g. the JMP estimates for Tanzania updated in April 2014) as many as fifteen data points are used to establish the trends in urban and rural water and sanitation.

The United Nations Development Programme (UNDP) also interacts with governments and statistical agencies to establish or clarify measures of progress towards the MDGs and, where necessary, undertakes reports of country progress on its own account. All of this has considerably improved the oversight of implementation and assessment of progress.

Changes in regulatory processes While private sector participation, or privatization (to give it its generic name), has not featured in the extension of coverage to meeting the MDGs, the overall character of the period since the MDGs were agreed has led to changes in the regulatory systems which seem to be laying the ground for private participation. The argument for these changes has generally been sector rationality, clarity of functions and efficiency of service, but the underlying determinants can be seen to be those of preparation for private participation. Essential to this logic is the separation of service authority (the political element) from the provider (a separate institution with responsibility for operations). This separation is the central feature of the sector-wide frameworks and other organizing frameworks which have provided greater participation by civil society, particularly women. Woven into the fabric of the new regulatory framework has been the devolution of responsibility for water provision to local government (from where outsourcing is possible), a corresponding decrease in the responsibility of the national state departments, and the acceptance (if not the achievement) of a less statist regimen with increased engagement of civil society.

Private participation – advocated but inoperative Privatization (a term which covers all kinds of corporate participation including outsourcing, contracting and transfer of ownership) was strongly advocated by the international financial organizations, but it was not a major feature of the time when the MDGs were first formulated. Although there were surprisingly few successful concessions or widespread outsourcing, there was a transfer of private models of management to the public sector, an orientation to the needs of business rather than people, and a divergence from the objectives of the MDG. The focus of the World Bank during this period was on the encouragement of private participation through agencies such as the Public–Private Infrastructure Advisory Facility (PPIAF) to provide technical assistance to governments in developing countries to create an enabling environment conducive to private investment, including the necessary policies, laws, regulations, institutions and government capacity (Marin 2009).

Most researchers are pessimistic about the role that privatization can play in achieving the MDGs because privately operated utilities are not well suited to serving the majority of low-income households. Since many of the barriers to service provision in poor settlements can persist, whether water and sanitation utilities are publicly or privately operated, it is argued that 'there is no justification for international agencies and agreements to actively promote greater private sector participation on the grounds that it can significantly reduce deficiencies in water and sanitation services in the South' (Budds and McGranahan 2003: 87). Although these researchers argue that there is no inherent contradiction between private profits and the public good, the experience of privatization in developing countries is not one of contribution towards meeting the MDGs. Case studies often describe poor procedures, corruption and the displacement of the necessary attention to the improvement of capacity and management in the public sector.

The lack of progress in terms of privatization (with significant setbacks in countries such as Bolivia) has forced the political leadership in developing countries to concentrate on the improvement of public capacity rather than the passing of responsibility and resources to the private sector. Despite this, corporates are constantly seeking to take profitable advantage of scarcity through the private ownership of possibly the most important substance for human life (Versace 2013), efforts which create strong levels of public opposition.

Trends in deprivation: Africa vs southern Asia

In reviewing progress towards the water and sanitation MDG targets, the two regions of Africa and Southern Africa can be usefully compared insofar as both were substantial MDG regions which had among the lowest initial coverage and challenges in both water and sanitation delivery combined with a basis for comparison over time and within sectors (such as urban and rural). Although they have very different population figures, 914 million people in Africa in 2012 and 1,726 billion people in southern Asia, the comparison is not intended to be one of direct numbers but of direction, rate and quality of change in each region. The challenge in meeting a target has two major dimensions: first the change in delivery capacity (which includes funding, administrative systems, procedures for learning and innovation, sectoral innovation and hardware) to provide coverage and secondly the changes in population size and migration which can appreciably expand the problem to be solved.

Table 11.1 provides details of the numbers of people gaining water and sanitation coverage in urban and rural areas in the two selected MDG regions. Rural water is taken as an indicator of the level of achievement and, by implication, the distance to traverse in progressing towards the MDG.

By 2012 southern Asia had increased provision of improved water sources to rural people by 325,661 million (Column 3) and raised its

TABLE 11.1 Numbers of people gaining coverage, water and sanitation over two periods: 1990–2000; 2000–12 (thousands)

		Starting point, rural water	Additional urban	Additional rural	Additional urban sanitation	Additional rural sanitation
S. Asia	1990–2000	65.4%	25,158	208,369	73,125	106,473
	2000–12	76.0%	34,504	117,292	32,306	153,137
	TOTAL		59,662	325,661	105,431	259,610
Africa	1990–2000	34.9%	10,111	62,531	29,388	23,245
	2000–2012	42.1%	19,537	51,229	71,754	44,361
	TOTAL		29,648	113,760	101,142	67,606

Source: www.wssinfo.org/data-estimates/tables/ plus additional author's calculations. (The author is aware that it would have been preferable for the two periods not to overlap, but three data points have been available and include most countries. These three points are used here and in subsequent tables and figures)

level of rural water coverage from 65.4 to 89.3 per cent, an increase of 24.8 per cent. The region reached the MDG target of reducing the population without an improved water source by 50 per cent. Africa had increased its provision of improved water sources to rural people by 113,760 million and raised its level of rural water coverage from 34.9 to 52.5 per cent, an increase of 17.6 per cent. At this point it was not yet approaching the starting point of southern Asia in 1990 (65.4 per cent). Nor did it meet the MDG target of reducing the population without an improved water source by 50 per cent.

TABLE 11.2 Levels of service and rates of change in southern Asia and Africa (%)

Region and period	National rate of change	Urban end point	Rural rate of change	Rural end point
Southern Asia				
1990–2000	0.88	92.1	0.88	76.0
2000–12	0.89	95.7	1.11	89.3
Africa				
1990–2000	0.69	83.0	0.72	42.1
2000–12	0.78	85.0	0.87	52.5

Source: Author's calculations from data downloaded from www.wssinfo.org/data-estimates/tables/

In Table 11.2 a range of data is provided which is indicative of the basic trends in the improved water coverage across time periods and sectors. Particular attention is paid to the rate of change as the optimal measure of the ability of delivery systems to improve over time, in comparison to the total numeric or percentage coverage. The rural rate is most indicative of change towards meeting the needs of the greatest number, and the poorest, of the population. This is not to ignore the acute needs of the extensive urban 'shacklands' in the most environmentally vulnerable cities of these two regions.

The national rate of change (Column 1) indicates the overall rate of progress towards universal coverage; in southern Asia this is fairly stable at 0.9 per cent per annum over the two periods and has risen appreciably in Africa from 0.7 to 0.8 per cent over these periods. Even at the end of the second period, Africa has still not reached the rates of change of South Asia at the baseline of 1990. The figures for increased urban coverage are more modest, which indicates that the urban/rural dichotomy is being reduced. Over the two periods (Column 4), in both areas the proportionate change in coverage has been greatest in the rural areas, rising from 76 per cent in 2000 to 89 per cent in 2012 in southern Asia and from 42 to 53 per cent in Africa. By comparison there was less change in the urban sector.

Trends in access in Africa

The greatest insight into uneven development, and the potential of the delivery system introduced with the MDGs, can be drawn from the situation in the African region. This is where the MDG strategy has faced its greatest challenge and where the potential for change has, accordingly, been the greatest. The questions to be answered are: has the MDG strategy led to accelerated rates of change and, in particular, has it led to an acceleration of rates of change between the two MDG phases?

The data on African countries herein has been compiled on the following basis; the regional data has been downloaded by country from the JMP database on the standard measures of water and sanitation and three data points accessed – those of 1990, 2000 and 2012.[4] Figures 11.1, 11.2 and 11.3 to follow present this data in scatterplots to illustrate change by country from the threshold of coverage in 1990. Since the rural population is generally the largest

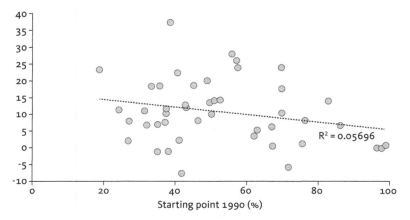

11.1 Rural water: change over the MDG period, 1990–2012

proportion of African populations, and represents the greatest numbers in need, rural water coverage has been used as the benchmark. While urban shack settlements often have the most acute need and problematic water systems, they represent a smaller proportion of the population in need.

Figure 11.1 above plots the aggregate progress over the entire MDG period to 2012 against the starting point in 1990. The percentage progress is the difference between the percentage coverage in 1990 and in 2012. The trend line indicates weak evidence of equitable growth with the countries with lower thresholds having somewhat greater growth over the period. At the one extreme (with starting points of 80–100 per cent coverage) three countries have very low growth, but those countries with the greatest challenge (with starting points of 20–40 per cent) show diverse results ranging from negative to more than 35 per cent change.

A number of countries have not changed, made negligible change or regressed. The very low levels of change are most evident among the countries which have high starting points in the 90 per cent coverage levels (where additional change is not desperately needed) but also in a number of countries below the 50 per cent starting point in coverage. The threshold range 40–60 per cent is possibly of greatest interest: there is a considerable range but most countries are clustered between 10 and 30 per cent improvement in coverage over the period.

Given the average starting point for Africa rural water of 42.1 per cent, the necessary average percentage increase for it to reach the MDG is 29. Such progress is well beyond the actual change achieved and the JMP concludes that only nineteen out of fifty African countries are on track to reach the MDG target (JMP 2012a).

Rates of change Figure 11.2 below presents a scatterplot of the rate of change in rural water coverage over the period 1990–2012, plotted against the threshold starting coverage point in 1990. While an equitable model of change would show a trendline declining to the right, the opposite is found. In comparison to the figures measuring the percentage increase since the starting point, which declines with every decile, the trendline for the annual rate of change shows a rising line from left to right. In other words the rate of change for every decile, tracking from the lowest starting coverage point to the highest, is increasing. A decline in inequality among countries would show the highest rate of change in those with the lowest starting point. This, then, is a line showing growing, not declining, inequality.

Since the average starting point for Africa is 42.1 per cent, the necessary annual rate of increase for it to reach the MDG would be 1.32 per cent. Such an average is, however, not readily represented graphically, and a dotted line charts the necessary increase in rates of change with the following points: 1.82 per cent for those countries with a 20 per cent starting point; declining to 1.36 per cent for

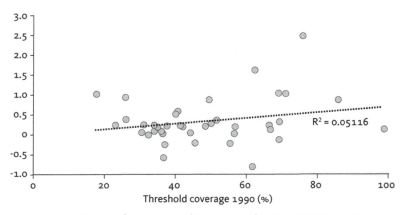

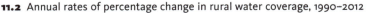

11.2 Annual rates of percentage change in rural water coverage, 1990–2012

countries at 40 per cent; and declining further to 0.45 per cent for those starting at 80 per cent coverage. The large number of countries starting between 20 and 60 per cent rural water coverage, which are clustered at the annual rate of change between 0 and 0.5 per cent, are not within striking distance of the target – even worse are those countries which have not managed to increase coverage at all over the period.

Accelerating or slowing? Figure 11.3 below shows differences in the rates of change attained in two periods, 1990–99 and 2000–12. The highest level of change would indicate the greatest benefit to countries from the expertise and support given to national programmes of water and sanitation, the lowest the opposite. Most countries have benefited more over time although some have not. Again equitable change with growing capacity over time would be represented by a sharply declining line showing the most challenged countries with the greatest change over the two periods. The slight decline of the trendline from left to right indicates that the countries with the lowest starting coverage benefited more during the second period (2000–12) than during the first. This trend does not nullify the data in the previous figure on national rates of change over the period 1990–2012, which indicated lower growth rates among those with the lowest starting coverage point. Rather it confirms that countries with the greatest challenge have benefited most from the duration of the international development represented by the MDG strategy.

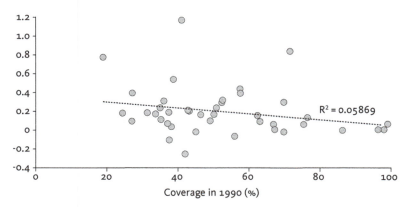

11.3 Annual rate of percentage change over two periods: 1990–99; 2001–12

Relative and absolute deprivation

Despite the MDGs being cast as benefiting the poor, the evidence from social surveys indicates that all the people benefit from improvements in level of service. Analysis of the data provides evidence of inverse equity hypothesis (Victora et al. 2000) in which those at the greatest risk are the least likely to benefit from interventions; or its corollary, that those who benefit from one intervention are likely to benefit from the next. While this conclusion was drawn from public health interventions, the hypothesis can equally be applied to the data from varying levels of access to water services.

Analysis of the survey data from thirty-five countries in Africa (representing 84 per cent of the region's population) on drinking water coverage by wealth quintiles and urban and rural residence, based on population-weighted averages, finds that poorer people are at a disadvantage in accessing drinking water. Access to the most basic, and each successive higher level of service, is found to be inversely proportional to wealth. Inequality appears socially entrenched.

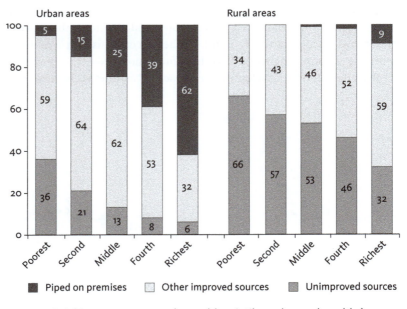

11.4 Drinking water coverage by wealth quintiles, urban and rural (%)

Significant differences are evident between the poorest and richest fifths of the population in both rural and urban areas. At one extreme, 94 per cent of the richest quintile in urban areas use improved water sources, and over 62 per cent have piped water on their premises. At the other extreme, 61 per cent of the poorest quintile in urban areas use improved water and 5 per cent have piped water on their premises. In rural areas, piped water is non-existent in the poorest 40 per cent of households (the first two quintiles), and less than half of the population have access to any form of improved source of water.

These distinctions between all levels – the very poor, the poor and the better off in generally poor communities – are not simply analytical but also relate wealth inversely to susceptibility to disease. A study of two communities which experienced cholera in the epidemic of 2000/01 in South Africa (Hemson et al. 2006) found that in distinction to the poor, the poorest had a significantly higher incidence of cholera and also an ongoing experience of diarrhoea in the post-epidemic period.

While the policies to provide higher levels of water coverage are generally 'pro-poor', as in the poorest are included in their design, for a number of reasons the poorest are the last to access improvements at all levels of service.

Six findings

The main findings from the analysis of the data on changes in water coverage, particularly changes in access to rural water over the period 1990–2012, are:

1 A comparison with other regions which have low levels of coverage shows that Africa is lagging behind. It started with a low level of coverage and progress in the rate of change has been modest, in comparison to southern Asia, for example.

2 The MDG approach has had very uneven results in the African region; the most challenged countries (those with the lowest threshold coverage) generally have had the lowest growth rate. This indicates that delivery is not pro-poor but, rather, reflects the existing inequalities experienced by the urban and rural poor.

3 Delivery on MDG7 targets in Africa shows many contradictions. In the rural areas, the number of people gaining access to water

has declined: 62.5 million gained access in the period 1990–2000 but the number dropped to 51.2 million in the period 2001–12. The numbers gaining access in urban areas (although modest) increased over these periods.

4 Despite the increase in the number of beneficiaries over time, the levels of service in the urban areas are not progressing. While water coverage is increasing, the preferred level of service 'piped on premises' is available only to a declining proportion of the urban population and is static in the rural population in Africa.

5 Rates of delivery have improved over time, but the process is slow and not on a trajectory towards universal coverage. The international mobilization, represented by the MDG strategy, has not resulted in accelerated results among the most challenged countries, i.e. those with the lowest level of coverage. The rates of change in Africa are lower than in other regions in both phases of the MDG. Despite this, the strategy has brought more change in the past twelve years than in the previous ten, and a start has been made in the reduction of the uneven implementation between water and sanitation coverage.

6 In an earlier period sanitation lagged considerably behind water delivery. This situation has now improved but, even though the rate of coverage in sanitation is increasing, there are actually growing numbers of people with improved water but without improved sanitation.

The evidence is that the MDG strategy has helped ramp up the overall proportion of the population entering the 'improved' water sector in the most challenged countries over the period 1990–2012. However, it has not achieved anywhere near the percentage rate of water coverage needed to approach the MDG target and it has not disproportionately benefited those most in need. It has benefited the most challenged countries in the second phase rather than in the first phase.

The politics of delivery

The commanding authority of the MDG, which is supported by international monitoring and evaluation, has had quite complex interactions with, and impacts on, some countries. For many countries there had not previously been explicit political commitments to provide water and sanitation to the population; it was frequently dependent on political loyalty or at the convenience of the elite. The MDG potentially introduced two lines of politics – the front rank of presidential statements and electioneering promises and a second rank of 'internationally encouraged' political commitments to health services and social and economic priorities in line with the MDG. The politics of MDG commitments were not necessarily part of electioneering politics at the national level; the two could run on somewhat parallel lines. However, this could change dramatically with the emergence of social movements or during periods of civil unrest.

The controversies in reporting on successes and failures in the delivery of services at a time when these issues were the subject of social movement contestation, and headlined in media, illustrate how difficult monitoring and reporting can become, even in a democratic country. Where governments have found it inconvenient to have public reviews, reports have been withheld and national targets and commitments obscured or even denied. With regard to the MDG, its international standing, and the research backing provided by the UNDP, have undoubtedly forced disclosure of failure as well as of success. While political commitments can be freely made or haphazardly withdrawn by politicians, the MDG, with its UN ties, must subscribe to an international reporting system.

In South Africa, for instance, the relatively expansionary and celebrated Reconstruction and Development Programme (RDP), which provided a set of concrete targets with dates for universal access to a limited service and incipient plans to redress the inequalities of apartheid, was set aside in 1996 for a conservative macroeconomic policy with ad hoc arrangements for social reform within line departments (Bond and Khosa 1999). Subsequently, under the Mbeki presidency (1999–2008), a set of targets were set for a range of delivery priorities and the presidency established its own monitoring and evaluation unit. The targets were for shorter time horizons and for more comprehensive achievements than those of the MDG. In water delivery, for instance, the target was to provide comprehensive access to piped standpipes, or a higher level of service, by 2008 and improved sanitation by 2010.[5] When each date was reached and the target not met, the dates were moved forward. With the change of presidency in 2009, all the specific targets disappeared from the presidency website and were replaced by generalized commitments without deadlines.

The first country report of the review of progress towards meeting the MDG in South Africa (as well as its own national targets) had found South Africa falling short in particular health-related measures, and was not made public. Following the change in presidency, the report on progress abandoned the more ambitious national standards and deadlines and accepted the MDG as a South African goal without reference to the previously set national targets (although additional provision such as 'free basic water' was mentioned).[6] The open reporting on the MDG has been a significant advance on previous presidential 'progress reports'.

Bottom-up perspectives

The analysis of statistics of water delivery in this chapter is complemented by the case studies in Part Two: the broad sweep of survey data here engages with concrete local observations. These cases are invaluable in relating the broad theoretical aspects of water systems and natural resources to the wide-ranging and diverse practices in communities. The emphasis is largely on the need for good governance and the way in which its effectiveness is qualified or reinforced through participation of national agencies at the local level, the role of women in water management, and through the embryonic forms of rural local government. The chapters in Part Two contain original insights and data which is not readily available and is particularly penetrating and thorough in the examination of gender issues and in the ways in which functionality[7] can depend on simple technologies and systems and local initiative.

The main focus of Part Two in terms of the broad water and development problematic is on groundwater access and on availability of drinking water for communities, which fits the hydrological realities and the overriding concern to achieve the MDG. There are also insights into the technical issues in the provision of, and access to, water. These provide a much needed bottom-up perspective on national and international policies. Here are water systems which are relatively isolated, small-scale, with limited local maintenance and uncertain financial support and with responsibility exercised by the rural people themselves. This data from the field marks advances, identifies problems and provides the evidence for many of the policy recommendations made in conclusion.

IWRM in the rural context While IWRM considers the multiple dimensions of the water resource, interactions with land and water and the interrelationships between environment and socio-economic uses of water, rural water management covers only a fairly narrow range of this spectrum. The broad conceptual approaches of IWRM are generally considered at a national or watershed level, for instance, and may seem rather remote when viewed at the village level. Rural populations are not really involved, far less integrated, into resource management. Water governance, as discussed in the case studies of Part Two, appears elementary and touches mainly on the social use or human access to safe drinking water. Other elements such as adequately meeting basic needs, quality, environmentally secure use which does not impair renewability, accessible information, democratic institutions (identified by Gleick 1998 as necessary to sustainable water use) are less in evidence. Water committees and incipient local government are not integrated into whatever institutional arrangements for IWRM may exist.

There could, however, be greater integration if there were greater decentralization – the placing of responsibility for water services at the local level – leading to inter-village and regional coordination of resources and services.

Governance: local and national The main issues which emerge from the case studies in Part Two are those of effective management of water infrastructure, functionality, gender and social systems. The model of rural communities taking responsibility for water management comes from the International Drinking Water Supply and Sanitation Decade (IDWSSD) in which community-based management is given the responsibility for oversight and management of costs, maintenance and repairs. This apparently enabling community ownership model places responsibility on to some of the poorest on earth to participate by funding their own services.

The good governance model currently in operation in most African rural communities seems to be centred solely on community-based organizations. Local government is not generally mentioned when people discuss women's participation, operations or maintenance.

Actual water governance appears to be managed by water users' committees which have front-line responsibility, supported with some technical capacity and sustained with unsure local revenue. They are relatively underdeveloped and are judged to require continued 'sensitization' in gender relations.

These studies do not point towards synthesis and cohesion but rather to a rudimentary level of service with uncertain technical support. Governance is derived from village solidarity, women's support and the interaction with the agencies which are available. The costs and challenges in providing external support tend to reinforce the community management model as technical support is very expensive in terms of both time and travel.[8]

Gender and water governance There are two levels in good governance which are well developed in the case studies above, namely those aspects pertaining to gendered participation and achievable sustainability. Good governance depends on effective participation of rural people to ensure accountability and effective use of resources. Two of the case studies find that half the population – women – are not allowed to contribute to improving governance except in an ancillary role as audience or supporter of activities undertaken largely by men. The evidence of closely observed social and institutional interactions in rural communities, and considerable local knowledge, demonstrates that equitable participation goes beyond the necessary question of equity and development of women's capacity, to ensuring responsive and effective local water management.

The chapters on women as water keepers and on participation in governance (Chapters 7 and 8) examine a contradiction at the centre of rural water systems. While women are allotted the burden of collecting and making water available in their households, they are not equitably represented in water management. Basically men take the reins of management and women take the responsibility for water collection and distribution. Their participation is essential to good governance at the local level but it is limited and restricted at an organizational level, largely reduced to being an audience to male performance. It is particularly acute at leadership level, notably with regard to specialized leadership roles such as secretary, treasurer or chair. Women are also absent in the technical roles of operations and maintenance.

A clear example of the disarticulation of policy and practice is found in relation to the requirement for WUCs to have equal representation of women and men. Although regulations prescribe an equal proportion of women on these committees, this is rarely achieved. Such equitable participation, if practised, would ameliorate or even resolve the dysfunctional division between the managers and the carriers of water; between male community leaders and women.

The reasons for women's lack of participation are complex. The answer, in part, is possibly that while women are aware of the opportunities, they may feel that they are not sufficiently empowered to move readily into leadership positions, may fear not performing well, or may not seek additional responsibilities with the time available. Possibly also the gendered distinction between 'hard' and 'soft' work in technical activities and maintenance still has sufficient purchase to block progress. Other studies confirm the problem of available time and uncertainty about taking on decisions with men (Whitmill 2013). Participation is a burden as well as an opportunity. Despite this, those who do participate gain greater self-worth and social recognition (Hemson 2002).

Studies in other African countries confirm the positive outcomes of women's participation in water committees and governance, management and water point functionality (Whitmill 2013).

Social and technical perspectives Since most of the rural water systems in Africa are small-scale and dependent on local resources and management, the emphasis has to be on local governance. Decentralization has many advantages but can place the greatest burden on the poorest strata, especially in terms of available funds for operations and maintenance. The case studies develop the connection between community-based management systems'[9] tenuous external support and the functionality of water supply. The evidence of the difficulties experienced by WUCs in collecting fees for maintenance shows the struggle in communities to provide the necessary funds to ensure functioning services. This issue is discussed in a number of the case study chapters, but in some detail in Chapter 10, specifically in relation to the maintenance of hand pumps.

The weakness of women's participation in water management ties into associated issues of feedback, technical capacity and financial contributions. Feedback from users with regard to the functionality of pumps and the water system more generally is essential for appropriate maintenance to be undertaken, and the usefulness of a functioning water system is an inducement for users to contribute to maintenance.

The intersection of national roles and responsibilities, district capacity and local need is a challenge. While the operations and management seem basic and simple, the local and national networks of health authorities, development officers, community organizations and technical agencies appear as complex and uncoordinated systems. Yet good governance depends on such coordination. The case study in Chapter 5 on integrated management of water services in Uganda presents a vast array of acronyms, positions and roles which are not necessarily synchronized in practice.[10] Here is evidence that the necessary intersection of the many departmental responsibilities (including health, education, local government, water, natural resources and public works) necessary to constitute good governance at the local area is not readily achieved.

Good governance is weakened by the two poles in the framework for water services – the national departmental pole and the community management one – not being well articulated. A study of functionality in Ghana (Duti 2011) describes the universal system of community-based management in rural Africa, whereby communities are made responsible for the full cost of operations and maintenance. It concludes that it is becoming obvious that communities struggle in providing sustainable water services and that priority has to be given to developing local government capacity to provide the necessary external support to the WUCs.

In African rural areas the need for safe drinking water is acute and dysfunctional water systems are a clear threat to health.[11] The ability of water systems to function consistently throughout the lifecycle of the infrastructure is the measure of good local systems, the right technology and external support. The effectiveness of water systems is strengthened by oversight by national agencies to review operations and maintenance. In Chapter 6 the technical support units in Uganda which provide the most direct support are examined and found to be clearly wanting. There are tensions between these units and local government in terms of responsibility for water services, which diffuse their effectiveness. Although the community-based management model has been adopted generally in developing countries, the authors conclude that it is failing in practice, as government is not taking the necessary steps to ensure its effectiveness.

The issue of oversight is often regarded as one of the weak links in the overall management of water systems in Africa. Two chapters speak to this problem. Chapter 5, for instance, provides evidence that there is oversight with regular (but not frequent) checks. It also presents evidence of a relatively high level of functionality in rural Ugandan water systems over several years. In comparison to estimates of 35 per cent in sub-Saharan Africa (Harvey and Reed 2007) or between 30 and 40 per cent of rural water systems in developing countries not working (Evans 1992), the figures for Uganda are between 20 and 25 per cent of systems not working. Possibly as important as the figures themselves is the process of review and oversight which identifies problems and plans for interventions.

A rigorous review of functionality of EU-sponsored water projects in sub-Saharan Africa conducted by the European Union auditors has found that few projects met the needs of recipients and that some 30 per cent of the projects were unable to ensure successful operation of the installations because of financial difficulties, a failure to build ownership and insufficiently developed technical skills (European Court of Auditors 2012).

This latter point is taken up in Chapter 10 on the functionality of water pumps, which defines functional sustainability as 'the availability and reliable operation of a hand pump (water supply service) over a significant period of time with minimal maintenance interventions'. This definition fits the context of weak technical support by placing minimal maintenance at the core of functionality. When the wear of piston seals was identified as the single greatest cause for maintenance, an innovation was tested. A thin layer of wear-resistant material was applied to the nitrile rubber piston seal in the pump system and was found to enhance the capacity of the material to resist wear. This innovation has minimized maintenance interventions and resulted in a raised level of functionality.

The question of sustainability of water services is usually set in the context of settlements. Indeed, improved water services can provide a pole of attraction to more remote households, drawing them into larger settlements as people seek access to necessities. The case of agro-pastoralists, as examined in Chapter 9, points towards changes in migratory patterns and constrained choice under the conditions of climate change and changing patterns of landownership. It presents the centrality of water as a natural resource for pastoralists and their cattle and their adaptation to changing patterns of seasons and social relations. Chapter 10 also provides perspectives on the impact of climate and socio-environmental changes on population movement and settlement.

The evidence from these cases is that the articulation between the villages and local and national government structures is weak. The impression is that the big decisions on extending new systems, broadly improving functionality and achieving the MDGs are conducted in an altogether different sphere. And it is not clear at all that there are any links between these political levels.

Sustainability: climate change and responses

In the language of policy and implementation, sustainability has generally been cast in a financial frame – in terms of capital costs, cost recovery, costs of operations and maintenance and willingness to pay. However, it is clearly evident that the financial aspects are just one element among many in actually meeting social needs, including those of the poorest, effectively providing for local and regional governance, and in accessing stable and replenishable natural resources.

The day-to-day functioning of water systems (summed up in the term 'functionality') is a matter of concern for communities, public health services and the operators of health systems. This level of functionality is often known but poorly measured in rural areas, and there are complex reasons for water systems breaking down, ranging from seasonal factors such as drought to lack of fuel for pumps (see Chapter 10). Rural populations, particularly those dependent on stand-alone systems, are vulnerable to reversion to distant 'traditional' sources with unsafe water quality.

Sustainability in remote areas is heavily dependent on village water management, often with weak support from technical teams. Yet the development of water committees with effective participation and leadership, particularly from women, can help resolve the breakdown problem as well as lay the basis for the social resources for broader rural development. Training and capacity-building at the local level are universally identified among practitioners as weaknesses whose resolution (with selected technical innovations) could positively change rural underdevelopment (see Chapters 7 and 8).

In a sense these are the more practical, but lesser, dimensions of sustainability. Over time the great dimension is the variance and extremes in climate change which Africa will experience and which will bring new challenges in delivery and potentially erode the gains made in the existing levels of coverage. Although Africa has the advantage that barely 5 per cent of the annual renewable fresh water is used, there are challenges in the human, economic and institutional capability needed to develop water resource sustainably. Africa is vulnerable to existing variance in climate with extremely uneven rainfall distribution, both seasonally and geographically. Droughts can be devastating, and Africa is reported to be exposed to more recurrent droughts than any other part of the world (Alavian et al. 2009). These droughts bear heavily on economic growth in one third of African countries, destroying economic livelihoods and farmers' food (UNESCO 2012).

Climate change is anticipated to make the water resources drawn on for irrigation and services more vulnerable. Some two-thirds of Africa is semi-arid or arid and a third of the population (more than 300 million people) live in a water-scarce environment (ibid.). It has the largest number of water-stressed countries, and it is the case that climate change further increases stresses in many African countries and the Middle East, while it ameliorates stresses in parts of Asia (IPCC 2007). Groundwater resources in African regions are considered to be most vulnerable (Alavian et al. 2009) and this has important implications, particularly for the 75 per cent of the African population which relies on groundwater as their main source of drinking water (UNEP 2010). Although climate change produces effects on humanity which may also be benign or positive, these are not evidenced in a review of the literature as it relates to Africa.

Despite the gravity of the identified climatic factors and their effect on Africa, it is the poor management of water resources, rapid urbanization, degraded watersheds, and high levels of political conflict, all elements of adaptive capacity, which are regarded as increasing vulnerability within the population.

Post-2015 options

What policies and strategies would help drive future development in Africa? Here some policies and strategies are proposed, designed to accelerate delivery of water and sanitation services, particularly to the rural and urban poor.

Greater international assistance required: It seems unfair that this global region, which is grappling with the greatest challenges of economic growth, debilitating diseases such as malaria, epidemics of HIV/AIDS and Ebola, coupled with challenges in expanding public services, should not have greater assistance in improving delivery of basic water and sanitation facilities to the people. Decisive progress towards universal coverage, without additional assistance, seems impossible. At its most extreme, existing policies place the burden for capital expenditure and for operations and maintenance on the poorest countries and on the poorest of the poor within these countries.

At the same time, commitment to expanding expenditure by national states on improved water and sanitation facilities has to be publicly committed to and maintained. A recent report (Oxfam 2013) tracks (possibly for the first time) the spending by developing countries on meeting the MDGs. Although it finds that progress can be explained by recent spending, it also finds that the majority of countries are spending much less than they have promised, or is needed, to meet the MDGs or potential post-2015 goals. 'Fall in aid, low execution rates, and low recurrent spending all threaten to reverse existing progress' (ibid.: 1). The spending dedicated to meeting the MDGs among the poorest countries is a mirror reflection of the magnitude of international assistance provided. The Oxfam report notes that progress is threatened by the shortfall in spending on essentials, such as the maintenance of water facilities to preserve the level of change already achieved.

Effective health systems depend on functioning water systems: Clinics and hospitals require safe drinking water for the daily tasks of cleaning patients and disinfecting surroundings. Ebola has stressed, weakened and often rendered inoperative existing health systems, in much the same way as cholera has preyed on vulnerable water systems. One of the priorities in the health emergency caused by Ebola has been the recruitment of international volunteers who can set up water systems for treatment centres.[12] The maintenance of public health depends on durable water systems, serving both the health facilities and the communities. Health systems should, preferably, not have a separate water supply (as is often the case in rural communities) and the need for improvement should be generalized through the communities they serve.

Cost recovery cannot be the basis for extending services: Many of the existing policies and practices in water and sanitation delivery are 'demand-responsive', i.e. service delivery is conditional on financial contributions from the rural poor to capital expenditure and to the costs of operations and maintenance. These policies are deeply ingrained as the African Development Bank presents a water programme for the continent which has 'demand-driven financing' and 'demand-responsive approaches' at its core (RWSSI 2013: 11). Demand-responsive policies are different from what they imply; instead of being a ready response to actual need, they involve payment, or commitments to pay, prior to delivery. Such policies place the burden for delivery squarely on the shoulders of the poor, differentiate services between the poorest and the poor, and are unnecessarily parsimonious. Carried out rigorously, demand-responsive policies hamper progress and make the transition to policies of universal coverage unworkable. Funding of operations and maintenance is vital to the functioning of water systems, and policies for free basic water need to be considered throughout Africa to make sufficient safe drinking water accessible to the poorest.

Rethinking the local state: Throughout the global South, water and sanitation are becoming local or municipal-related services. In Africa, rural local government is often poorly developed, linked to traditional authorities, without a local tax base and inadequately funded. Despite this, the drive to improve water coverage, particularly in rural areas, has led to the development of new civil society groupings and incipient local government in the form of water, sanitation and health committees. These committees are often essential to the development of local capacity in rural areas to maintain water systems, which are often stand-alone schemes with only intermittent support from technical agencies. Frequently, these are durable forms of rural civil society which can give women some voice in an essential aspect of rural life. These committees deserve recognition and incorporation into statutory democratic rural local government. In combination they can then form the basis for the management of more extended water systems than the stand-alone schemes.

Wherever possible, regional schemes, providing piped water to communities, should be considered. It appears that stand-alone schemes are vulnerable to breakdowns of all types as communities are often isolated from technical support. Regional schemes, bringing together a number of villages, have the advantage of scale to engage technical support and provide safe drinking water in sufficient volume to communities.

As the numbers of water systems expand, the focus needs to turn to functionality. Although the community-based management model remains the basis for rural water management throughout Africa, it has structural weaknesses and needs to be integrated into local and district systems for effective management. Recognizing some of these deficiencies, the World Bank is encouraging the engagement of private contractors to operate water systems. Such 'delegated management' could arise from the separation of the operator from the water authority (the community or embryonic local government). This form of privatization, it is promised, will provide a 'sustainable service' (WSP 2010). However, the record of such privatization shows many new problems, not least in relation to the funding of such contracts. Improved functionality should be built around democratic forms of rural government which (through equitable share of revenue) can provide more of a base for resources to operate and maintain water systems.

New technologies: delivery and functionality: New 'right' technologies are needed to accelerate delivery while keeping operational and maintenance costs low. Solar pumps enable water systems to be free from dependence on diesel and are relatively cheap to maintain. Unfortunately they are often regarded as being less powerful, incapable of raising the head of water over 40 metres and less functional than diesel. While there are limitations on centrifugal pumps, ram pumps have been found capable of raising the head of water to 70 metres and of providing sufficient volume to transfer water from river level to storage tanks, thus providing gravity-fed water reticulation systems across a widely dispersed population.[13]

Although it has not yet been adopted, rainwater harvesting could be considerably extended if polymer water storage tanks were locally produced in rural areas (as is possible on specially designed trucks). Making drinking water accessible to the household (as in the case of water tanks) is a higher level of service in rural communities.

Information on the status of dispersed water systems is often poor and inaccurate. Innovative communication systems to pass information about problems in water systems in remote rural areas and to pass responses to rectify these are possible through existing text messaging services.

Shack settlements need intelligent provision: It is possibly most difficult to extend water coverage to shack settlements, the reasons being that the right of occupation is often not established, populations are dense and poverty in terms of income and resources can be greater than in rural areas. The population living in shacks is estimated to be set to double from an existing 200 million to 400 million by 2020 (UNESCO 2012). Close settlement should mean that water delivery could be undertaken through scaling up and extending existing systems to include shack settlements. This would be infinitely better than leaving the shack populations dependent on shallow wells which are readily contaminated by waste water and latrines. Urban water managers, who are often concerned about recovering adequate costs from such initiatives, need to assess the possibilities of pressure management to lower the total water loss to municipal systems and other ways of reducing costs as (hopefully) urban housing upgrading and economic growth over time reduce shack populations.

Better coverage can be a component of rural development: Electricity power generation is generally associated with the development of water systems beyond the rudimentary, such as improved springs and hand-operated water pumps. Water systems could be a starting point for improved access to information and the internet. Groups of scientists and architects in Germany and local African partners have been exploring SWING (Sanitation, Water, and INternet off Grid) initiatives and technologies with communities and local governments in South Africa, Tanzania and elsewhere as an approach to all-rounded development. The mobilizing concept is one involving local experts and local communities in relations of equality with scientific and developmental groups to bring the latest technologies and services to the most remote rural areas. Solar technologies have already been used to effect on a small scale to develop solar power, communal water houses, community halls and internet access.[14]

Conclusion

The achievement of MDG7 at the international level has been undermined by a number of factors, including a definition of safe drinking water which did not include the quality of water, very uneven progress, and the ongoing deprivation of millions in the poorest countries which have also had the lowest rates of change. The 2.3 billion who benefited from drinking water were largely in Asia, which had already seen marked progress in water coverage prior to the introduction of the MDG. The African region recorded a level of progress which fell well short of the goal of halving the population without access to improved water and sanitation. The evidence from the analysis is that, while delivery in Africa was somewhat accelerated in the second period of MDG, the processes were very uneven and some countries actually recorded a decline in coverage.

The comparative analysis of the southern Asia and Africa regions points to some of the underlying dynamics of a latecomer region's development of water systems through improvements in hardware, procedures for learning and innovation, and gains in sectoral innovation. It was anticipated that water systems would start with limited economies of scale and low-intensity learning but that the slow, long-run building of capability would, with a combination of supporting factors, lead to sustained accelerated delivery. The evidence is that those regions and countries of greatest need have historically seen the slowest progress. The rising tide of accelerated delivery in many developing regions has yet to raise substantial populations with the most acute need.

The low growth of higher levels of service in Africa, such as piped water on the premises, indicates that the stages of development have been unable to progress beyond the slow extension of existing infrastructure. Advances marked by technologies, allowing for extensive reticulation which could increase scale, are not yet in evidence. The various elements which would accelerate change, such as the commitment of additional international assistance, innovation in existing models of delivery, and the use of the right technology, have yet to constitute combined inputs and development.

In many regions of Africa the recent advance is challenged by new epidemics and by climate change. While considerable additional international assistance is needed to approach universal coverage, particularly in rural areas, the level of international commitment appears ambivalent at best. There is relative indifference to African dilemmas. There is a very evident burden on countries emerging from civil war, plagued by malaria and tropical diseases, and now crippled with Ebola, but the international agencies, which in previous eras have provided support, have been incapacitated through decades of austerity (Fink 2014). The water systems of Africa, in themselves, constitute a weak link in the chain against disease and provision of supplies to maintain existing health systems. There is a critical need for far greater assistance, a fact which, indeed, has been known for some time.

The post-MDG period needs to prioritize resilience to climate-change impacts on water supply, planning for improved access beyond the village in regional systems, renewable energy technology for water pumping, and new thinking in rural development and urban redress. This book would argue that a post-MDG strategy needs to focus on achieving the historic target of universal access to water and to improved sanitation. It needs to devise a development strategy which uses water initiatives to drive new rural development strategies as well as new urban developments.

Notes

1 Personal communication, Ronnie Kasrils, former minister of water affairs and forestry, South Africa.

2 The tracking of actual flows of financial assistance and national expenditure is extraordinarily difficult and the issue is returned to below.

3 The JMP uses linear regression to estimate data for a given year in a particular country even if no survey or census was carried out in that year, in order to be able to compare data across countries for the given year. WHO and UNICEF: 'Introduction to JMP methodology' on the JMP website, WHO, Geneva, and UNICEF, New York, www.wssinfo.org/definitions-methods/method/.

4 Where data on these dates is not available, the country data has not been compiled; this has excluded Cape Verde, Comoros, Congo, Eritrea, Gabon, São Tomé, Somalia, Lesotho and Seychelles.

5 www.sahistory.org.za/archive/2005-president-mbeki-state-nation-address-11-february-2005.

6 beta2.statssa.gov.za/wp-content/

uploads/2013/10/MDG_October-2013.pdf.

7 Functionality in water systems is the quality of being practically suited to operate continuously to meet the intended purpose.

8 In the author's experience, technical workers based at a rural centre find visits to remote water schemes demanding. The visits frequently involve starting work early, travelling considerable distances over poor roads, having no midday meal, working late into the afternoon and getting home late.

9 These were developed as the preferred management system in the International Drinking Water Supply and Sanitation Decade (IDWSSD) in the 1980s and are a common feature in developing countries. In Uganda these are specifically termed community-based management systems (CBMS) although another term used commonly in African countries is the Water User Committee (WUC).

10 The integration of governmental

agencies in IWRM is a central concern but, in addition, there are the interests of agriculture and industry which generally do not as yet seem fully integrated and regulated in IWRM in African rural areas.

11 The cholera epidemic in 2000/01 in South Africa was directly related to measures of cost recovery at the epicentre which led to taps being disconnected and the system breaking down.

12 www.cbc.ca/news/health/ebola-volunteer-work-not-for-everybody-canadian-doctor-says-1.2795628.

13 Information from design for water system for Mnxekazi village (near Mount Frere), Eastern Cape, South Africa, 2010. The author acted as project manager for a set of initiatives combining scientific bodies and implementing agencies to provide water services to remote areas without using fossil fuels.

14 Information from Communal Water House project, Jansenville, Eastern Cape, South Africa, and from communications with Professor Konrad Soyez, Potsdam University (2010–13).

References

Alavian, V., B. Blankespoor, A. V. Danilenko, E. Dickson, S. M. Diez, R. F. Hirji, M. Jacobsen, C. Pizarro, G. Puz and H. M. Qaddumi (2009) *Water and Climate Change: Understanding the Risks and Making Climate-smart Investment Decisions*, Washington: World Bank

Bates, B. C., Z. W. Kundzewicz, S. Wu and J. P. Palutikof (eds) (2008) 'Climate change and water. Technical paper of the Intergovernmental Panel on Climate Change', Geneva: IPCC Secretariat.

Bond, P. and M. M. Khosa (1999) *An RPD Policy Audit*, Pretoria: HSRC Publishers.

Budds, J. and G. McGranahan (2003) 'Are the debates on water privatization missing the point? Experiences from Africa, Asia and Latin America', *Environment and Urbanization*, 15(2): 87–114.

Duti, V. (2011) 'Tracking functionality for sustainability', Presented at the 2011 Annual Review Conference of the Community Water and Sanitation Agency held in Kumasi, Ghana.

European Court of Auditors (2012) *European Union Development Assistance for Drinking Water Supply and Basic Sanitation in Sub-Saharan Countries. Special Report No, 13*, Luxembourg: European Court of Auditors, www.eca.europa.eu/Lists/ECADocuments/SR12_13/SR12_13_EN.PDF.

Evans, P. (1992) *Paying the Piper: An overview of community financing of water and sanitation*, Delft: International Water and Sanitation Centre.

Fink, S. (2014) 'Cuts at W.H.O. hurt response to Ebola crisis', *New York Times*, 3 September, www.nytimes.com/2014/09/04/world/africa/.

Francis, D. and J. Bessant (2005) 'Targeting innovation and implications for capability development', *Technovation*, 25(19): 171–83.

Gleick, P. H. (1998) 'Water in crisis: paths to sustainable water use', *Ecological Applications*, 8(3): 571–9.

Harvey, P. A. and R. A. Reed (2007) 'Community-managed water supplies in Africa: sustainable or dispensable?', *Community Development Journal*, 42(3): 365–78.

Hemson, D. (2002) 'Women are weak when they are amongst men: the participation of women in rural water committees in South Africa', *HSRC Newsletter*.

Hemson, D., B. Dube, T. Mbele, R. Nnadozie and D. Ngcobo (2006) 'Still paying the price: revisiting the cholera epidemic of 2000–2001 in South Africa', *MSP Occasional Paper no. 10*, Capetown: Municipal Service Project.

Hemson, D., K. Kulindwa, H. Lein and A. Mascarenhas (eds) (2008) *Poverty and Water: Explorations of the Reciprocal Relationship*, London: Zed Books.

Hutton, G and J. Bartram (2008) 'Global costs of attaining the Millennium Development Goal for water supply and sanitation', *Bulletin of the World Health Organization*, 86: 1–80.

IPCC (2007) *Climate Change 2007: Impacts, Adaptation and Vulnerability. Contribution of Working Group II to the Fourth Assessment Report of the Intergovernmental Panel on Climate Change*, Cambridge: Cambridge University Press.

JMP (2012a) *Data and Estimates*, WHO/ UNICEF Joint Monitoring Programme for Water Supply and Sanitation, www.wssinfo.org/data-estimates/ tables/.

— (2012b) *Progress on Sanitation and Drinking-water – 2012 Update*, Geneva: WHO/UNICEF Joint Monitoring Programme for Water Supply and Sanitation.

— (2014) *Progress on Sanitation and Drinking-water – 2014 Update*, Geneva: WHO/UNICEF Joint Monitoring Programme for Water Supply and Sanitation.

Marin, P. (2009) 'Public–private partnerships for urban water utilities: a review of experiences in developing countries', in World Bank/PPIAF, *Trends and Policy Options*, 8.

OXFAM (2013) 'Putting progress at risk? MDG spending in developing countries', Research Report, Oxford: Oxfam International and Development Finance International.

RWSSI (2013) *Strategic Plan 2012–2015: Delivering basic water supply and sanitation to rural Africa*, Abidjan: African Development Bank.

UNEP (2010) *Africa Water Atlas*, Nairobi: Division of Early Warning and Assessment (DEWA), United Nations Environment Programme.

UNESCO (2012) 'Managing water under uncertainty and risk', *UN World Water Development Report*, vol. 1, 4th edn.

Versace, C. (2013) 'How to profit from the next big scarce resource', Forbes. com, 25 July, www.forbes.com/sites/ chrisversace/2013/07/25/how-to- profit-from-the-next-big-scarce- resource/.

Victora, C. G., J. P. Vaughan, F. C. Barros, A. C. Silva and E. Tomasi (2000) 'Explaining trends in inequities: evidence from Brazilian child health studies', *Lancet*, 356: 1093–8.

Whitmill, J. (2013) *Exploring Links between Gender Equity and WASH Sustainability and Effectiveness in Northern Ghana*, Atlanta: CARE.

WHO (1992) *The International Drinking Water Supply and Sanitation Decade, End of Decade Review*, Geneva: CWS Unit, Division of Environmental Health, apps.who. int/iris/bitstream/10665/61775/1/ WHO_CWS_92.12.pdf.

WSP (2010) *Sustainable Management of Small Water Supply Systems in Africa*, Practitioners' Workshop Report, October 6–8, Washington, DC: Water and Sanitation Programme, World Bank.

NOTES ON CONTRIBUTORS

Richard Bagonza Asaba is an environmental social scientist and lectures at the School of Women and Gender Studies, Makerere University, Kampala. Richard was one of the PhD students on the Water Is Life: *Amazzi Bulamu* Project, and has published two articles on gender and access to water in the *Journal of Gender and Water*. He has over ten years' experience of development projects and research and has undertaken various consultancies, including evaluation of development projects with governmental and non-governmental organizations in a Ugandan (and East African) context.

Narathius Asingwire is a senior lecturer and former chair, Department of Social Work and Social Administration, Makerere University, Uganda. His key areas of research include safe rural water, hygiene and sanitation. Alongside research, he has worked in a consultancy capacity in the areas of rural water and sanitation. His most recent publication is *Interrogating the Role of Social Work in Policy Reforms in Uganda: A Case of Demand-driven Approach for Rural Safe Water.*

Brian Corcoran is a lecturer in the School of Mechanical and Manu-facturing Engineering at Dublin City University, where he lectures on thermo-fluids, sustainable water systems and pneumatics. A graduate of Bolton Street College of Technology and of Dublin City University, he is a chartered engineer. His research interests include sustainable water systems, sustainable energy systems, high-purity water systems, wireless environmental sensors and lab-on-a-chip projects. He has collaborative links both nationally and internationally and a substantial research track record.

G. Honor Fagan is a professor of sociology at the National University of Ireland, Maynooth. She has previously lectured in sociology depart-ments in Northern Ireland, South Africa and the UK, and currently has research capacity-building relationships with universities in Uganda, Mozambique, Tanzania, Malawi and South Africa. Her research interests focus on human security, gender and development, and governance. She has published over twenty-six journal articles and book chapters and three books, including the prize-winning *Globalisation and Security: An Encyclopaedia.*

David Hemson has directed a university programme on social policy and served as research director with the Human Sciences Research Council (HSRC) in South Africa. His field of research includes South Africa, other African countries, and groundwater replenishment in Indonesia. He has conducted research in climate change adaptation, water policy, cholera, service delivery and impact evaluation and has provided project leadership in fourteen research projects in the HSRC. He has written numerous research reports, peer-reviewed articles and book chapters, and co-edited a book on poverty and water.

Consolata Kabonesa is senior lecturer and dean at the School of Women and Gender Studies, College of Humanities and Social Sciences, Maker-ere University, Uganda. Her research focuses on gender and human development, and her major research interests include water, agriculture, health (especially HIV/AIDS), technology (including ICT), and gender budgeting. Her recent publications have focused on gender in relation to e-learning, access and utilization of information communication technology, water, climate change, land rights, and conflict transformation. She has a PhD from the University of Illinois, Urbana-Champaign, USA.

Michael Lubwama is a faculty member in the department of Mechanical Engineering, Makerere University. His research interests include surface engineering of thin films deposited on elastomers, nano-bio-composite polymers/materials and second-generation biomass for enhanced energy services. He holds an MSc in mechanical engineering (with a specialization in sustainable energy engineering) from KTH Royal Institute of Technology, Sweden, and a PhD in mechanical engineering from Dublin City University. He was an 'Empowering the Teacher' fellow with the Centre for International Studies at MIT for the 2014 fall semester.

Gloria Macri is visiting researcher at Dublin City University. She was a Government of Ireland Scholar and completed her PhD at DCU in 2012. Her doctoral thesis focused on the process of shaping and negotiating the diasporic identities of Romanians in Ireland in online space. Her research interests include: diaspora communities; online communication; youth; and social media. She has had extensive involvement in various international academic research projects, such as the EU-EIGE project on Women and the Media in the European Union and MEDIVA, an FP7 (7th Framework Programme for Research and Technological Development) project on strengthening the media's capacity to reflect diversity.

Joyce Mpalanyi Magala is a development consultant and researcher with a background in sociology, women and gender studies. She has provided consultancy services at international and national levels to government ministries, NGOs and the private sector, employing qualitative methodologies and community-based research. She has a wealth of knowledge in sector policy and strategic planning, as well as institutional and organizational development, with a specific focus in the fields of water, sanitation, child health, gender and HIV/AIDS.

Lyla Mehta is a professorial research fellow at the Institute of Development Studies (IDS) at the University of Sussex and a visiting professor at Noragric, Norwegian University of Life Sciences. She uses the case of water and sanitation to address conceptual and empirical issues concerning scarcity, rights and access, resource grabbing, power/knowledge interfaces in policy debates as well as the politics of sustainability. She has worked on water management issues in southern Africa and studied the cultural and institutional aspects of sanitation in Ethiopia, Bangladesh, India and Indonesia.

Synne Movik is a researcher at the Norwegian Institute for Water Research, in the Water and Society division. Her work focuses on different aspects of water governance, exploring policy discourses, institutional structures, the politics of resource allocation, regimes of rights and access and how uncertainty and risks are dealt with. She is involved in a number of projects in Africa, Asia and Europe. She has a PhD from the Institute of Development Studies at the University of Sussex, which had its focus on water allocation reform in South Africa.

Sobona Mtisi is an independent researcher, with a background in sociology and demography, and holds a PhD in international development from the University of Manchester. He has over thirteen years' research experience in water governance and development in southern Africa. He has held research positions with the Water Policy Programme, CPI and with the Department of Sociology, both at the University of Zimbabwe, and Population Services International-Zimbabwe. His current research interest focuses on the contributions of water to growth and development in the context of climate change in Africa.

Firminus Mugumya is currently a lecturer and coordinator of the MA in Social Sector Planning and Management at the Department of Social Work and Social Administration, Makerere University, Uganda. Since 2010 he has been involved in research and writing on the governance and sustainability of community-based water management systems for rural safe water provisioning in developing contexts. His research in this area has mainly been carried out in Uganda and was funded by the Water Is Life: *Amazzi Bulamu* Project, leading to his PhD in 2013.

Ronaldo Munck is head of civic engagement at Dublin City University and visiting professor in Development Studies at St Mary's University, Canada. He is the founding chair of the Development Studies Association of Ireland and has written widely on development issues from a Southern and social movement perspective with an output of more than twenty books and over one hundred academic journal articles. Recent work includes *Rethinking Latin America: Development, Hegemony and Social Transformation*. He was a PI for the Water Is Life research project funded by Irish Aid.

Alan Nicol is programme director of the Global Water Initiative East Africa. He has a background in political science, international relations and development studies. He established the Water Policy Programme at the Overseas Development Institute in 2001 and has led work for a range of bilateral, multilateral and intergovernmental organizations. His current research interests focus on the political economy of trans-boundary river basins and water resources development in agriculture. Most recently he has developed the concept of 'water smart agriculture', particularly in relation to smallholder farmers in East Africa.

Áine Rickard is a researcher in the School of Geography, Planning and Environmental Policy in University College Dublin. Her current research focuses on international migrant labour in the developing world and how such workers experience development initiatives designed to increase their livelihood options. Alongside her research she engages in digital advocacy and campaigning to increase public awareness of issues of social inequality. Her background is in human geography and sociology.

Kimmitt Sayers holds a master's degree (research) in engineering science from University College Dublin. He is a senior lecturer in engineering at Dundalk Institute of Technology in the areas of mechanical design and sustainability. His primary research interest is technology enhancement through innovation and design. Prior to joining DkIT, he worked in consultancy, designing metal cast engineering components using CAD software, and he also worked in the die-casting industry. He served as a committee member on the Water Is Life project.

Anthony Staines is the first chair of health systems in the School of Nursing and Human Sciences in Dublin City University. A medical doctor, he originally trained in paediatrics, before switching to public health. He has published extensively on a range of topics in public health and epidemiology. Although primarily a methodologist, he works on health information systems and child health policy.

Larry A. Swatuk is associate professor in the School of Environment, Enterprise and Development at the University of Waterloo. He is also visiting professor at the Institute of Water Studies, University of the Western Cape, South Africa. His current research interests focus on the political ecology of natural resources governance and management, with a particular focus on water in Africa. He has published extensively, and among his recent publications is *Natural Resources and Social Conflict: Towards critical environmental security*, a volume co-edited with Matthew Schnurr.

Mavuto D. Tembo is a lecturer at Mzuzu University in Malawi. He holds a PhD in geography (in climate change and its adaptation). His research interests include climate change and adaptation, sustainable agriculture, water resources management and GIS (geographical information systems). He is particularly interested in how climate change is shaping food security, belief systems and water resources. He is endeavouring to go beyond conventional research approaches and apply qualitative GIS as a methodology in his research. He applied the methodology in his PhD research in the Makondo parish in Uganda.

INDEX